CHURCHILL'S DESERT RATS
IN NORTH-WEST EUROPE

CHURCHILL'S DESERT RATS

IN NORTH-WEST EUROPE

From Normandy to Berlin

PATRICK DELAFORCE

Pen & Sword
MILITARY

First published in the United Kingdom by
Alan Sutton Publishing Ltd in 1994

Republished in this format in 2010 by
Pen & Sword Military
An imprint of
Pen & Sword Books Ltd
47 Church Street
Barnsley
South Yorkshire
S70 2AS

Copyright © Patrick Delaforce, 1994, 2010

ISBN 978 184884 111 6

Printed and bound in Great Britain by
CPI Antony Rowe, Chippenham, Wiltshire

Pen & Sword Books Ltd incorporates the Imprints of
Pen & Sword Aviation, Pen & Sword Family History,
Pen & Sword Maritime, Pen & Sword Military,
Wharncliffe Local History, Pen & Sword Select,
Pen & Sword Military Classics, Leo Cooper, Remember When,
Seaforth Publishing and Frontline Publishing

For a complete list of Pen & Sword titles please contact
PEN & SWORD BOOKS LIMITED
47 Church Street, Barnsley, South Yorkshire, S70 2AS, England
E-mail: enquiries@pen-and-sword.co.uk
Website: www.pen-and-sword.co.uk

Contents

Introduction

First In, Last Out of the Battle

May your glory ever shine! May your laurels never fade! May the memory of this glorious pilgrimage of war which you have made from Alamein, via the Baltic to Berlin, never die. It is a march unsurpassed through all the story of war . . . *May the fathers long tell the children about this tale.*

These were Winston Churchill's dramatic words to the British 7th Armoured Division – his favourite – on 21 July 1945. They were spoken in the ruins of Berlin, to celebrate the final Victory Parade of the Second World War.

The Desert Rats, who took their name from the long-tailed African desert rodent, wore their insignia of the Jerboa with great pride.

As their GOC, Major-General L.O. Lyne DSO, wrote:

No division has contributed more to the downfall of the Axis Powers and to the total defeat of Germany. The Desert Rats saw service in the Middle East when Italy declared war on us in 1940. They fought with great distinction all through the long campaign which culminated in the victory of Alamein. They took a leading part in the pursuit of Rommel's defeated forces and in the final breakthrough to Tunis.

The division was the first British Armoured Division to land in Europe when it took part in the assault landing at Salerno. It served through the Italian campaign till brought back to England early in 1944 to prepare the great assault on Western Europe.

Churchill's Desert Rats is the story of the final campaign from Normandy to Berlin, told by dozens of individual Desert Rats – troopers and privates, sergeants, young troop leaders and company commanders. It was a terrible struggle in Normandy, followed by the Break-Out and Great Swan to liberate all of Northern France and Belgium. Ghent was taken, followed by months of dour fighting in the Peel country of Holland, the crossing of the Rhine and the fierce hot pursuit through Germany, the capture of Hamburg and the final entry into Berlin.

The roll-call of famous regiments was deeply inspiring: the Cherry Pickers (11th Hussars, Prince Albert's Own), 8th Kings Royal Irish

Hussars, the 1st and 5th Royal Tank Regiments, the Queens Infantry Brigade, 1/5th Queens Royal Surrey (Guildford), 1/6th Queens (Bermondsey) and 1/7th Queens (Southwark), the Sharpshooters (4th County of London Yeomanry), 1st Battalion of the Rifle Brigade, 3rd and 5th Regiments of Royal Horse Artillery, the Norfolk Yeomanry 65th Anti-Tank Regiment RA and the Skins (5th Inniskilling Dragoon Guards), who joined in August 1944.

The German army regarded the Desert Rats as the élite of the British Army. Indeed Monty thrust his three desert divisions, including the 7th Armoured, straight into Operation Overlord to push out of the initial vital bridgeheads. But many of the Rats – quite rightly – thought that they had done far more than their fair share of fighting. They knew all about dying in the desert and in Italy and, having survived, felt little inclination to die in the Normandy bocage, outgunned in their Cromwell tanks by mighty Panzers – Tigers and Panthers – and the deadly 88mm A/Tank gun. After all there were another dozen British and Canadian divisions waiting in the wings untouched by the scars of war.

This is a story of courage. If you know at first hand of all the dangers from snipers, mines, Nebelwerfers, Panzerfaust, 88mm guns and Panzer fire, it takes enormous guts and instinct for survival to keep pushing down the centre lines. In their long final eleven-month campaign the Rats took grievous casualties. The Sharpshooters in Normandy and the Queens Brigade in Holland had to be merged, even disbanded, because of their losses. The division was stretched to the very limits of endurance but still, as Monty put it, 'they were in at the kill'.

Churchill's Desert Rats is dedicated to the memory of the thousands of Rats who are buried in well-tended, green-pastured cemeteries.

I was fortunate to fight with 11th Armoured Division, the 'Black Bull', from Normandy to the Baltic with 13th RHA, and then on their disbandment, I moved in late 1945 to spend eighteen months with the Desert Rats as a troop commander in 3rd RHA. In all the great battles in north-west Europe the Black Bull and the Desert Rat fought side by side against a ferocious determined foe. We won.

If there are errors of names, dates and places, they are mine alone. At the end of the book I have referred with many thanks to the score or two of Sharp End soldiers – usually with sand in their shoes – who have made this book so interesting.

CHAPTER ONE

The Old Soldiers

The First World War song, 'Old soldiers never die, they only fade away', may have been applicable to the Desert Rats, but their own motto was 'An old soldier is a cautious soldier, that is why he is an old soldier.'

Made famous by Jon's 'Two Types' cartoons and loaded with battle honours they arrived back in the UK from Italy on 7 January 1944. A race apart with brown faces (and knees), to many people they appeared rude, cocky and arrogant – a law unto themselves. They spoke a foreign language with strange words like shufti, shai, maleesh, imshi, sayeda, buckshee, and of course ackers and bints! They sang peculiar songs such as the haunting Wehrmacht marching song 'Lili Marlene', albeit with unusual and vulgar words! Their army costume was bizarre – gaudy coloured silk scarves, brilliant pullovers, and a peculiar array of headgear. Their officers wore scuffed 'brothel-creeper' suede shoes, highly coloured corduroy trousers, and some sported luxuriant moustaches and carried fly whisks. They all claimed still to have sand in their shoes – in East Anglia. The pale-faced British army who had not yet soldiered outside Britain winced at the arrival of these jaunty, swashbuckling Desert Rats. But war-weary Britain made much of the victors of Alamein, Tobruk, Benghazi, Tripoli, Mareth and Tunis, and more recently Salerno, Naples and Volturno.

> Monty had a little *div*
> He called the Desert Rats
> And now they are going home
> They'll all put on their hats.
>
> They'll all wear hats of different kinds
> So you cannot tell by that
> You'll only know they're Monty's boys
> By their little Desert Rats.

Divisional doggerel!

Sergeant Major 'Knocker' Knight of 'B' squadron 5th RTR suggested to Trooper Norman Smith that he might be shot as a spy as he was not wearing regulation uniform. He *did* wear his tank beret and army trousers, but shoes instead of boots and a leather jacket and coloured silk scarf instead of conventional battledress top. One tank commander sported a black silk top hat, and passing his brigadier, raised it most elegantly as a salute. Trooper Duce was a gunner/mechanic with 8th Hussars and noted: 'No trouble spotting the difference between the old hands and replacements. For one thing they were about ten years older; also they were deeply tanned. In addition they all wore the Africa Star Medal Ribbon. Young replacements were treated with complete indifference at first and during off-duty hours they tended to keep to themselves . . . I was glad to be with these people. They seemed to ooze experience.'

Gordon Johnson wrote: 'I was transferred as a wireless operator along with 250 eighteen-year-old reinforcements from 5th Royal Inniskilling Dragoon Guards to 5th Royal Tank Regiment on their return in Jan 1944 from Italy. After the stricture of a cavalry regiment, the 5th were a new world with scant respect for Authority, Military Police and Americans, not necessarily in that order! We were issued with Cromwells which would hardly keep out the rain, and Fireflies which were some use.'

For the first few months of 1944, after some welcome home leave, the division found themselves temporarily billeted in the black fenlands and blasted heaths of East Anglia. A far cry from the winds and dusty sands of the desert, but alas there were few pubs or cinemas. The Nissen huts in that cold winter were only just preferable to tents and bivvies. Conditions were such that graffiti appeared on walls saying 'No leave, no second front.'

Major John Edney, later DAA and QMG of 131st Queens Brigade, wrote: 'We all considered that we were by far the best division of the British Army and every man was proud of it. When we, together with 51st Highland Div and 50 Div left the 8th Army, its real backbone returned to England for the last and greatest battle. . .'

A friend of Norman Smith, 5th RTR, who was a sapper major in Italy, said that when he first went up to the fighting among the Desert Rats 'they had a special aura about them which you could not help noticing.' Norman was told that in peacetime the regiment had been known as 'The Shitty Fifth', as their ceremonial guard turnout at Buckingham Palace had been sloppy. Perhaps the RTR colours are apt – brown, red and green (through mud and blood to the green fields beyond).

Major-General 'Bobby' Erskine DSO was particularly irked at having to surrender some members of his highly experienced, well-knit team. His GSO1, Lieutenant-Colonel Pat Hobart, went to the Guards Armoured Division and his OC Signals was also posted. On 27 January Brigadier 'Bolo' Whistler, CO of 131st Queens Brigade was posted to 3rd British Division. Major John Edney wrote:

Maurice Ekins of the Royal Fusiliers was the new Brigade commander. He had not been out of England during the war and had a peacetime attitude to soldiering and an adherence to the rule-book. He would

Major-General Bobby Erskine
DSO, GOC 7th Armoured
Division.

look at us at times *as if we were from another planet.* With our battle
experience, he must have realised that we had the edge on him. Even
later on in battles it took him a long time to learn and fortunately he
did not stay very long with us.

On 3 July after three weeks in Normandy, he was replaced.

The GOC addressed all divisional officers on 11 February at Mumford
cinema. He told them of the coming invasion of Europe, their role as
immediate follow-up division after the initial landings and the training
programme ahead. The armoured regiments would have to go north to
Kirkcudbright in Scotland to do their gunnery training and maintenance.
After their brisk two months in action in southern Italy with Sherman tanks
it was of course inevitable that the division would be re-equipped with
Cromwell tanks. One Sherman Firefly equipped with the new 17-pounder
gun was a distinct bonus. Most squadron HQs also employed two
Cromwells armed with 95mm howitzers.

Trooper Duce wrote:

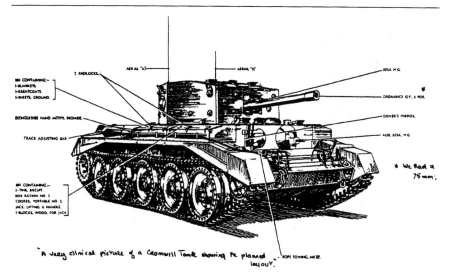

A Cromwell tank, with points of interest marked.

The Cromwell (heavy cruiser) tank was the first real advance in design and technique that our people had come up with. The Rolls Royce Merlin converted to tank use was called the Meteor, produced 540 bhp at governed revs coupled to the Merit Brown epicycle gearbox and Christie suspension system, 77mm max-armour plating, 75mm dual-purpose gun, plus secondary armament of two heavy base machine guns . . . The Cromwell was also very fast with power to spare, even with governors fitted to keep speed down to 40 mph. This was still some speed for a 28-ton tank and in the breakout from Normandy even wheeled vehicles were pushed to keep up with them. With regard to tank guns the Germans always seemed to be one step ahead of us. When we had the 2 pdr, they had the 50mm in their Mk IIIs and 75mm in Mk IVs. Now we had the 75mm and 17 pdr, the enemy had the 75mm long special and the formidable 88mm on their massive Tigers, the Panthers taking the special 75mm. Good as the Cromwell was, it was no match for any of these enemy tanks in a tank-to-tank situation in gunpower alone, apart from the thinner plating, but then neither was the Sherman really. The Cromwell's strong points were its speed and reliability.

The 8th Hussars were officially an armoured reconnaissance regiment but having identical equipment of Cromwells and Stuarts, were regarded as the fourth armoured regiment.

Norman Smith, 5th RTR, had definite views on their new Cromwells, having just got used to the Sherman. The driver's escape hatch was covered

'C' Squadron 5th RTR with Cromwells, training for the invasion. They are pictured in Shakers Wood, Brandon, Norfolk.

by the turret when the gun was in certain positions: 'Our lads were not going to stand for that.' The other defect was that the armour around the turret was perpendicular, thus considerably reducing the chances of AP shot glancing off. Sloping armour (glacis) was the ideal with some chance of shot bouncing off and not penetrating.

Corporal Peter Roach was initially with the recce troop of 1st RTR.

The new Humber scout cars we condemned as soon as we saw them, too little armour, poor across country and a driving position which was almost impossible to leave in a hurry. Where were our beloved Dingos? Then the first of the Cromwell tanks arrived. This was the crunch for this was to be the strength of the unit. There was gloom. A vehicle recognition class was taken by our OC, in which we questioned him about thickness of armour, weight of projectile and muzzle velocity of the respective tanks, ours and the Germans. He was an honest man and when he had finished, there was silence. Each sat quietly brooding. Again we were to be hopelessly outgunned and after our brief period of equality this was a bitter blow . . . [Later] new hatches were devised and fitted to enable the driver to escape with some alacrity – to men who had watched their friends incinerated, this improvement helped morale.

Monty came to see his favourite division on 16 and 17 February and visited and inspected every unit on a bitterly cold, snowy day. 'The great man stepped out, waved and peeled off his sheepskin flying top so that we could all get a good look at his medal ribbons,' noted Trooper Norman Smith. 'He wore two badges in the black tank beret he sported, the Royal Tank Regiment badge and the General Staff badge.' 'Tankies' disapproved of him wearing the black beret and RTR badge to which he was not entitled! A week later the monarch came to see that rare species – Desert Rats in England. Sergeant Harry Ellis, 15th LAA Regiment RA, recalled that HM King George VI inspected all four gunner regiments at Sandringham: 'The 7th were very experienced fighting men and we felt we had been selected to take part in the coming invasion because of our experience.' The Cherry Pickers were inspected on 24 February by Monty, Ike and Tedder and were entertained in the Mess with port and plum cake.

When young Bill Bellamy rejoined the 8th Kings Royal Irish Hussars after dysentery had put him in hospital, he reported to the adjutant in West Tofts camp near Thetford, Norfolk. 'To my horror I found that the 15 cwt truck allocated to me was driven by the same trooper, Bob Weir MM, who had greeted me when we arrived in Benghazi. He saluted me most respectfully and then said "A little fucker like you needs protecting, I'll look after you."' Weir was eventually kicked out of the regiment, but then won a DCM for extreme bravery while serving with the 5th Dragoon Guards, the Skins!

The next VIPs to visit the division were a Russian delegation who stayed for lunch with the 8th Hussars. The Russian general sat next to Colonel

'A' Squadron 8th Hussars, June 1944. Left to right: 'Goon' Gadsby ('C' Squadron), Bill Evans, Bill Talbot-Hervey, Bill Bellamy, Dallas Barnes, Tony Hind, 'Piff' Threlfall, Mike Brown.

'Cuthie' Goulburn, who during lunch pointed to the Balaclava battle honour embroidered on the tablecloth in front of him and said: 'We celebrate that as a great victory, General.' 'So do ve Colonel,' replied the Russian general, 'So do ve!'

During that cold winter and spring large scale exercises called 'Shudder', 'Shiver' and 'Charpoy' took place.

Brigadier Herbert, on Monty's staff in May 1944, saw 7th Armoured Division troops driving by Monty's HQ at Southwick heading for Farnham:

> I felt the troops were not altogether right. Now two or three people came up to me and said "Do you realise that these people are out of hand?" They were responsible senior fighting soldiers and they were really worried about it [indiscipline]. And I went out and had a look and I agreed. They were not under control – they were forcing people off the road, assing about generally – *in a way that experienced troops going into battle would not behave!* I mean they were the Desert Rats, the most famous division in the British Army, and they were fed up and

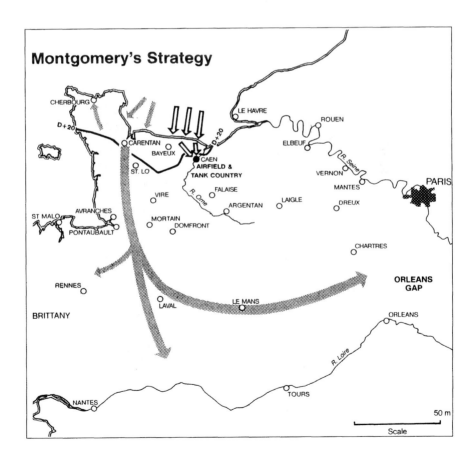

irresponsible. So that there was some reason to be uncertain as to whether everything was all right or whether it wasn't!

Colonel Duncan Riddell, formerly with the Desert Rats in North Africa, wrote of them:

> They were an experienced division; perhaps too experienced. They had seen a lot of war and a lot of death. Most of the other units unlike 7th Armoured and 51st Highland Division had spent the war training in the UK. To units like the 11th Armoured and 15th Scottish, war was still an adventure, and they were eager for the fray – for a while at least. 7th Armoured and the 51st Highland had long since realized that war is a nasty, bloody business!

Later that month the division left their concentration in Norfolk and moved into immediate invasion areas to complete tank and vehicle waterproofing, the Queens Brigade with all the gunner regiments, sappers and RASC to West Ham and Brentwood near the London docks and the 22nd Armoured Brigade to Ipswich. Divisional TAC HQ arranged themselves in Ashley Gardens near Victoria Station to finalize shipping plans, study intelligence reports, prepare maps – and just possibly visit the fleshpots of Soho. On 28 May the GOC briefed all officers in the

Skins prepare their tanks, June 1944.

Brentwood garrison cinema. The 22nd Armoured Brigade plus 5th RHA (with their Sexton-Ram SP 25-pounders) were to land first on 7 June (D+1) and, assuming that 50th (Northumbrian) Division had secured a bridgehead and captured Bayeux, move down the Bayeux to Tilly-sur-Seulles road towards the vital Mont Pinçon.

The prime minister and Monty had the utmost confidence in their three desert veteran divisions – at first. Churchill wrote to Marshal Stalin on 7 June 1944:

> There was a tank engagement of our newly landed armour with 50 enemy tanks of the 21st Panzer Grenadier Division late last night towards Caen as the result of which the enemy quitted the field.
>
> The British 7th Armoured Division is now going in and should give us superiority for a few days. *The question is how many can they bring against us in the next week.*

CHAPTER TWO

Morale and Reputation

Lieutenant-General Brian Horrocks wrote in his autobiography:

As the leaders take the most risks they tend unfortunately to become the first casualties and as more and more of them are killed or disappear into hospital, so the offensive power of their unit wanes . . . The problem of what might be called divisional psychology requires constant attention in war. A division may go into its first battle well-trained and full of enthusiasm but lacking in front-line experience [this certainly applied to 11th and Guards Armoured Divisions]. If it can have a quick success when it is still at the peak it will probably develop into a magnificent fighting formation. But some divisions never recover from a first unfortunate battle *or* from being left in the line too long. To decide on the right moment at which a division should be pulled out of the line for a rest requires nice judgment on the part of a superior commander.

During 1944 Winston Churchill wrote to the War Office (CIGS and Secretary of State for War):

It is a painful reflection that probably not one in four or five men who wear the King's uniform ever hear a bullet whistle, or is likely to hear one. The vast majority run no more risk than the civil population in southern England. It is my unpleasant duty to dwell on these facts. *One set of men are sent back again and again to the front*, while the great majority are kept out of all fighting, to their regret [well, perhaps!].

Lieutenant-Colonel Mike Carver (to become Field Marshal Lord Carver), himself a desert veteran commanding 1st Royal Tank Regiment with 7th Armoured Division, noted:

In the regiments which had been in the Middle East as many as half and often more than that had been doing it for four years. Many who had been brave as lions and still were prepared to be on occasions, either had lost their nerves – they usually went fairly soon – or had a pretty shrewd judgement as to what risks they could take and still have a fairly good chance of surviving.

The Desert Rats, who were extremely battle-weary before D-Day, were now to face severe criticism.

Lieutenant-General Brian Horrocks, perhaps Monty's ablest Corps Commander, wrote later in 1944:

> Another disturbing feature was the comparative lack of success of the veteran 7th Armoured and 51st Highland Divisions. Both of them came again later on and finished the war in magnificent shape, but during the Normandy fighting they were not at their best . . . The danger signal comes when the troops begin to say 'Is nobody else fighting this war?' The 7th Armoured and 51st Highland Division, *after being lionised in the UK*, came out to Normandy and found themselves faced with an entirely different type of battle fought under different conditions of terrain. And they began to see the difficulties all too clearly. A racing enthusiast once described this condition as 'like an old plater who won't go in the mud'. All the more credit to them that they eventually staged a comeback and regained their Middle East form.

After the 11th Armoured Division under General 'Pip' Roberts had smashed 12 miles through the German front at Caumont in less than thirty-six hours, Monty wrote to the US General Simpson at the start of Bluecoat that 7th Armoured had simply failed to push out its flanking shield in time:

> I fear I shall have to remove Erskine from 7 Armoured Div. He will not fight his division and take risks. It was very easy in the desert to get a bloody nose and a good many people did get one. The old desert divisions are apt to look over their shoulders and wonder if all is OK behind or if the flanks are secure and so on. 7 Armoured Div is like that. They want a new General who will drive them headlong into and through gaps torn in the enemy defence – not worrying about flanks or anything . . . We want Generals now who will put their heads down and go like hell.

When Major-General G.L. Verney took command of the division in Normandy on 4 August 1944, he wrote:

> Two of the three divisions that came back from Italy at the end of 1943, the 7th Armoured and 51st Highland, were extremely 'swollen-headed'. They were a law unto themselves: they thought they need *only obey those orders that suited them*. Before the battles of Caumont I had been warned to look out for the transport of the 7th Armoured on the road – their march discipline was non-existent. Both these divisions did badly from the moment they landed in Normandy. They greatly deserved the criticism they received . . .

Major-General 'Pip' Roberts, who commanded the dashing 11th Armoured Division, the Black Bull, which was an outstanding success in the Normandy-Baltic campaign wrote: 'Monty's principle of including *experienced* formations and units in the invasion force was *unsound*; much better results would have been achieved if *fresh* formations, available in England, had been used in their place . . . I noticed on several occasions the differences in dash between formations which had been fighting a long time and those who were fresh.' (Letter to Liddell Hart, 1952.)

Peter Roach served in the recce troop of 1st RTR and wrote:

We were sure of ourselves, with an inner calm that was often taken as conceit, but was a very different thing. We had mainly come to terms with our life and with the many faces of death . . . There seemed no need for enthusiasm and histrionics. *We took unkindly to learning new techniques* for we all knew that death was the lot of every one of us whether in the near future or in our old age. [And later] There was a feeling that because we had done well in the past this was no reason that we should be expected to carry the burden now. There were too many men who had done enough to warrant an easier passage.

During the eleven month campaign Monty, acutely disappointed by the division's *initial* performance, changed the 'management' frequently. Three GOCs, seven brigade commanders, two CRAs and a hundred officers cross-posted just before Operation Bluecoat – all to little effect.

Field Marshal Rommel criticized the British Army for always chopping and changing their commanders. He was probably right! Peter Roach again: 'The regiment [1 RTR] was tired, yet like an old war horse at the smell of powder, it raised its head and would not be left behind.'

In the first three weeks in Normandy the division suffered 1,149 casualties.

CHAPTER THREE

An Armoured Division's Role in Battle

When Rex Wingfield joined 1/6th Queens he was given a very good brief by his new 'muckers':

The job of an armoured division is a highly specialised one. It is a spearhead. The point is three regiments of tanks and in close support of each of them is a company of the 1st Rifle Brigade in halftracks (and carriers). The blade is you, riding in Troop Carrying Vehicles (TCVs) – three battalions of infantry. You now belong to the 1st/6th Queens Royal Regiment. You also belong to 131 Lorried Infantry Brigade of the 7th Armoured Division. An armoured division probes and pushes its way through or around opposition. It does not bash blindly ahead. It does not stop to 'mop up'. It moves on and hopes to God that its supplies last out, or catch up. The limit of the advance is the limit of those supplies. An armoured division is basically restricted to main roads but it can use good firm tank-country. Tanks make their way ahead. If they meet machineguns they deal with them. If they bump anti-tank guns or anti-tank ditches – it's the infantry's job to deal with those. Anti-tank guns are cleared by infantry flank attacks. Infantry also clear and hold anti-tank ditches until AVREs (armoured vehicles Royal Engineers) bring up tank bridges or 'fascine' tanks to fill up the ditch. At night the tanks laager on some prominent feature or natural obstacle such as a hill or river. Round them in all-round defence are the infantry. During the night supply columns battle their way to you – we hope! By next day your TCVs have brought up an *ordinary* infantry division to relieve you and on you go again! From dawn to dusk you have rocket-firing 'Tiffies' constantly circling round – and all the division's artillery to play with. We don't have to worry much about wood or street cleaning. That's not our job. That's for ordinary infantry divisions – very costly in men. If *our* tanks go and play with someone else we're taken out of the line because we're not strong enough to hold anything.

Tactics

Lieutenant-Colonel Mike Carver (later Field Marshal), who commanded 1st RTR in Normandy, wrote about the problem of tank-infantry co-operation. He made the point that in the desert, tanks and infantry had tended to operate *independently*, generally with far from satisfactory results. Despite the fact that the 'virgin' 11th Armoured Division had trained for three years in Britain in close tank-infantry deployment (under the eagle eyes of 'Hobo', Major-General Hobart), in the great Goodwood battle their GOC General 'Pip' Roberts was ordered by the Corps commander to deploy – desert fashion – his armoured brigade and his infantry brigade in *parallel*. To be rather cynical, it is often true that many generals still fight their *last* war campaign. Certainly Monty and his Corps commanders at first used desert warfare tactics in Normandy, with little success. In practice close tank-infantry co-ordination needed a great deal of firm but tactful direction, since tanks frequently attracted shelling by Nebelwerfers or 88mm airburst, like moths to a fire. On one occasion Norman Smith, 5th RTR, remembers:

> One of the nearby infantrymen, a big gingery Scot from the Queens, came over and said, not entirely jokingly, 'Why don't you tankies piss off and leave us in peace for a bit?' The next morning we were quite surprised to see none of our tanks had suffered a direct hit [from the evening stonk] but some of the infantry had been killed and wounded from shells dropping in their slit-trenches.

Many 'tankies' wrote of the sheer discomfort of fighting a tank war. Drivers, co-drivers and gunners (who *had* to sit) longed to stand up, and commanders and wireless operators/gun loaders yearned to sit. Usually the crew needing to urinate used empty shell cases and threw them out of the tank. For more serious business one would leap out with tank spade, dig a little hole (depending on incoming fire), squat over it, replace the divot and leap back into the tank. Sleeping became impossible and crew slept standing up (and then fell over) or fell asleep on their little seats, resting their heads where they could. The squadron radio net kept everyone more or less alert. 'We were like Pavlovian dogs, switched on the moment our call sign came over the air!' recalled Norman Smith.

Reconnaissance

The 11th Hussars, the famous Cherry Pickers, were undoubtedly the finest armoured car recce regiment in the British Army. They had served in Mersa-Matruh in 1935, Palestine in 1936–8, Mersa-Matruh again in 1939 and were proud to have been first into every captured town in the long desert campaigns. They were in action again on 11 June 1944. From long experience they knew the importance of getting the armoured car patrols along the roads in front before the enemy had time to recover his balance sufficiently to put out his roadblocks with their support of anti-tank guns or Bazookas. Two or three cars would inevitably be knocked out by AP. It was difficult to extract the driver, and fifty-four graves marked the blackened trail of burnt-out cars from Normandy to Hamburg.

Queens' Lorried Infantry Brigade

Rex Wingfield, who joined 1/6th Queens just before the Great Swan, described how the lorried infantry went to war:

> Two RASC drivers took it in turns to drive each massive TCV vehicle. They were top heavy and yawed frighteningly at speed, particularly when cornering. Usually they were cold and draughty, but when the canvas screens were folded down a warm cosy fug built up as the infantry inside dozed, played cards, ate their 'compo' rations en route and smoked incessantly. The air sentry sat on the roof, his feet dangling down from the circular lid for the A/A Bren gun. Inside there were two rows of tip-up seats facing inwards and a central row facing out in alternate directions. The TCV was high-sided, and the sides were un-armoured, which made it highly vulnerable to *any* enemy activity. The two doors at the back opened outwards with a mounting step on left and right.

The Queens Brigade travelled hundreds of miles in their mobile 'homes'. It was better than marching.

Artillery Support

Two famous experienced Royal Horse Artillery regiments – the 3rd and the 5th – had provided the division with a precise avalanche of protective shelling since the early days in the desert. The 3rd usually supported the Queens with their towed 25-pounders, and the 5th the 22nd Armoured Brigade tankies with their Sexton-Ram SP 25-pounders. During the campaign they collectively fired 550,000 rounds, equivalent to thirty rounds per gun per day, although in Normandy some of the crisis-battles demanded up to 400 rounds per gun. Their quick, accurate, brutal firepower was greatly feared by the Wehrmacht.

The Picture of War

Major Creagh Gibson commanding 'A' Squadron, 5th Inniskilling Dragoon Guards, wrote home to his father giving a clear picture of the war as it had affected them up to mid-August:

> August 14th 1944: We came out of the line last week after some weeks of battle. I will endeavour to give you an account of our daily life but it is difficult to be descriptive because of security. I cannot say which formation we are in, although it is probably quite clear to the Boche.

The battle divides itself into two different types; one when we are working with a similar formation to ourselves and the other when supporting infantry. Armoured battling has been on a very small scale on our sector because of the very enclosed country. There is no doubt that the Boche has made good use of the terrain. He has proven himself to be clever, subtle and crafty. A few determined men, well sited and camouflaged and manning an anti-tank gun, can give an armoured regiment a very bloody nose in a very short time. They lie up in the ditches and hedgerows and cannot be seen. The first indication of their presence is when a leading tank is knocked out. Even when this happens, you cannot tell from whence the shot came. They seem to use some smokeless powder and there is no flash. They also employ many snipers who have very accurate rifles with telescopic sights. They play havoc with the crew commanders who frequently have to have their heads out of the turret to observe. These snipers are very brave and continue shooting for a long period after the forward troops have passed. Many are caught but it is certain that some get back through our lines to fight again. The general method of advance in this sort of country is to attach a squadron of tanks to a battalion of infantry. The infantry try to ensure that there are no nasty people manning anti-tank guns or carrying bazookas. The tanks deal with machine-gun posts to protect the infantry. The co-operation between the two arms is difficult but we are getting better at it.

On a typical day we get out of our protective trenches at about 0430 hours and 'stand to' till just after first-light, which is between 0530 and 0600 hours. We are usually only a field away from the infantry who hold the line at night. As soon as it is light enough each vehicle crew cooks breakfast which may consist of anything from tinned soya sausage to tinned bacon and beans with bread or biscuits and tea. It makes a very good meal and everyone is quite ready for it. It is often the only cooked meal of the day. There may already be one or two troops of tanks in support of the infantry and these have to be relieved. The advance begins through the thick countryside until a strongpoint is met.

During the past week, prisoners have been coming in readily but not before they have been soundly shelled. Each pocket of resistance has to be dealt with. Artillery fire is called down and tanks deploy to get in a shot from a flank. We have excellent artillery support which can be called down on to targets only a hundred yards ahead. The enemy dig very narrow slit trenches which give them excellent protection, but their casualties are very high. They also dig in their tanks and these are a devil to deal with. They can only be dealt with by an armour-piercing shot and when a tank is brought into position where it can observe, so can *it* be observed. Rocket-firing Typhoon aircraft are often called for to deal with them. Provided the target can be identified, they can usually destroy a tank. The aircraft comes down in a steep dive. The combined roar of the engine and the rocket has a devastating effect upon the morale of the defenders.

I have spoken about 'being in the line'; in fact there is no line. Pockets of resistance are left behind which have to be cleared. This pushing, probing and clearing up goes on throughout the day and until dusk when we form what we call a 'loose laager', i.e. groups of tanks dotted about. Our casualties have really been very light. Those we have suffered have nearly all been caused by mines, shelling or mortar-fire. We are perfectly protected inside our vehicles but you have to get out sometimes and it is then that chaps get caught.

Mine Clearing

Rex Wingfield, 1/6th Queens, describes this dangerous task, which all front line troops had to undertake from time to time. It was known as Potato Picking.

We spread out lying on our stomachs, and took out our bayonets. They were nasty looking things like a meat skewer, and they had an end like a screwdriver. They looked horrible. Worst of all they were damned short. Inch by terrifying inch we moved forward going through the drill. Bayonet upright held above the ground, swing forward, swing back, swing left, swing right. That tells you whether there are any trip-wires around. No? Grip the bayonet lightly but firmly at an angle of 45 degrees to the ground and prod gently. If you prod straight down, you won't know what hit you. If you find a mine dig all around it and watch for any connecting wires. Render safe by shoving nails into the plunger. The Army Drill book always assumes that an infantryman had half a ton of nails in his ordinary essentials. But those bayonets were damned short. A shout from the right and a nasty flat cheese of a Teller mine was found – and another and another. We found a belt about two hundred yards long and twenty deep, a mixture of Teller anti-tank and S-mines. An S-mine was a pleasant little toy, which shot 4 feet into the air and then exploded about 300 ballbearings as well as its own casing into a nasty scythe cutting down anything in its way. Slowly, carefully, with death three inches from our pale faces, we prodded, located and rendered them harmless, every minute cringing for the huge flash which would be the end of Eight platoon. We cleared the minefield. It took six hours. The tanks ground slowly through the white tapes and into the fields.

The Other Side of the Hill

The Desert Rats in June 1944 thought that they were the most experienced division in the British Army. Rommel had placed his second, even third-rate divisions to defend the Atlantic Wall of concrete bunkers, minefields and beach 'horrors'. His well-trained Panzer, SS and Panzer Grenadiers were in reserve inland. The II/987th Grenadier Regiment was issued with these 'Combat Rules for the Coming Battles' (translated):

1. A loud forceful 'Hurrah' is one of your best weapons. It paralyses the enemy's will to fight, makes your battle more easy. By a loud 'Hurrah' you deceive the enemy as to your own strength.

2. When you are not shooting or observing, your proper place and that of your weapon, is under full cover. Your weapon belongs outside only when you are shooting.

3. Even if you have already had heavy exertions, dig in all the same and camouflage yourself. Renew your camouflage *often*! Better no camouflage at all than bad camouflage.

4. Even if no-one is shooting from the enemy's side, conduct yourself as if there was an enemy sniper 100m away from you. If the enemy does not shoot that is because he is observing your position in order to be able to fight you all the more effectively.

5. In positional warfare win superiority of fire by well-armed rifle fire.

6. Shoot as calmly in battle as on the range. Even in a big attack 'letting fly' is *not* sufficient. You must destroy each individual enemy deliberately, especially enemy commanders, MG crews, wireless operators, forward observers, all soldiers equipped with binoculars.

7. Single enemy soldiers will only be shot at with rifles. Six men are no target for a LMG or for artillery. Shoot only at identified targets and not senselessly into the blue, or you will have no ammo left when you need it.

8. If you have won a small success, do not imagine the war is won, do not worry about enemy prisoners or wounded but prepare for the counter-attack.

9. If you are wounded do NOT scream for 'Stretcher-bearer'. You will drive all your comrades crazy and will receive no assistance anyway until it is your turn.

10. If you are always ready for gas, no gas can surprise you. Don't flap.

11. Even in a critical situation do not lose your calm. It is only the man who gives up who is lost. Have confidence in your own strength, your skill and your weapon.

No wonder the PZ Grenadiers fought like demons in the bocage – highly skilled demons!

The German tank commanders on the defensive adopted brilliant camouflage techniques with dug-in, hull-down Tigers and Panthers disguised as buildings or clusters of bushes, even haystacks. The old desert hands never mastered the art of camouflage in the dangerous green pastures and woods of the Normandy bocage.

The Armoured Divisional Strength

During Operation Goodwood an analysis of unit strength was as follows (number of officers in brackets):

1st RTR, 694 (43)
5th RTR, 682 (37)
4th County of London Yeomanry, 609 (41)
1st RB, 843 (31)
8th Hussars, 702 (46)
11th Hussars, 772 (57)
1/5th Queens, 803 (32)
1/6th Queens, 842 (38)
1/7th Queens, 830 (35)
3rd Ind M.G. Coy Northumberland Fusiliers, 214 (9)
3rd RHA, 667 (37)
5th RHA, 667 (37)
65th A/Tank Reg Norfolk Yeomanry, 754 (33)
4th Field Sqn RE, 262 (9)
621st Field Sqn RE, 246 (7).

Total *fighting* strength of the division was 9,587.

CHAPTER FOUR

Arrival – 'We Knew it was War'

In the event the division's invasion of Normandy went more or less to plan. Brigadier 'Looney' Hinde and the advance recce party of 22nd Armoured Brigade landed on D-Day with HQ 50th Division, charged with finding an assembly area for the main arrival on 7 June. The 11th Hussars sailed on the *Bradford City* from Millwall Dock and landed on Juno beach, Courseuilles-sur-Mer, on 9 June. They then motored to Ryes, 14 miles to the west. The Queens Brigade in support arrived a few days later on the 12th. To many of the eighteen- and nineteen-year-old soldiers the landing was a momentous occasion. Even the old Africa hands had not seen so much seawater before!

Trooper Norman Smith, 5th RTR, had a difficult beach landing. The LCT discharged his Cromwell too far from the beach:

> We had the engine running already and drove off and down into the drink; far too deep, far too deep. The first wave tore through all the ropes holding our bedding on the back; the second wave swamped the specially built up air-intake shute on the back of the tank. We were drowned. The engine stopped and we had water over the whole of the hull and lashing around the turret. 'Knocker' Knight, our tank commander, a short fair, square-shaped man from the north of England, leaped down into the water, opened up the flaps and pulled 'Ianto' Evans, our driver, and Billy Bilton, the co-driver, out. A few yards away a vehicle hit a mine and men and debris were blown into the air. Shells were still coming over . . . there were many marine commandos lying dead on the beach.

Trooper Albert Mitchell, with the Norfolk Yeomanry, wrote of the landing: 'The odd shell hitting the water here and there. Little or no German air activity. Tanks, vehicles going ashore in a steady unbroken stream. I thought "we are ashore in strength, they have lost now." I was frightened but so excited – but no trouble getting ashore.'

'We landed in mid-afternoon with no opposition and were ashore in about 10–15 minutes, but we knew it was war. The sea was supporting the bodies of so many British soldiers on a gentle swell and I remember thinking that we had had it cushy – those chaps were alive yesterday and had made it easy for us,' were 8th Hussar Sergeant Bertram Vowden's remarks. He was impressed by the smart CMPs in their red caps directing all traffic quickly through cleared minefields.

Lance-Corporal Harry Hopkins, 'A' Company 1st RB, wrote:

We transferred to LCTs just off Arromanches, dropped us near to the beach. My job as section leader was to lie on the half-track bonnet and as soon as we left the water to pull the waterproof sheet off the front. We then later laagered in a field. The only people we saw were three French girls wearing German jackboots. They didn't appear to be overjoyed at seeing us. The following morning was the picture of what war was really like. Amongst the devastation of a small village was a farmhouse with the front wall missing. Everything inside appeared to be intact. Outside the farm were two British scout cars with all the occupants dead. Upstairs in the farmhouse an elderly couple lay dead in the bed. They appeared to be asleep; it was obviously the blast that had killed them.

Trooper Geoff Ferdie, A2 Echelon of Able squadron 5th RTR, wrote:

I was on the LCT which carried two tanks and six three-tonners full of ammo. A craft very similar to a river barge but with a drawbridge in the bow. There was no accommodation for the tank or crews and no cooking facilities. All the food was cooked in the bows of the boat on a petrol stove. Everything we ate or drank tasted salty, except the self-

Skins on LST 416 waiting for the tide to go out.

heating soup and cocoa which was a God-send. Captain Dixon, who was in another craft, was in a terrible condition, green from ear to ear and wanting nothing better than to die quickly. At light (on 7 June) the scene was one which I shall never forget. The sea within half a mile or so of the shore was literally packed with craft of every conceivable size and shape ranging from the large LSTs to tiny infantry assault boats, all queuing up to disgorge their loads. Behind us could be seen HMS *Warspite* and a number of cruisers occasionally firing at some unseen target miles inland. In due course we disembarked and saw our first German prisoners who were returning to England. After a drive of several miles inland with the crews sitting on the outsides of their tanks we parked round the edge of a large field near Bayeux, ripped off all the waterproofing and camouflaged the vehicles. It was funny to be alive when one has half expected to be killed on the beaches. We could not understand why there was no noise of fighting and shelling.

'The most extraordinary sight', Christopher Milner, 1st RB, remembers, 'was watching aging tramp steamers, high out of the water, with their propellors thrashing, charging up and gradually sinking into place to form the Mulberry (why so called?) artificial harbour.'

The Queens Brigade had sailed on 4 June from Tilbury Docks on the MVs *Cameronia* and *Leopoldville*, with their transport on MT No. 24. They sailed via Southend, Spithead and the straits of Dover and arrived at Gold beach, east of Arromanches, west of La Rivière, and the brigade concentrated around Pouligny, north-east of Bayeux, on 8–10 June.

Derrick Watson, then Intelligence Officer with 1/5th Queens Royal Regiment, wrote:

I was in charge of a group of odds and sods vehicles on a LCT captained by a very young sub-lieutenant in the Wavy Navy, who treated me with very great respect. The boat approached a long stretch of golden sands completely deserted. No Beachmaster with megaphone. No taped corridors as we had been led to expect. Ramps down – move off – and the convoy crossed the sands without incident and halted briefly to remove the waterproofing. The exit from the beach was a country lane bounded by high hedges. We drove along this lane, the sun shining, the birds singing, perfect peace. I wondered at the time whether we had been landed in Spain, whether I should be charged with desertion . . .

Bill Bellamy's 8th Hussar troop was split over two craft, TT 111 and TT 114, which sailed from 'Bumper quay' in Gosport harbour. He was aged twenty and in charge of forty-three men and fifteen soft vehicles. He remembered:

The tanks of 'A' Squadron 8th Hussars landing on Gold Beach, Le Hamel, 9 June 1944.

Our LCT drew into line with several others which were being marshalled by a very busy corvette, itself off-loading infantry into smaller landing craft. The sea seemed to be full of wrecks and flotsam with stranded ships, apparently stuck in the sand, all around us. Our captain was having difficulty in finding a way through all these hazards, but I was more thrilled by the sound of guns on shore. This really was war. [The landing into three foot of water proved no problem. Once on the beach, Bill tried to stop and check that all his troops were ashore] . . . but an angry Beach-Marshal waved me on. I told my driver, Corporal Fry, to slow down and I shouted back that I must collect my troop together. '*Not* on *my* beach, sonny' came the reply as he thumped the side of the vehicle and on we drove. As we got into the dunes I noticed the first evidence of battle with burnt-out vehicles and general débris mixed into the German barbed wire entanglements. These bore the sign 'Achtung Minen' – I hoped there were none left on the road!

Peter Roach, 1st RTR, recollects his arrival off the Normandy coast: 'At night we were almost halted and we could hear firing from the shore and the assembled naval craft. There was the rumble of bombing and occasionally the sky was lit with tracer spraying upwards like some giant firework. With the grey of morning we gazed in fascination at the vast throng of craft assembled off the beaches.'

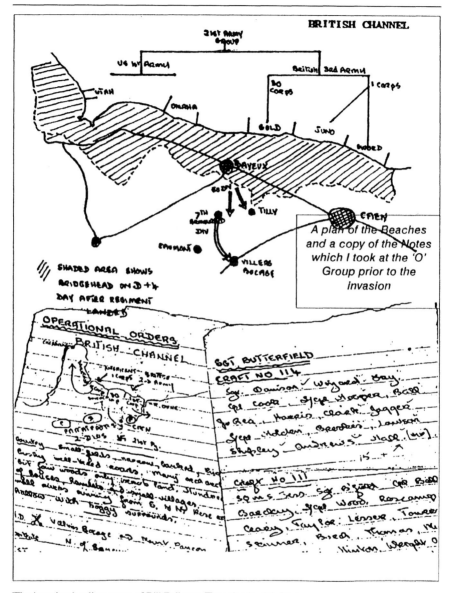

The invasion landing notes of Bill Bellamy, Troopleader 8th Hussars.

Private Albert Kingston, 1/7th Queens, wrote:

We landed on 10 June and I was surprised to see so little destruction. The countryside was very green with high hedges running along little roads. Some of the roads had hedges which were more than twelve foot high and so thick you could not see through them. They were good

8th Hussars drive out from an LCT into 3 ft of water, 9 June 1944.

defensive positions and the units that had been fighting in this sort of countryside deserve every credit. It must have been a real hell. There were lots of little cemeteries we passed as we moved up the line. Four or five graves in a group – an infantry section perhaps or a Sherman crew – because the place was littered with knocked-out Shermans. And some of them stank. There was more than likely bodies still in them.

A silver trumpet accompanied Lance-Corporal James Kay as he jumped into 3 ft of water and waded ashore. He had played it in the 1/7th Queens unit dance band, which had given concerts all over East Anglia. For the next five months, instead of 'Reveillé', 'Cookhouse', 'Jankers' or 'Lights Out' he would be playing the 'Last Post' over the Queens' burial parties.

Rex Wingfield, with 1/6th Queens, recalled later in August 'the squat miracle of Mulberry Harbour, first the blockships, their funnels and masts jutting from the calm water, then the huge concrete caissons. The low sandy shore with stunted grass springing from the dunes. Gap-toothed holiday villas flaunted their shattered emphasis.' Wingfield's craft tied up at a monstrous, floating pier; each end had great steep poles and the pier moved up and down as if it was on giant pistons, then the troops marched along the long steel pontoon bridge to the shore. 'The thing that strikes one most strongly,' Tom Ritson, 3rd RHA, wrote home, 'is our enormous superiority on the sea and in the air. On the way over we never saw a Jerry ship and one never needs to look up at the planes. The Germans come over a bit at night and then there is an awful noise – but mostly our guns.'

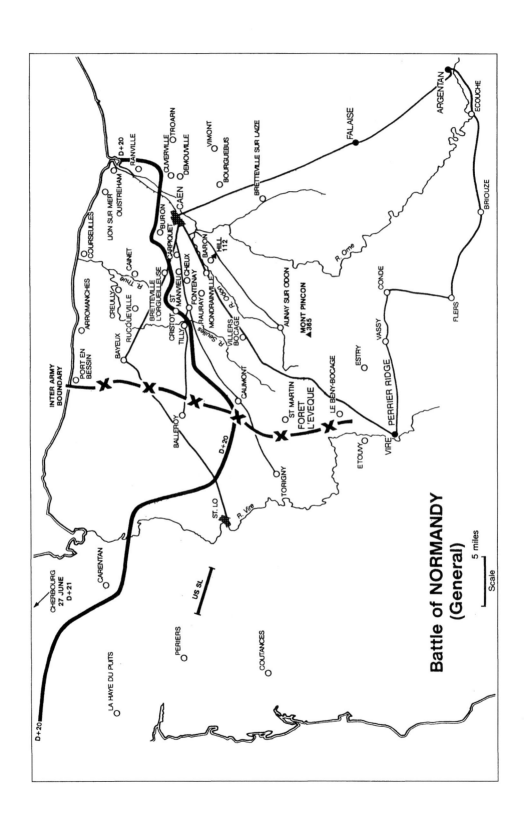

Battle of NORMANDY (General)

Although 50th Division had captured Bayeux and had advanced south on the Tilly and Caen roads for about 3 miles, Monty's objective of taking Caen had not been achieved, and it would not be captured for many more blood-thirsty weeks. So 5th RTR were the first into action supporting 56th Brigade, closing out enemy pockets at Sully and Port-en-Bessin.

Certainly not the desert and not even their short Italian campaign through small thick orchards, vineyards, narrow roads, hills and rivers, had quite prepared anyone for the problems of fighting in the Norman bocage country. Small fields lined with tall, thick hedgerows on top of strong 3 or 4 ft earth banks made superb defensive country. Woods and copses sheltered snipers. Anti-tank guns commanded the narrow winding roads at short range. Tank crews soon found out the hard way that a crew member needed to scout and recce and have a 'shufti' round each corner. 5th RTR had some nasty fighting, destroying four 88mm guns and two others, at the cost of two tanks and six casualties, including Captain Noble, 5th RHA. Lieutenant Garnett's tank was boarded by enthusiastic PZ who were only just repelled. Trooper Geoff Ferdie recalls:

'A' squadron moved to a pocket of resistance at Sully where they had sharp encounters with a battalion of German infantry and an SP. The terrain was very bad for tanks with narrow sunken roads winding among thick hedges and copses, and visibility in all directions very limited. It was not pleasant to see one's friends going into action not knowing who was to come back and an hour or two later to hear the sharp crack of high velocity guns and the rattle of machine-guns including the unmistakable Spandau. After dark I took up petrol and ammo lorries to the tanks.

The local opposition had been identified as 352nd Infantry Division and 12th SS Division on the left front.

For the next three days, 10–12 June, the armoured brigade was ordered, together with 56th Brigade under command (2nd Essex, 1st South Wales Borderers and 2nd Gloucesters), to make a determined attack. 4th County of London Yeomanry (the Sharpshooters) led on the left towards Tilly and Juvigny with 5th RTR on the right parallel through Blary, Ellon and Folliott, towards Verrières. 1st RTR was in reserve guarding the bridges over the river Seulles. 1st RB in their carriers and halftracks were to support and combine with 4th CLY and 5th RTR, backed by 3rd and 5th RHA, 86th Field Regiment RA, 64th Medium Regiment RA and the anti-tank M-10s of the Norfolk Yeomanry.

The German defences included Panther and Mk IV and V tanks, Mk IV flame-throwing tanks, road blocks, snipers and plenty of infantry. In the villages of Bernières-Bocage, Buceels and Jerusalem, the division suffered its first serious casualties. A platoon of 1st RB was written off and 5th RTR lost five tanks, while sixteen men were killed. Cromwells, Honeys and even

Sherman Fireflies were knocked out despite massive artillery support. The Panzer Lehr, theoretically a training division but in practice highly trained, had held its defensive line between Tilly and Verrières fairly comfortably, helped by excellent defensive cover of small fortified hamlets and woods, and had caused the division considerable losses in men and tanks. It was an unfortunate start.

Trooper Geoff Ferdie recalled: 'near Verrières A squadron suddenly "bumped" a number of German tanks in an orchard. The Jerries had the advantage of surprise and we suffered casualties including two tanks brewed up and a number of killed and wounded. By now we felt we were really in the war.'

We sailed from Felixstowe and landed on the morning of the 7th [June 1944] and were soon in action. A German officer was brought in [remembers Gordon Johnson, 5th RTR], the Major sat him down with a mug of tea, I began to think it was an odd war, but it transpired they were both at Oxford. Our letters were censored after a fashion by our troop officers, an A squadron driver used to write home in Welsh, that beat the system! All the reinforcements were so naïve. My closest friend, Dennis Huett, and his crew decided to go and look for their crew commander who had disappeared (a desert man?). He had gone Bomb Happy. They walked over to a barn some 200 yards away. They walked into a Tiger that we were looking for. The usual 'Hande Hoch'. They were told to keep quiet till some infantry came up to fetch them. My friend pointed out that it was the lap-gunner (Callaghan)'s 21st birthday! The German disappeared into the turret and came up with a bottle of wine and the comment 'We cannot let that pass unnoticed!' Gordon was sent to find out why they were not answering the radio, discovered the situation and set all world records as he ran back to safety!

Signalman Peter Knight, 1/5th Queens, wrote after the first battle for Caen: 'Very tough going – noticeably a lot different from the Desert. I believe we had more [men] deserting than at any previous time, including people who had won medals in Africa.' But Rex Wingfield, 1/6th Queens, was told on his arrival: 'You are now in the finest Battalion in the British Army. The Seventh (AD) already has a reputation. It's up to you not to tarnish that reputation.'

The Queens Brigade, who had taken up defensive positions on 11 June round Nonant, were ordered on the next day to outflank Tilly from the west and occupy Juvigny. So 1/5th and 1/6th Queens plus 1st RTR attacked at dawn down the Folliott–Verrières road. Captain Blessley, 1/6th Queens, was killed in an attack on Verrières and, under heavy enemy fire, the Queens withdrew and concentrated near Jerusalem. It was their first fighting in the bocage and they found 'fields of all sizes and shapes, none large, bounded by thick hedges, usually with bank and ditch. Hedges growing thorn and hazel, full of taller oaks, poplars and limes, all very enclosed. In mid-summer the tall crops made defenders always invisible. Many sunken lanes made good tank obstacles of great assistance to the defending tanks and guns.'

During this hard-slogging three day battle Trooper W. Hewison with 'C' squadron 1st RTR, wrote home:

> Hope the people at home aren't thinking we're doing nothing in this Tilley-sur-Seulles sector. The Yanks may appear to be doing wonderful work in capturing Cherbourg but only because we are holding down 5 crack Jerry divs (including the 7th's old sparring partner the 21st and 15th Panzer divs – also the Panzer Lehr and the Adolf Hitler Youth div). The Yanks have 2 divs on a hell of a front. But they are doing well. I shall scream if I hear any more Italian or North African tales! Haven't had mail for 8 days now. Hope that Mustang pilot baled out but I think he left it a bit too late. That's the 7th crash I've seen here. [Hewison commented on his CO's promotion (Lieutenant-Colonel Michael Carver) to take over 4th Armoured Brigade.] Hope new CO is as good a soldier. [Hewison acquired temporary girl friends throughout the campaign.] Lucille's blue eyes in Bayeux. She'll just look at me and I'll buy the shop. French are getting more stingy. A woman *demanded* 2 tins of sardines for ½ kilo of butter. Christ! Managed to get a couple of eggs.

In action more or less continuously, Peter Roach, 1st RTR, wrote:

> As we moved out of laager before it was properly light and did not come back until it was dark, one of the great troubles was lack of sleep. Our hours for rest were reduced to something like four, of which time had to be given to refuelling, loading ammunition, dividing up rations and doing a guard duty. Another problem was the mathematical division of a fourteen-man compo food pack between tank crews of four and scout car crews of two – when everyone was tired and tetchy.

Gunner Harold Swain with 65th A/Tank Regiment RA (Norfolk Yeomanry) joined his regiment in Normandy shortly after D-Day: 'I was then told that we were part of the famous 7th Armoured Division or the Desert Rats. I felt very proud as I was a very young soldier just twenty years of age.'

Early on in Normandy Alan Moorehead, perhaps the best war reporter, fighting in his tenth campaign, wrote in *Eclipse*: 'There was a kind of anarchy in this waste, a thing against which the mind rebelled, an unreasoning and futile violence. We hid in the grey dust and waited for the shelling to stop. There seemed no point in going on. This was the end of the world, the end of the war, the final expression of man's desire to destroy. There was nothing more to see, only more dust.'

Rex Wingfield saw 'the German POWs, shuffling wrecks just following the Bren-gun carrier in the lead. They were past caring, figures bowed with fatigue, ragged uniforms, weary, hopeless battle-drugged bodies, glassy staring unseeing eyes, grey and bloodshot, stared into the grave.' Hitler's children.

The 8th Hussars CO had ordered Bill Bellamy to report in person to the GOC, 'Bobby' Erskine, that they had arrived safely and were ready for battle. On arrival at Divisional HQ:

> I felt rather important and romantic, a slight 'Hero of Peninsular War galloped in with Vital Message' feeling overcame me. 'I have the honour to report, Sir, that the 8th Hussars have landed and are in harbour at Sommervieu' I said, standing stiffly to attention after giving him my best and most punctilious salute. 'Good God, man' said the General, 'I don't want any more bloody tanks, give me 131 Brigade.' I certainly sensed that he was a worried man.

On 10 June the GOC was more confident and reported back: 'only 4 tanks lost that day. I never felt serious difficulty in beating down enemy resistance.' These words were a hostage to fortune.

CHAPTER FIVE

Villers-Bocage – Defeat, a Draw and Victory

Monty now decided to step up the war of attrition around Caen. On 10–11 June 51st Highland took a terrible beating east of the River Orne battling against 21st Panzer, 346th, 711th and 716th Wehrmacht Divisions. So Dempsey sent Bucknall's XXX Corps, spearheaded by 7th Armoured Division, into a gap between Villers-Bocage and Caumont, advancing by minor roads between Balleroy and the valley of the River Avre. The order of battle was for 8th Hussars to lead followed by 4th CLY and 'A' Company 1st Rifle Brigade plus 5th RHA. Then came 1/7th Queens, 5th RTR and the rest of 1st RB. The Americans had been reported fighting just to the west in Caumont, which had been heavily bombed by the RAF and was burning furiously.

On the afternoon of 12 June the advance set off through the villages of Le Bas Mongard, Trungy, St Paul-du-Vernay and Ste Honorine-de-Ducy. For 2 miles all went well.

Lieutenant-Colonel Cuthbert Goulburn, 8th Hussars CO, wrote in his diary: 'We are all beginning to think we have obtained a complete breakthrough.' But Livry, 3 miles north-east of Caumont, was defended and held out until 2000 hrs. 8th Hussars were then ordered to go east-flanking. 'A direct advance up the road is the only way . . . off go Talbot-Hervey's troop. After two or three minutes we hear an anti-tank gun fire about three shots. Hervey goes off the air . . . shortly afterwards Hervey's troop corporal returns in his tank, very shaken and in tears to say both leading tanks had been brewed up.' Bill Bellamy recalled: 'The sad news from A Squadron that Bill Talbot-Hervey was dead, as were many of his troop and Douglas Rampf was seriously wounded. This made a great gap in the friends . . . for the first time the war became more bitter and personal.'

The next day, the 13th, was to turn out even more bitter. Alan Moorhead wrote in *Eclipse*:

Here we were in this first week of the battle exploiting a possible breakthrough with very little opposition, an armoured brigade in front and the infantry coming along behind in lorries. It was exciting to be on the move at such a pace. We bypassed Tilly-Bocage where the Germans were still holding out and early the following morning [13 June] the tanks ran through to Villers-Bocage. It was a neat little crossroad town. The central square. The church. The restaurant called 'Vieux Puits' which was famous for its tripe and its *Escalope à la Normande.* Just over a thousand inhabitants. The tanks roared through to the slopes beyond. The infantry followed in single file along the side of the road and presently we were all standing in the central square together.

At 0430 hrs on the 13th Lieutenant-Colonel Viscount Cranley, commanding the Sharpshooters, led the division from Livry eastwards through Briquessard and Amaye-sur-Seulles, and swiftly and peacefully into Villers-Bocage, the main objective. 'A' Squadron 4th CLY and 'A' Company 1st RB went through the town at 0800 hrs and moved north-east towards the high point 213 on the main road to Caen. J.L. Cloudsley-Thompson, 4th CLY, recalled:

Villers-Bocage is a fairsized county town, there was no sign of the enemy, so we drove straight along the main street. The Brigadier [Looney Hinde] and the Colonel went forward in their scout cars to join the leading troops. A Squadron had got right through and RHQ which I was commanding were just leaving the town when the rear tanks of A Squadron burst into flames and the crews baled out. Every RHQ tank began to reverse.

The Rifle Brigade platoon commanders were called forward to the head of the column for an 'O' group. By 0900 hrs the motor platoons without their officers were being exhorted by those behind to close up head to tail at the side of the road to enable another CLY squadron to pass through them. Flank visibility was less than 250 yards. At 0915 hrs Sergeant O'Connor of Bruce Campbell's platoon suddenly reported two or three Tiger tanks moving parallel to the column about 250 yards away. They swung north and engaged the vehicles standing in the road. The *last* tank of 'A' Squadron 4th CLY was hit and set on fire, another tank went up and then it was the turn of the 'A' Company RB's halftracks which were set on fire one by one. Two more Tigers started firing from due south near the outskirts of the town and seven more Cromwells and a Firefly of the 4th CLY were knocked out. Sergeant Bray got a 6-pounder A/Tank gun into action and claimed two enemy halftracks and one armoured car before a Tiger knocked his gun out and drove down the road machine-gunning the ditches.

Harry Hopkins, 1st R B, also recalled his experiences at Villers-Bocage:

On D+ 6/7 we were told the Brigade were going to thrust quickly through the countryside to a place called Villers-Bocage. There we were to position ourselves on a hill and stop the German armour getting through to Caen. When we arrived at the crossroads at the bottom of

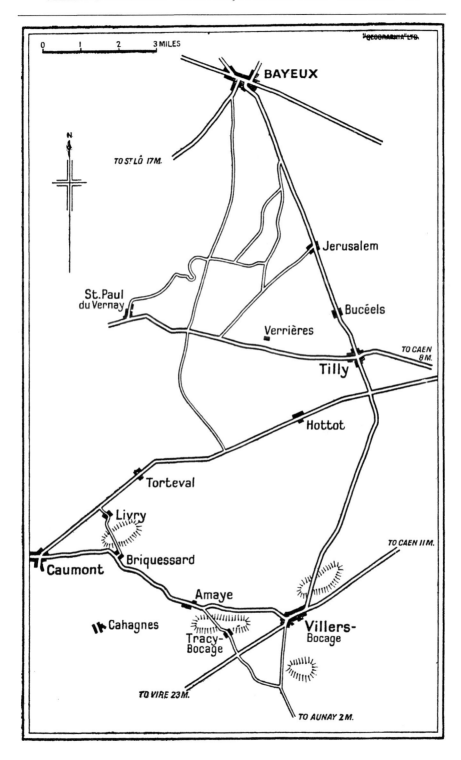

0   1   2   3 MILES

"GEOGRAPHIA" LTD.

N

BAYEUX

TO ST. LÔ 17M.

Jerusalem

St. Paul
du Vernay

Bucéels

Verrières

TO CAEN
8 M.

Tilly

Hottot

Torteval

Livry

TO CAEN 11 M.

Briquessard

Caumont

Amaye

Cahagnes

Villers-
Bocage

Tracy-
Bocage

TO VIRE 23 M.

TO AUNAY 2 M.

the hill, the Officers went forward for a briefing. It was very quiet, more like manoeuvres. Someone gave the order to close up and we relaxed in the sun beside our halftracks. Suddenly there was a loud bang and the front vehicle went up in smoke. The next vehicle to 'brew-up' was one near the rear thus blocking any chance of escape. Casualties were mounting as other vehicles were destroyed. Three of my section along with myself crept along a ditch and managed to escape.

The four Riflemen hid in a chicken coop overnight and eventually made their way back to their depleted battalion. A few days later: 'The officer and several NCOs were killed by snipers in the cornfields and I was wounded when the "moaning minnies" came over.' After being hospitalized in Rotherham Harry Hopkins rejoined the RBs before 'Market Garden'.

Although half a dozen Sharpshooter Cromwells were dispersed in two fields near the crossroads at Point 210 it was clear that the joint force 4th CLY/1st RB were taken totally by surprise by a savage, (initially) single Tiger tank attack! Lieutenant Michel Wittmann, commanding No. 2 Company 501st SS Heavy Tank Battalion of 1st SS Panzer Division was camouflaged in a little wood north-east of Villers-Bocage. No. 1 Company under command of Captain Mobius was on their right. Wittmann had recorded an astonishing 117 tank knock-outs on the Russian front. Just after 0900 hrs Wittmann knocked out the *rearmost* of the Sharpshooters' Cromwells and with his next AP shot destroyed a Sherman 17-pounder Firefly in front of it. Peter Roach, 1st RTR, wrote later: 'We believed the tale of the CLY who were ambushed in a cutting beyond Villers-Bocage. A Tiger tank had come over the top of the cutting and knocked out the first and last vehicles. The commander had then appeared from his turret, taken off his hat and bowed to the remainder, such was the feeling of immunity given by this great gun [88mm] and armour.'

A German photograph of the disaster at Point 213, Villers-Bocage.

It was slaughter. The Sharpshooters had bunched their tanks together and 1st RB's carriers and halftracks made easy targets. Wittmann machine-gunned the Riflemen despite vain attempts with 6-pounder A/Tank guns and Piats to tackle him. Wittmann then advanced towards the town along the Caen road and destroyed four more 4th CLY Cromwells. At 1030 hrs Viscount Cranley spoke for the last time to Brigadier Hinde on the wireless. He then told his tank crews: 'Burn your tanks and get out.'

Instead, at 1300 hrs, Captain Mobius with eight more Tiger tanks appeared with infantry support and took prisoner all the survivors between Point 210 and 213. Captain Christopher Milner, 2 i/c 'A' Company 1st RB, and thirty riflemen escaped to tell the tale. The 4th CLY squadron leader Major P.M.R. Scott MC was killed and Viscount Cranley and many others taken prisoner. That was the end of the first stage of the battle of Villers-Bocage – a humiliating defeat for the Desert Rats.

Christopher Milner noted afterwards that *if* 11th Hussars (under Corps HQ) had been available to reconnoitre ahead of the division on the 12th and 13th June towards Point 112 and then Point 210, it is possible that their fast scout cars would have detected 501st Waffen SS Heavy Tank Battalion – and possibly avoided or lessened the actual disastrous action with 4th CLY and 'A' Company 1st RB.

Major I.B. (Ibby) Aird, CO 'B' Squadron 4th CLY, described the second separate battle that took place in the centre of Villers-Bocage:

> For a short time all seemed quiet and then the most indescribable confusion broke out. Up the street in front Lt Ingram's Honeys and a half dozen halftracks of the RBs were burning. The RHQ tanks started to move *backwards* down the narrow street. As they did so Spandaus opened up from the windows above and the street began to fill with smoke and noise of falling slates, punctuated by the sharp crack of an 88mm. Out of the smoke trundled a German Tiger tank. Major Carr, the 2 i/c, fired at it with his 75mm but heartbreaking and frightening the shots failed to penetrate the side armour even at this ridiculous range. Almost immediately his tank was on fire, he himself seriously wounded and members of his crew killed or wounded. The Tiger went on to shoot up the Shermans of the 5th RHA OPs with their poor wooden guns, the IO's scoutcar and the MO's halftrack.

Brigadier Hinde had said that the town must be held at all costs. Major Aird now assumed command of the sadly depleted Sharpshooters and with 1/7th Queens arriving with their A/Tank guns, the joint force put tanks, infantry and A/Tank guns (plus Piats) covering all roads leading into the main square.

At about 1400 hrs the second battle for Villers-Bocage really got under way. 1/7th Queens had debussed at St-Germain just beyond Amaye. 'D' Company under Major P.C. Freeman, 'C' Company under Major E.M.

French and the carriers under Captain J.A. Beard now did yeoman service. For four hours in drenching rain the infantry dispersed into houses and every street corner with Piats, protected by an out-gunned Cromwell or 6-pounder A/Tank gun, the Queens and Sharpshooters hunted and were hunted. Tigers, Mk IV and Mk V tanks prowled round the town – four were knocked out by the Queens A/Tank guns or by Piats all at close quarters.

The Intelligence Officer of 1/7th Queens told his opposite number at 1/5th Queens (Derrick Watson): 'He was on the first floor of a shop in the centre of the town discussing how to deal with a German tank – drop a blanket soaked with petrol on top of it is one method advanced in Infantry Training Courses. Fortunately he said the tank settled the matter by charging through the shop window, so they made a hasty exit at the back.'

Private Albert Kingston, 1/7th Queens, recounts:

We were in the town centre, a little square and not much else. There were a few shops open, cafés I think and we were just standing about waiting for orders when we heard the sound of gunfire coming from the road out of town. There seemed from the noise to be a big battle going on and presently we saw black clouds of smoke in the air. One of our soldiers said they were tanks blowing up. All of a sudden our anti-tank platoons were ordered into action - to take post. The ammo trucks were driven into side streets and all the rifle sections were told to take up positions in windows of houses on the 'enemy' side of the village.

Lance-Corporal 'Jimmy' Kay, who at one time was firing his Bren gun from a church in Villers-Bocage, wrote:

We entered the town in complete silence when all of a sudden we were shelled and fired at by Spandaus which caused absolute havoc among our troops. The frightening sight of Tiger and Panther tanks was somewhat removed from the days of playing a trumpet in a dance band! Spandaus were firing from house windows and there was the clatter of roof slates falling and of breaking glass. The Tigers seemed to be unstoppable and the guns of our Cromwells seemed to have no effect on the giants. This had been a gruelling battle and many of our lads were lost.

Private Kingston continues:

There were several loud bangs which were our 6-pounder A/Tank guns going off and then one very loud explosion . . . a Bren carrier of ammo went up. [A German tank fired an AP shot that went all through Private Kingston's 'house'.] The firing seemed to spread . . . Jerry infantry were working their way into the town. Then there was some more tank gun fire, some machine gun fire and then dead silence. We waited . . . The street was a mess. Bricks and rubble all over the place. A couple of hundred yards up the road was the biggest tank I have ever seen. It looked undamaged. One of our 6-pounders was lying on its side just opposite our house.

Many acts of bravery were recorded. Lieutenant Bill Cotton MM and his troop took on three Tigers although his tank equipped with a 95mm howitzer gun was no use at close quarters. Sergeants Bramall and Lockwood played hide and seek and eventually set fire to a Tiger and a Mk IV. *Les pompiers* (the fire brigade) appeared as in a French farce to try to put out the flaming German tanks. Fierce fighting took place near the railway station and 'A' Company 1/7th Queens, particularly CSM Baker, distinguished themselves. But with more German infantry from Panzer Lehr and 2nd Panzer Grenadier Division arriving and amidst heavy shelling, the decision was taken at about 1800 hrs to call it a day. Under a heavy barrage of smoke and HE, co-ordinated by the CRA of American 155s plus 3rd and 5th RHA 25-pounders, the two companies of Queens and two surviving CLY squadrons were evacuated westwards back to the villages of Amaye-sur-Seulles and Tracy-Bocage.

The second battle was a painful, confused, but honourable draw. About fifteen heavy German tanks had been knocked out and their supporting infantry given a bloody nose. But during the day the division lost twenty Cromwells, four Fireflies, three light tanks, fourteen halftracks and fourteen Bren carriers. The Sharpshooters had twelve officers missing, three wounded and eighty-five ORs missing, killed and wounded – a dreadful blow. Major 'Ibby' Aird now took command, and reorganized and revitalized RHQ and the two surviving squadrons. The 1st RB had three officers and eighty ORs missing or killed in action and 1/7th Queens had forty-four casualties. Other units also incurred losses that day, including 5th RHA and 1/5th Queens. Since 50th Division had not made any progress on the left (eastern) flank and there was a gap on the right between the Americans assaulting Caumont it was clear that the Desert Rats were now exposed on both flanks. But as Sergeant Stan Lockwood of 'B' Squadron 4th CLY said: 'We felt bad about getting out. It made it seem as if it had been such a waste.'

The third battle of Villers-Bocage took place the next day. The division was now esconced in a defensive box or 'island' on high ground east of Amaye-sur-Seulles waiting until relief came from 50th Division fighting towards Tilly. The box was 2,000 yards east to west and 1,500 yards north to south. The 1/5th Queens and 4th CLY were in the south-west corner, 1/7th Queens to the east, 1st RB facing north. All of 22nd Armoured Brigade with 8th and 11th Hussars plus 5th RHA were concentrated, every wood and orchard congested with transport, tanks, guns and troops – perfect targets for artillery and aircraft! However, the joker in the pack was the powerful 5th AGRA and 186th US Field Artillery Battalion with a massive fire capacity, lurking in the wings to the west and north.

Panzer Lehr, after their triumph in Villers-Bocage, now launched a series of vicious counter-attacks on what they must have imagined to be a disheartened target.

Major Bill Apsey MC, CO 'I' Company 1st RB, temporarily under command of 5th RTR, recounts:

> Denis Matthews and his platoon took up positions to our right front facing north, Geoffrey May and his platoon covered the area behind Matthews facing north-east. The area was thick with hedges and trees. Enemy MET was clearly visible and within range of our mortar. I sent Sergeant Barrett forward to OP and within minutes he was relaying targets. From then on the mortar hardly stopped firing. When we ran out of bombs we obtained further supplies from the other companies. Sergeant Barrett and his team were magnificent and he was justly awarded a bar to his MM.

A rather large American liaison officer nicknamed 'Butch' attached himself, and although it was his first time under direct fire proved invaluable. In one crisis, Bill Apsey said: 'Pity we cannot blast that bloody wood off the face of the earth.'

'We sure can Major, I'll lay on an AGRA [target].'

'OK old son, let it rip.'

For five minutes all hell was let loose. The wood virtually disintegrated before their eyes and the infantry of 2nd SS Corps, recently in Russia, were

Monty awards a bar to the Military Medal to Sergeant Barrett 'I' Company 1st RB, after the Villers-Bocage battle.

written off. All the two survivors could report was trees, men, legs and arms flying in all directions and hundreds killed.

5th RTR moved out to threaten the outskirts of Villers-Bocage. At 1100 hrs 'C' Company 1/7th Queens withstood a determined attack that 5th RHA stonked on open sights, often at 100 yards' range. The South African, Lieutenant H.T.R. Large, was killed in this action, but heavy enemy mortar fire on 1/7th Queens continued for some time. Near Amaye 1st RTR met the 11th Hussars and confused fighting took place around Cahagnes and Briquessard with determined Wehrmacht infiltrating through the orchards and copses.

The Corps commander, Lieutenant-General Bucknall, gave orders for the division to withdraw towards the Briquessard area since enemy were now evident south *and* north of the box! But at 1800 hrs a strong attack came in on the west side of the box against 'A' Company 1/5th Queens, where Major R. Elliott did splendid work. Thirty heavy tanks and a whole brigade of Panzer Grenadiers were reported in action. 'C' Squadron of the Sharpshooters extracted some revenge by brewing up two Mk IV tanks and mowing down advancing Panzer Grenadiers coming through the orchards. 1st RB were shelled and 'I' company lost Geoffrey May and CSM Jefford, while Gerald Pritty was wounded. Later they had some stiff fighting plugging the gaps between the two Queens battalions. The Norfolk Yeomanry's A/Tank guns brewed up several German tanks and 1st RTR's sector was attacked. Peter Roach wrote: 'Back down the radio went the message "Able 5 is brewing". The battle went on.'

Again 'G' battery RHA, with massive assistance from the Corps Artillery (AGRA) and the American heavies, fired DF targets – even Royal Navy ships joined in to defend the perimeter. It was a close range battle and pinpoint targets inflicted enormous damage on the enemy. Reliable estimates were about eight hundred casualties and twelve Mk IV tanks. For four hours the determined enemy counter-attacks were massively contained and they broke off and retreated at 2000 hrs. At half past midnight the tired, bruised Desert Rats moved out of their defensive island back through the short night. 2nd Panzer in their turn had lost the third battle of Villers-Bocage.

Corporal M.R.M. Matthews with the recce troop of 1st RTR remembered how 'their Mk IV Stuarts and Humber scout cars under command of Capt. B. Young suffered inevitable casualties while working the close country round Villers-Bocage and Caumont. Capt. Young & Lt. Elgar were both killed on the same day. Capt. Jack Storey came from A Sqn to take over command. The recce troop was now known as 'Jack's Boys'.

'After four days continuous fighting around Villers-Bocage,' wrote Trooper Geoff Ferdie of 5th RTR, 'A Sqn came back with the regiment to La Moulotière. All the crews were worn out after three nights without sleep and being continually sniped during the day when they ventured to put their heads from the tanks.'

Gordon Johnson's 5th RTR Cromwell was hit in the engine compartment either by an 88 or a Panther's 75mm. The tank spun round and 'brewed'. Gordon was wounded, picked up by the neighbouring Americans, jeeped to Casualty clearing, boat to Southampton, and thence by train to Worcester. Temporarily adopted by the US Army, an American general arrived at Gordon's bedside with his minions. 'On behalf of the President of the United States and the people . . .', taking a purple heart from the ADC's purple cushion. Gordon (naively?) interrupted and said 'I think there must be some mistake.' The general snatched back the medal with the comment: 'A goddammed Limey . . . thanks, feller' and moved to the next bed!

Colin Thomson, armoured car driver with the Cherry Pickers, recalled:

> My troop penetrated as far as Cahagnes where we saw a large concentration of enemy armour moving towards Villers-Bocage. Round the corner of a narrow lane came a German 8-wheel armoured car. Its commander descended and began to walk down the lane towards our officer's vehicle, obviously believing we were Germans. It wasn't until he came within 100 yards that his suspicions were aroused. He dropped his binoculars and bolted into the thick hedge. Our lead gunner let go. The Jerry vehicle went up in a cloud of smoke.

Lieutenant Derrick Watson, Intelligence Officer with 1/5th Queens, recalled how in their defensive box 'enemy tanks were seen and heard to be forming up. Almost immediately the forward companies were attacked by two battalions of Panzer Grenadiers. Owing to the terrain it was a close range battle. I recall a battery of 5 RHA cheek by jowl with Bn HQ engaging the enemy infantry over open sights with airburst and Bren guns.' Also: 'I clearly remember Pte Baldwin, the company cook and a crack shot standing on top of a 3 ton lorry bringing down a German sniper who had foolishly climbed a very tall tree. This brought forth a great cheer from the ranks.'

In the two days' fighting in and around Villers-Bocage 1/5th Queens took forty-two casualties including Captain V.G. Tweedie and Lieutenant Randolph Churchill, and 1/7th Queens had 128 casualties.

Gunner Harold Swain wrote: 'Their Tiger tanks knocked out three of the four guns in our troop and we lost a lot of our comrades either killed or taken prisoner, but we managed to survive.' Gunner Roy Edmundsen, 'C' Troop 257th Battery 65th A/Tank Norfolk Yeomanry, recalls how after their landing at Arromanches French villagers draped flowers over their guns, but their adjutant took a dim view and ordered the gunners to discard their floral tribute. Roy admired his CO Lieutenant-Colonel Stewart:

> It was as if he was leading the Charge of the Light Brigade. We were under heavy fire most of the time round Villers-Bocage. Paddy Hart and I were on the Bren gun much of the time. Sergeant Bland brought in some German prisoners and we handed them over to a Canadian

officer with 1/5 Queens who led his men with a gun in EACH hand. On the same day he was wounded and the Queens adjutant killed. [Later] Our battery CO Major Ditchfield was killed coming up the road in his jeep. [Roy was badly wounded by a shell.] Paddy got help. I was put on a stretcher on a jeep and taken back to the RAP, then brought back by 45 Marine Commando to Gosport.

Every regiment suffered losses as the young leaders became casualties. Bill Bellamy, 8th Hussars, wrote:

[I] heard that Mike Browne, another of my friends and a very capable Troop Leader in A Sqn had just been killed. I was devastated, that was three out of the five Troop leaders in A Sqn killed or wounded in two days of action. I had hardly assimilated this news when Jack came over and told me that Philip de May with whom I had shared all the excitements of the journey out to join the Regiment in Egypt had just been killed by the shelling within the leaguer. War does not allow much time for mourning.

Peter Knight, 1/5th Queens signaller to Major Burton, 2 i/c, helped recce positions for the planned withdrawal: 'We had to wait until dusk to withdraw under the RAF bombing raid on Villers-Bocage. At about 8 pm the Brigadier 131 Queens Bd stopped at the X roads and told our 2 i/c what a wonderful job 1/5 had done with its recent counter-attack.'

Derrick Watson remembered 'the supporting infantry slumbering exhausted on the hulls of the Cromwells in many cases too far gone to waken or dismount when they reached safety of their new harbours'.

Sergeant George Stimpson, 'C' Squadron 5th RTR, recalled that his troop of Cromwells was 'in reserve just behind Squadron HQ. All morning there had been skirmishes when German infantry tried to close in and later two Panther tanks appeared on the scene. These were driven off by the Firefly tanks but in view of the increasing show of enemy strength, 10 troop were ordered forward to give positive support.' Later that day George:

was struck by the apparent inactivity of the adjacent tank and said to my driver 'Slip', that was his nickname, go and have a look at it. He soon shouted back 'They've buggered off'. So I told him to look for damage and try to start it up which it did first time. We removed the compo rations, there was no shortage of food but old desert campaigners always use a bit more. One of my crew drove the abandoned tank back to Squadron HQ. I handed the tank back to its original crew commanded by a 2nd Lt. After a while he came over and said 'Sergeant, someone has taken our rations and brewing up kit.'

'Where did you *leave* the tank Sir?' I said. No reply. 'Perhaps there are Panzer Grenadiers enjoying a good strong brew and eating mixed fruit pudding.'

Private Bill Hinde had joined 1/6th Queens just before D-Day:

Most of us 18 year olds we still had bumfluff. The two Harris brothers, I knew from Bermondsey, got their lot in the first week – virgin soldiers, one was 19, the other 18. It seemed to most of us we would *never* get out of Normandy. We were taking on all the Panzers to make it easy for the Yanks. Mind you the 12 SS were young buggers, still arrogant when POWs. After they had been sniping our chaps, our blood was up it did not take much to shoot the buggers – no worry about the Red Cross Convention.

'The disaster', wrote Christopher Milner, 1st RB, 'to A company reforming in orchards six miles BEHIND the lines, was caused by a single German lone tank; first shot was direct hit on OI lean-to, four killed but a miracle that I survived.'

Meanwhile 100 RAF Lancasters bombed and destroyed Villers-Bocage, inflicting civilian casualties, flattening the town, blocking all the roads and just possibly killing a few Wehrmacht. Under cover of darkness the exhausted division withdrew 4 miles north-east to positions east of Caumont.

General Dempsey, the Army Commander, said to Chester Wilmot, the journalist and author: 'This attack by 7th Armoured Division should have succeeded. My feeling that Bucknall [Corps Commander] and Erskine [GOC 7th Armoured] would have to go started with that failure. By this time 7th Armoured Division was living on its reputation and the whole handling of that battle was a disgrace.'

But by any standards the defensive battle of the 'box' was a success: the Germans were given a beating and 2nd Panzer Division's attempt to counter-attack between the British and American armies had been rudely thwarted.

CHAPTER SIX

Bocage Fighting – 'the Quick and the Dead'

Training in East Anglia was no preparation for the dangerous hazards of fighting in the unique Norman bocage country. A paradise for the defenders, there were woods, copses, rivers and streams, winding, undulating narrow country lanes and, notably, the huge thick hedgerows around most of the small rectangular fields. Up to 12 ft of hedge atop an earth rampart perhaps 4 or 5 ft high meant that snipers, bazookamen, A/Tank guns, even tanks, could hide in the midsummer foliage. Artillery barrages and Typhoon cab-ranks could not *pinpoint* targets. The only advantage to the Allied marauders was a negative one! The *long distance* killing power of Tiger, Panther and 88mm gunners was rarely invoked. For the tank man 'life depended very often', Norman Smith, 5th RTR, recalled, 'on a fast and accurate target identification, sighting, loading and firing. Truly it is said that there are the quick and the dead.'

The German defenders employed superb camouflage tactics, whether they were infantry or armour. Anyone who fought in the bocage country in June, July and August 1944 will never forget it.

For the next two and a half weeks – until 31 June – the division took up a mainly defensive role in the Norman bocage. 22nd Armoured Brigade were in reserve around Ste Honorine-de-Ducy, 4 miles north of Caumont. The Queens Brigade and 1st RB held a line 2 miles south-east at La Palmerie, Livry and Le Pont-Mulot. 8th Hussars had a mobile role covering the eastern flank, La Butte north to St Paul-du-Vernay, which 50th Division were holding.

The enemy front west and east of Anctoville was strongly held with their tanks also in reserve. Both sides patrolled strongly and Nebelwerfer and artillery fire harassed the Queens by day and night. 'Stand to' was always at 0415 hrs and 2215 hrs. Regular shelling, mortaring and sniping took its daily toll. On 17 June two battalions of 304th Panzer Regiment attacked 1/6th Queens in the evening. 8th Hussars and the MGs of Northumberland Fusiliers helped break up the attack on Briquessard, but the Hussars lost five Cromwells and suffered twenty casualties. The RHA regiments fired DF targets, which finally drove the PZ back. But desert veterans of the Queens became casualties. Lieutenant-Colonel Forrester was wounded by a shell, Major R. Elliott and Major Borret and sixteen others were killed or wounded. Derrick Watson recalled the PZ attack:

Major Elliott o/c A Coy asked for a tank to be sent up in support of his men pinned down in slit trenches. I was ordered to direct the tank up to his position, so I climbed up, gave orders to the tank commander through the turret. We crashed through the hedges in great style and charged up to the trenches with engines roaring and me clinging to the turret. The men raised a great cheer in greeting. Shortly afterwards the CO visited A Coy and was heard to tell [Major] Russell Elliott 'You will defend this position to the last man and the last round.' The CO returned to Bn HQ and was greeted with the radio message. 'Major Elliott has just been killed.' Spontaneously the CO said 'He can't be – I've just spoken to him.' Russell had been killed by a shell bursting overhead in a tree. He had led his company across 2,000 yards of minefields at Alamein, survived the drive to Tunis, the landing at Salerno, the drive across the Volturno and the Normandy landings. As they said in the First World War 'His number was on it.' [A roving Tiger tank was causing problems and] Brigade whistled up an M4 – a self propelled 17-pounder on a tank chassis commanded by a rather jolly lieutenant (Norfolk Yeomanry) – a weapon which looked most impressive and turned out to be so. Some 20 minutes later the lieutenant, even jollier, described how he had stalked the Tiger up and down the hedge and knocked it out. Sure enough I went to inspect it – a grisly sight, burnt out with the tank commander's body draped over the turret, minus the jacket.

On 19 June the BBC Home Service broadcast a radio programme about the division, and on the 22nd Lieutenant-Colonel Rankin arrived to take over command of the unlucky Sharpshooters.

Jack Geddes of the 4th CLY wrote:

I have worn the same clothes for seven days running as have we all but I know they must take us out of battle soon, for we are beginning to reach the limit of our endurance. We must come out of battle to lick our wounds and re-equip. God! . . . but in Normandy the days are long. It is still summer – the long evenings stretch for ever and the nights are too short.

The imperturbable Brigadier 'Looney' Hinde announced that 'no further purely armoured breakout was contemplated, that 7th AD was in reserve and a hard slogging infantry battle lay ahead, supported by armour'. He was quite wrong. When Operation Goodwood took place the armour and infantry – desert fashion – fought their own separate battles.

Meanwhile Bill Bellamy, filling a dead man's shoes like so many other twenty-year-olds that June, became a troop leader in 'A' Squadron 8th Hussars. The gunner and wireless operator in the Cromwell were also aged twenty. His troop sergeant was Bill Pritchard:

a solid and capable man who had previous experience in the desert. He was philosophical about it all and was very welcoming and supportive of me. Piff Threlfall, my Squadron Leader, had fought throughout the desert campaign with great distinction. To me he was a demi-god, totally unflappable and I was always prepared to listen to him. I trusted him implicitly and was quite prepared to risk my life for him if he should demand it.

Bill distinguished himself by berating his colonel, Colonel 'Cuthie', and Brigadier Hinde, when they visited his front line troop, because they carelessly strolled diagonally across the fields and thus gave away the 8th Hussars' positions!

A new arrival to 1/5th Queens from the Ghurkhas, and more recently an instructor with the Army Small Arms Training School, was Major 'Jack' Nangle. Brigade Intelligence wanted a fighting patrol sent out to bring back a prisoner for identification:

I was leading the patrol along the hedgerow when I heard the click of a bolt being drawn back, so using my 'Instinctive Pointing Sense', I fired a burst from my Sten gun in the direction of the sound. There was a groan and a rush of feet. On investigation we found a German lying dead behind a Spandau. My burst had hit him between the eyes. This showed the value of the IPS!! . . . so the patrol hoisted the corpse and I grasped his hands round my neck in front of me.

Derrick Watson recorded that Nangle was awarded the MC for this patrol: 'It raised the morale of A Company and the battalion. Of particular comfort was the discomfiture of Brigade Intelligence when they received the gruesome remains. They were not amused.' Watson also recalls:

a daring visitor who made the hazardous trip behind a DR from the safety of Rear Echelon to Bn HQ. This was a Private Buggs whose official duties were to bring a load of bumf for the Adjutant to sign. He also brought the post up. He also milked the cows in the neighbourhood. This meant a plentiful supply of milky porridge for breakfast. The Adjutant believed Buggsy should be mentioned in despatches for these duties but the CO said there was no provision in King's Regulations.

Two sad things happened on 26 June in the bocage campaign. 1st RB lost three officers killed that day from shelling – Major Dorrien Smith, Captain G.S.W. Talbot and Lieutenant James Caesar. And at 0500 it was learned that 4th County of London Yeomanry would soon fight their last battle and were to leave the division, take their tanks to Carpiquet aerodrome and amalgamate with their sister regiment 3rd CLY. This would be the end of a long valiant run through the desert and Italy – loaded with battle honours. Their replacement would be the dashing, famous (but recently untried) 5th Inniskilling Dragoon Guards.

By 22 June 1st RB had lost fourteen officers and 163 other ranks in fifteen days of fighting in the bocage. At Le Pont Mulot they received a large draft of reinforcements from the 8th Battalion 60th Rifles.

The 1/5th Queens in late June were positioned on reverse slopes just north of the shattered village of Livry, in an area that was bocage at its worst. The infantry, no longer lorried, living in slit trenches in the rain, suffered a steady drain in casualties from shell and mortar fire and occasionally from snipers. All the time enclosed in the damp prison of the bocage, the lines of sight bounded by a hedge 200 yards away. At night there was the constant anxiety of patrolling through close hedges, which were often mined to pin down or identify an elusive enemy.

These were Derrick Watson's memories of that time.

Later in the campaign Rex Wingfield wrote:

Waiting for action is frightening but once the battle or the patrol starts, fear vanishes. In battle so much is happening at once, you're so busy that you haven't time to be scared, you haven't even time to think. You do things instinctively. But at night or in some pause in the battle you have got time to think. The mate you saw go down. The tank which 'brewed up'. The shell which stuck in the ground two feet away and failed to go off. When Ted fell, did he try to break his fall? If he did, it probably meant that he was only wounded, but if he seemed to sag at the neck, knee or ankle you knew what that meant. You look into the dusk. A solitary man is digging a trench. You watch him carefully. If he digs slowly and apathetically you know his mate is dead.

On the last day of June the weary division was pulled out of the line as the American 2nd Armoured took over the sector. June ended with a lot of wet weather and Bill Bellamy recalled 'always living in thick glutinous mud. This made the simple business of living so much more difficult. The mud got into the bedding because as we huddled together for shelter under the waterproof covers we couldn't help treading on other people's bedding in our efforts to reach our own. Cooking became a dreadful chore and nothing ever seemed free from wet and filth.' Meanwhile Cherbourg had fallen to the Americans on the 24th and 50th Division was battling on the left (eastern) flank and took Tilly, but the enemy still held Hottot.

At Cully near Coulombs on 1 July W.E. Mason with 13th Medium Regiment RA, part of 8 AGRA, which often supported the Desert Rats, recalls:

While I was waiting for the main body of RHQ to arrive I had a chat with some men from the armoured division. They were able to give me some eyewitness accounts of actions against the Germans. The future looked very black after this discussion! We were in an orchard in a hollow and in front of the guns. Consequently found it very noisy especially when we fired a large barrage into Carpiquet aerodrome. [And later:] We had some bad luck at Le Mesnil Patry for Capt. Jones of B Troop and his signaller disappeared into the blue. Capt. Kerr had a nervous breakdown. Capt. Eve of C Troop was buried by a shell and had to be dug out. Capt. Williams the Adjutant had a nervous breakdown and was posted. In the section Dave Cutts injured his foot when riding his motorcycle, Signaller Key had trouble with his ears. Both went to hospital.

Mason and Co. went to a cinema in the village of Marcelet and saw a film with Lana Turner in it, and he and his mate played a game of 'Spoof' or 'Sevens'. His friends Signaller Free and Corporal Shan were accused of looting in Fresnay, but 'Jumbo' Free talked the Provost Marshal out of a charge! 'Normandy Stomach' was a violent form of diarrhoea from which many troops suffered, caused by food infected by flies that had fed on the corpses of the long-dead cows to be seen in every field.

Major B.E.L. Burton of the Queens described the next period, 1–18 July:

We always lived in the open. Houses and barns were used as recreation rooms but all troops slept out. For the most part we leaguered in fields and orchards tucking ourselves away in any available cover. Slit trenches were dug. When the weather was fine and warm it was lovely and very healthy. In wet weather bivouacs had to be improvised out of ground sheets and gas capes but it was not really possible to keep the bedding dry. Food in the early stages consisted of compo packs containing rations for 14 men for a day. Everything was tinned and ready cooked, only requiring heating – contents varied but one got very tired of 'compo' after a time. When the 'build up' allowed, field service rations including fresh meat, bread and tea were issued instead. There is no doubt that the rations were very good. The cigarette issue averaged fifteen a day. Mail from home came regularly and quickly. The homeward mail at first was slow. Companies went regularly by turns to Bayeux for baths and cinemas. But also we had training infantry with tanks – *a careful slow system of co-operation in bocage country.*

Rex Wingfield with 1/6th Queens later noted:

We had never seen inside of a tank before, so we climbed into the Cromwell. The turret was very small, packed with guns, amongst odd food and of course cigarettes. Only dwarfs could find room to move in there. The crew must be contortionists or deformed. On a Cromwell sit between the turret and the exhaust in the middle. Too near the turret, the wireless static, words of command and loading would drown out noise of incoming shell or mortar bomb. In that case lie flat in the middle as shells burst up and outwards.

He reckoned Sherman Fireflies were difficult to climb and lodge on.
Of that seventeen day rest period Bill Bellamy, 8th Hussars, wrote later:

The weather started to improve and we spent our days training with 131st Queens Brigade in the art of infantry/tank co-operation. Most of them hated tanks, considering them to be noisy, smelly, absolute give-aways to their positions and a large target which drew enemy fire. Despite this we got on very well together and forged a degree of understanding which was to prove very valuable in the months ahead. During the period of our stay at Jerusalem we set up a Squadron Officers Mess and brought the mess three-tonner up from Echelon. It was a great benefit to us all, as we learned to talk about our ideas, experiences and problems under relaxed conditions.

Bellamy also met officers from 5th RHA and 1st RB with whom the 8th Hussars often found themselves in the same Battle Group.

On July 1st a sad and gory episode took place [recalled Leslie Gosling, 3rd RHA]. We were just about to hand over to 2nd US Armoured Division. 'M' Battery was firing intensive scale; we thought we were pretty slick and could have 3 or 4 rounds per gun in flight at the same time. The 25-pounder gun breech was knocked open *before* full recoil and the next round slammed in. Unfortunately the No. 4 was poised to reload, but holding a round with a defective 117 fuse, the breech struck the cap and a premature detonation resulted. One man only of the six man detachment survived and he lost a leg at the thigh. The rest were splattered, and it was not until the next morning that the No. 1's head was seen suspended in the trees above.

During this time out of the line Trooper W. Hewison, 1st RTR, one evening (3 July) 'heard pipes playing tonight – went over dozens of fields to find them. At last saw a lone piper pacing back and forward – a captain of the CLYs. Whilst I was there he played a lament, a Strathspey and a march. I asked him to play "Mushlochy Bridge" and he did. I'm sure if I ever go to Hades I'll find a Scotsman playing a reel round the Devil.' Later, on the 13th, 'New CO [Lt-Col E.H. Gibbon, as Col Carver had been promoted to command 4th Armoured Bd] had a shufti at the ranks and grinned inanely all the time but doesn't seem a bad bloke. Came into Len Dauncey's crew as a lap gunner.' The regiment was in laager for a fortnight. On the 17th 'Big push going in today or tomorrow. 8 Corps & 12 Corps in the line with 30 Corps in reserve. The Geordies say they will be in Paris in a week. I wonder.'

Until 17 July the division remained in the orchards around Jerusalem between Bayeux and Tilly. In this uneventful period many officer changes were made among the senior officers. Lieutenant-Colonel J.H. Mason took over command of 1/6th Queens and Lieutenant-Colonel M.F.P. Lloyd assumed command of 1/7th Queens. Brigadier E.C. Pepper from the Bedfordshire and Herts became OC 131st Queens Brigade, Lieutenant-Colonel J.B. Ashworth OC 1/5th Queens. Many reinforcements – 2nd and 3rd 'flights' – arrived for the depleted Queens battalions, but they remained well under strength.

CHAPTER SEVEN

Operation Goodwood – 'We're in the Wrong War'

Monty desperately wanted to break the apparent stalemate even though the Canadians were fighting in Caen by 10 July. Rommel had fortified thirty of the small villages and hamlets south and south-east of Caen and had accumulated most of his crack divisions there – 21st Panzer, 16th GAF, 271st and 272nd Infantry and 1st, 10th and 12th SS Divisions. Operation Goodwood was to be the textbook 'African Desert' style breakthrough. A massive aerial bombardment would 'take out' most of the immediate defensive posts, supported by huge artillery barrages. Because of the shortage of infantry (7th Armoured had taken 1,000 infantry casualties during June), there were to be no integrated armoured and infantry attacks. Moreover the rolling cornfields south-east of Caen were admirable 'tank country'. This was a double-edged weapon because it meant that the vastly superior German tanks – Tigers and Panthers plus 88mm guns – would have a field day (which they did). Three armoured divisions would, in theory, burst through Rommel's defences and maybe reach Falaise, 20 miles due south of Caen. The immediate objectives would be for 8th Corps with 11th Armoured leading to head for Verrières, Guards Armoured towards Cagny and Vimont, and 7th Armoured towards Garcelles and Secqueville.

The task of assembling and routing 61,000 officers and men plus 870 tanks and 980 armoured vehicles across modest little bridges, through deep minefields, overlooked by artillery OPs in the Colombelles factories, and within easy range of the Luftwaffe, was, to say the least, extremely daunting. Before the Sharpshooters' last battle, in which they would have two officer and four OR casualties, Colonel Rankin wrote:

> I think no-one came away from this conference [at HQ 8 Corps] without a feeling of the deepest gloom. No-one thought there was the remotest chance of getting to Falaise. No-one felt that passing three Armoured Divisions over one bridge could lead to anything except chaos and we all knew the bulk of the German armour had been concentrated in the area S and SE of Caen.

On 18 July 4th CLY was the last regiment of the three divisions to cross the river en route for Hubert-Folie.

On 17 July the Queens Brigade moved to St Gabrielle east of Bayeux, and early on the morning of the 18th along the immensely crowded roads to Blainville, north-east of Caen, and then with the rest of the division across the River Orne in blinding dust.

Private Robert Boulton, with a carrier platoon of the Queens, wrote later: 'All I remember of Goodwood is sitting for most of one night in a traffic jam waiting to cross a bridge and the non-existent Luftwaffe being very existent. When we did cross tanks and trucks were on fire all over the place. The dust was absolutely choking.'

At 0600 hrs every man in the three armoured divisions noted with awe the huge armada of Lancasters and other bombers which, in theory, were going to knock out every village in the way of the great tank attack.

General 'Pip' Roberts, GOC 11th Armoured, wrote of the battle:

About this time (about 1100 hrs) I suddenly saw Brigadier 'Looney' Hinde, who was commanding 22nd Armoured Brigade. He had been making a little recce and I thought 'This is good, we will soon have 7th Armoured Division to take over the area between us and Guards Armoured.' But not at all: when he reached me he said 'There are too many bloody tanks here already.' I was staggered and before I could explain that a lot of the tanks he had seen were *knocked out*, he had disappeared. And I may say 7th Armoured did not put in an appearance before 5 pm. There was some story going round afterwards that they could not get through Cuverville and Démouville, but do not appear to have tried the route which both we (11th and Guards) took and that *must* have been the route that 'Looney' Hinde took because there was no other. I cursed both my old division and my old brigade.

[Later] I managed to get a word across to Bobbie Erskine that I was disappointed that 'Looney' Hinde did not seem to want to get into the battle. He did not agree with this but I think the message got home. It in no way interfered with the good relationship between Bobbie and myself.

On the first day 11th Armoured had suffered 336 casualties; the Guards lost 137 and 7th Armoured 48 casualties.

By nightfall on the 18th, mainly because of the awful logjam of traffic, 7th Armoured only had 5th RTR in action near Cuverville, where they had a nasty skirmish losing six tanks and twelve men, but claiming two Mark IVs themselves. While the Guards tried to get into Cagny, which had received 750 tons of RAF bombs, 5th RTR eventually cleared Grentheville on the morning of the 19th and took eighty prisoners. Corporal Peter Roach described how 'we came to another flat stretch with knocked out Cromwell tanks extending right away to the ridge in front. Delay, frustration, ignorance of what was happening . . . On again through the slow long day. The fighting was fiercer now.' Later the driver of the tank in front was hit in the head and Roach helped pull him out through the small hatch. 'The light was going slowly and the air warm. I sat on the top of the tank as we ate cold rice pudding from a tin. I looked at my hands gory with dried blood and brains.'

Major Bill Apsey MC, 1st RB, was:

> shocked to see so many brewed up tanks of the Fife and Forfar Yeo and Northants Yeo. . . . Our casualties were mounting from shell and mortar fire but we couldn't get them back so carried them with us. 'I' Company took over Grentheville from 8 RB (11th Armoured Div) and were shelled incessantly. We moved forward in the morning to clear the line Soliers and Bourguébus with supporting tanks and artillery. Two platoons moved into Soliers and started to clear it. All went well so I left the gunner and tank OPs who were with me to catch up with the leading platoons. I remember walking towards the crossroads and suddenly found myself sitting in the road. My leg looked a mess but no pain. Almost immediately I was on my back with my left arm useless. Damned mortars – you could never hear them coming. Somehow I crawled to the side of the road and was then conscious of a blow in the back. Third time lucky! Fourth time? Suddenly silence and my batman, Rifleman Jackson and others rushed over and put me in the back of a tank. A jab of morphia, swig of Scotch and I was on my way to the RAP.

Bill Apsey was badly wounded and invalided out of the army. 'In the ambulance were two tank boys horrendously burnt, both died on the way back. My fighting war was over after three years and three times wounded, I had against all the odds survived. I still ask myself, Why me?'

That night the Luftwaffe was out in force. The 11th Hussars, who suffered three officer and twenty OR casualties in Goodwood, were bombed, as Trooper Colin Thomson reported: 'A German anti personnel bomb blew its splinters forwards and sideways about one inch from the ground. From that moment it was standing orders that everyone slept below ground. It was a fearful sensation hearing the bombs coming down, whining and screaming towards your shallow foxhole which seemed dreadfully exposed and inadequate.'

On day two of Goodwood, 19 July, General Dick O'Connor, the Corps commander, had a conference at 1200 hrs at General Roberts' TAC HQ. His plan was for 11th Armoured, who had lost 126 tanks the day before, to take Bras on its little hill at 1600 hrs and then the neighbouring village of Hubert-Folie. And at 1700 hrs 7th Armoured would perform the major role of completing the capture of Soliers by 5th RTR, Fours by 1st RTR, and then Bourguébus, while the Guards Armoured were to attack Le Poirier and then Frénouville. Bourguébus ridge was the main stumbling block as it was heavily defended by seventy-eight 88mm A/Tank guns and tanks.

That day 1/5th Queens moved from Giberville, which had been taken by the Canadians, dug in round Grentheville and found a battery of abandoned Nebelwerfers, notorious for their terrific noise and blast effect. 1/6th Queens had dug in astride the road and railway south of Giberville, and 1/7th Queens were in the village of Démouville, both villages having been painfully cleared by 11th Armoured the day before. Prisoners were taken from 1st SS Panzergrenadiers and 16th GAF Division and the Luftwaffe dropped butterfly anti-personnel bombs on both villages at night. Private Robert Boulton wrote:

> Our carrier section pulled off the road just opposite the dressing station of the 1/5th Queens [who had twenty-five casualties during Goodwood], who were doing an attack. A long and continuous stream of casualties were coming in. I remember saying there would be nothing left of the Bn if this went on much longer. Worse still there was a poor lad who had most of the bottom of his back blown away. There was nothing to be done for him so he was just put outside on a stretcher. The poor devil screamed for about two hours. Morphine seemed to have no effect. He was pleading for some one to finish him off. Our sergeant had been in the war from the start and even he was white and shaken.

The 8th Hussars were harboured in reserve in a large open field near Démouville. Bill Bellamy noted: 'We were called to Squadron orders and ordered to prepare to go up to Fours, a village about 2 miles to the south and support 1/6 Queens. On 20 July Ifs, Bras and Hubert-Folie were occupied and patrols pushed on as far as Verrières, held by up to 100 tanks of 1 SS PZ Div, a battle Group of 2 Panzer and 272 Infantry Division.'

1/7th Queens, who sustained twenty casualties, including two officers, reached Bourguébus by the evening and 1/6th Queens stayed in Grentheville, Soliers and Fours. Peter Roach described the Queens:

> marching solidly through the village went our infantry company – slow obvious steps, no hurry, no eagerness, no fear. A bevy of shells fell and with them one man, now with one leg. His comrade behind stopped and bent over him and then straightening up, undid his gas cape from off his pack and spread it over the peaceful figure. Quietly and with barely any disturbance to their movement, they had passed through the village.

5th RTR and 'I' Company 1st RB occupied Soliers and then pushed into Bourguébus at 1800 hrs on the 20th. They destroyed two Tigers and a Panther for the loss of one Cromwell, and then, going in again the next day, by midday had captured two Panthers intact and destroyed another Tiger without loss. Later in the day, despite very heavy shelling, they set another Panther on fire.

Norman Smith, 5th RTR, wrote:

We moved into Bourguébus where we lost another tank. Sgt 'Pluto' Ellis, commander of one of our Fireflys with my friend Harry Ireland as his main gunner, then knocked out two German Tiger tanks and one Panther tank, one of which he spotted through his binoculars about 600 yards away, seeing just the 88mm gun sticking out beyond a haystack. He got Harry to fire his AP shot straight through the haystack and we all watched the thick black plume of smoke as the Tiger burned. Pluto was a cool customer, short, stocky with black hair and dark unshaven impassive face.

Meanwhile 1st RTR and 'C' Company 1st RB had occupied Fours against considerable enemy fire from Nebelwerfers, anti-tank and field guns. Trooper Bill Hewison with 'C' Squadron 1st RTR, wrote in his diary:

Came up to regiment from spare crews in Major Dingwall's tank as gunner. God help them! Thunderstorms and very heavy rain – the whole area a quagmire. We're in the wrong war – this must be 1917. Feet haven't been dry since, but you get used to it. Heard 3 RTR [in 11th AD] lost ALL but 8 of their tanks. Mosquitoes another pest at night more exasperating than Jerry 'manglewurzels' [Nebelwerfers, also known as sobbing sisters]. Am bumps all over face and head and arms with the blighters. Bloody annoying.

The armoured brigades of VIII Corps were now withdrawn out of the battle to refit and absorb replacements for casualties. On the afternoon of the 21st the Queens were relieved by 8th Canadian Brigade in torrential rain and moved back to Cuverville and Giberville. The rest of the division concentrated near Démouville. On the 22nd 1/7th Queens were badly shelled by 105mm guns and strafed by ME 109s, killing their adjutant.

George Stimpson, 5th RTR, now had a new troop commander, a rather tall full lieutenant called Baker, fresh from England. After forty-eight hours of standing upright in his Cromwell, but not with his head exposed, he reported sick to the MO who diagnosed 'Tank Commander's Feet'. He was evacuated, never to be seen again. Just after Goodwood Stimpson's Able tank, 10 Troop was ordered to clear a farmhouse. Their Cromwell bashed down the gateway in the wall to avoid mines and ran into a gas ambush. 'I ordered my crew to put on their respirators and reported to the Squadron leader we were being attacked by gas.' Their tank had landed on and squashed about fifty large glass containers of ammonia belonging to a fertilizer-minded Normandy farmer!

'After Goodwood,' wrote Private Bill Hinde, 1/6th Queens, 'Jerry made a couple of counter-attacks but the Div and Army Arty [artillery] made short work of them. He got nowhere near our positions at that time – thank God we had all that artillery to back us up.'

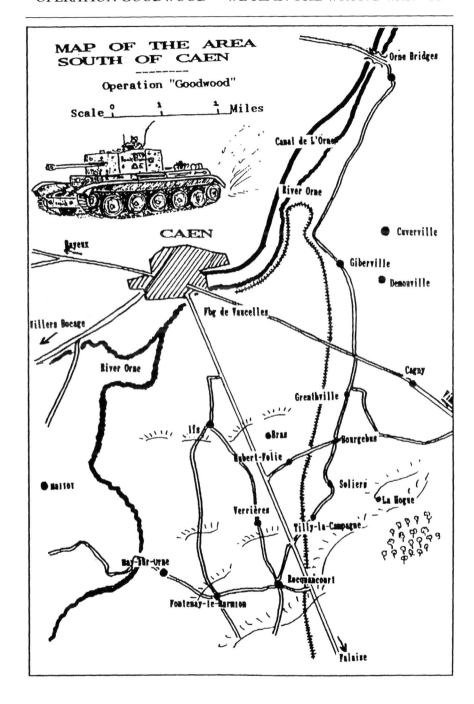

Goodwood ended in heavy rain and tears. Monty's grand slam tank attack had failed to break Rommel's defensive ring. Although most of the fortified hamlets and villages had been taken out by the massive RAF bombardment, sufficient survived, particularly on the Bourguébus Ridge, to give VIII Corps a bloody nose. Thirty square miles of rolling Normandy countryside had been won – at a dreadful cost. The 493 blackened Sherman and Cromwell tanks were replaced more or less overnight, but the hundreds of young leaders were not so easily replaced. 7th Armoured suffered 200 casualties (1st RB forty-seven, 1st RTR thirty-eight and 5th RTR, 1/5th Queens and 11th Hussars about twenty-five each). But they had given the German high command a terrible fright and drawn the bulk of their divisions away from the American front – an honour totally unappreciated by those who fought at Goodwood. And at great cost Caen at long last was captured. It was ironic that the day before Goodwood started Field Marshal Rommel was severely wounded. He would have been proud of his army, which held its line with incredible, stoical bravery.

CHAPTER EIGHT

Operation Spring – 'Shell Happy Now'

The front line soldiers knew little of the external dramas. Rommel's wounding, the 20 July bomb plot to assassinate Hitler, or the SHAEF brass's lack of enthusiasm for Monty's bravado handling of Overlord – to date! Now over a million men were ashore – 591,000 British and Canadians and 770,000 Americans. It was clear from the astonishing array of support service crammed into the fields behind the front line that, as usual, the thin red line of infantry (14 per cent) and tanks (6 per cent) fighting in the hedgerows were bearing the painful brunt. *Plus ça change, plus c'est la même chose*! Sightseers came to Normandy: the King, the Prime Minister, General de Gaulle and every possible Whitehall warrior. And of course the journalists. 'We heard that in England (and in America)', wrote Norman Smith, 'there had been quite a lot of complaint in the newspapers. Why had the advance in Normandy slowed down? Were we getting bogged down like in 1914–18? Were we, in short, really trying quite hard enough?'

The losses by now in front line troops were appalling. 15th Scottish had already lost 5,354 casualties, 3rd British nearly 7,000 and the three British Armoured Divisions, each with only two brigades, about five thousand men. And by the end of July the Americans had taken 100,000 casualties, of whom 85 per cent were PBI or 'grunts'.

On 25 July the division was put under command of 2nd Canadian Corps. Operation Spring was, in effect, a continuation of Operation Goodwood, a combined infantry and armoured attack down the main road south of Caen towards Falaise. 2nd Canadian Division were on the right flank advancing towards May-sur-Orne, and 7th Armoured Division in support of 3rd Canadian Division were heading for Verrières. The usual air bombardment and heavy artillery barrages came down ahead on to Rommel's carefully fortified villages. On Verrières ridge 1st SS had 100 tanks and a Battle Group from 2nd Panzer waiting for the Canadians. It was a familiar story. The Canadian Black Watch, the Fusiliers Mont Royal, and the Calgary Highlanders were soon torn to ribbons.

In their final action 4th CLY distinguished themselves. Fireflies under Captain Bill Cotton advanced to Pt 72, west of Hubert-Folie, and, with the aid of a Typhoon cab rank, destroyed five German tanks and SPs. 1/5th Queens moved towards Beauvoir farm and 1/6th and 1/7th Queens were north of Ifs. Ernie Pitt and George Campbell were stretcher bearers with 1/5th Queens. 'South of Caen we had some stretcher cases to deal with and I said I would take them back to the RAP on a Brengun carrier. I laid on the back to hold them on, got about two fields away when a shell came over knocking me off and shrapnel going right through my leg. I got picked up by a Canadian tank.'

Trooper William Hewison, 'C' Squadron 1st RTR, kept up his diary:

July 25th. Most of the lads shell happy now – specially the old 8th Army wallahs. They can see an end of war in sight. They want to make the last lap.

July 26th. Yesterday was a very black day for the regiment went into action and had a proper balls-up. Partly due to the impossible task given to us and partly due to new CO. He's not much use. All No. 5 Troop except its Firefly brewed up – Thomson and Smalley killed. Boak wounded in shoulder through HE and Fishes went slap-happy and Musdes is missing. Nothing known yet of 6 or 8 troops. 7 troops Firefly must have got it because Syd Chamberlain was seen wandering around slap-happy. Stan Greenough, George Smith, Nick have apparently done the bunk towards Caen. About the 8th time Stan's baled-out. He's absolutely slap-happy now. Johnny came through OK but is more shaken than he cares to admit. All the Regt going slap-happy if nothing is done. We've had about enough. No RAF over. 88s and SPs ringed the ridge and the Squadron hadn't much of a chance. Got 4 Tigers in the morning. B Sqn hasn't suffer'd as bad but have lost some tanks. RBs and Queens knocked up. Ken came up last night with a bombed ammo lorry, driver done the bunk, had shrapnel in eyebrow. Mr Boak acted marvellously guided Johnny's tank back for about 100 yards before he blacked out. Blighty for him. Jack Malsery couldn't get Thomas or Ginger Smalley out because of the 'brew'. Ginger Adcock got an eye missing. I'm praying to God that I'll come through all right. Won't at this rate. Wish we still had Micky and [Major] Dingbat. They between them would see us through. Our tank will probably be repaired for to-morrow – wish it would take a fortnight. The 8th Army lads say this show worse than the Knightsbridge duffy. B & C Squadrons amalgamated owing to losses. Our lads have done grand work – killed hundreds of German infantry and claim several panzers & SPs. 'C' Sqn alone held up Jerry counterattack after Canadians had been driven back from 2 villages.

But Private Robert Boulton, 1/5th Queens had a different perspective after the brutal fighting by Canadians and 7th Armoured to take little Verrières. 'Our feelings towards the enemy I find surprising. We felt nearer to them than to civilians. We did not hate the general run of the German army – but the SS were another matter! You didn't think you would survive if taken prisoner by the SS. I do know that some SS did not survive being taken prisoner by the British!' That day, 26 July, 1/7th Queens, whose CO Lieutenant Colonel Lloyd had left after three weeks, now under command of Major W.D. Griffiths, were in the Troteval farm area. The Queens were to spend four days dug in under heavy fire, which caused heavy casualties.

Bill Bellamy's 8th Hussar squadron at first light on the 27th was ordered to support 1/6th Queens advancing towards Rocquancourt. In the early morning dark he spotted a troop of Cromwell tanks deployed up ahead. They were drawn up in line ahead on the top of a hill and turned out to be three knocked out Canadian tanks with the red maple leaf on their sides and with their dead crews inside. It was a long hot day and his troop were the accurate target for Nebelwerfer bombs, which 'landed plump in the centre of the Troop area at least one directly on the back of my tank and one on the front glacis plate of Bill Pritchard's. It gave us great confidence to see that they had caused so little damage.'

The following day, some 600 yards to the rear, 'another sunny warm day and the sky seemed to be full of Typhoons strafing the enemy positions. It was a fantastic sight to see them suddenly dip their noses and power down towards an unseen enemy. When they were some 2,000 ft up they released their rockets, continued on down, firing their cannons as they went, before swooping up again to rejoin their "cab-rank".'

Norman Smith, 5th RTR recalled:

> I was now [26 July] back on 'Knocker' Knight's tank. We had advanced through some trees dividing one field from another when a number of well-hidden German 88mm anti-tank guns on the slopes to our right opened up on us and other tanks in our troop. We saw tanks on both sides of us take direct hits and burst into flames. Armour piercing shells were just missing us. 'Knocker' gave the order to speed up and superbly swung the tank round in an arc to avoid the gun that was hunting us. He got a sight of exactly where it was from its muzzle flashes as it fired at us. 'Knocker' guessed the range correctly, gave us the order to load HE and got our gunner laid on it. Our second shot knocked the gun out before he got us.

But George Onions' tank was hit and he was wounded by a well-camouflaged Panther. Geoff Waterson, another Desert man, was badly burnt and 'Yam' Taylor, the driver, and Ken White, the wireless operator, were killed. 'Yam' had served on the north-west frontier in India and survived the Desert and Italian campaigns, only to leave his bones in Normandy.

On the night of 26/27th counter-attacks came in on Verrières which were dispersed by 3rd and 5th RHA firing DF targets. Eventually at great cost Verrières and Tilly-la-Campagne were taken by the Canadians. From 26 to 28 July the division remained in defensive positions with 5th RTR in support of 4th Canadian Brigade at Verrières, 4th CLY astride the main Caen–Falaise road, 1st RTR in reserve and the Queens Brigade holding the triangle Tilly, Soliers and Hubert-Folie, often attacked by fighter-bombers at night. 1/5th Queens positions took 1,500 shells each day, mainly 150 and 210mm, and thirty Nebelwerfer stonks, causing heavy casualties in the Beauvoir farm and Ifs area.

As Colin Thomson, 11th Hussars, wrote later: 'I have read a fair bit about Normandy and how we "lost our dash" or how the infantry went to ground rather than pressing on. Where, I wonder, were the people who wrote this? Do they realise just what the British Army went through?' 7th Armoured lost 400 casualties in the period 15–28 July.

Finally, on 28 July, the Queens Brigade was relieved by 9th Canadian Brigade and the division was ordered back to rejoin 30 Corps in the Caumont sector. On the 29th 4th CLY departed sadly to leave their tanks at Carpiquet aerodrome and the Skins – 5th Royal Inniskilling Dragoon Guards – fresh from England under command of Lieutenant Colonel J.E. Swetenham, joined the division.

In his book *First In, Last Out* Corporal John Pilborough wrote that, on meeting up with the division:

To these veterans of the desert and the bridgehead we must have looked very raw recruits. En route to the harbour area we passed some tanks of the 8th Hussars. Their crews carrying the stains of battle, tired and dirty, regarded our fresh paint and enthusiasm a little dubiously. A begrimed and bearded driver put his head out at one halt and asked 'What mob are you?'

'Skins' we answered.

'Never 'eard of 'em' he said, and sank back into the dark and oily depths. The remark summed up the attitude of the Division towards us. We were green troops; no sand in our shoes.

Corporal Syd Swift, 'B' Squadron of the Skins, was:

ordered to collect Sherman 17 pdr Fireflies from Carpiquet Airfield near Caen. My crew was to be Smith 33 (driver), Smith 10 (operator) and Jack Riggs (gunner). We were greeted by shelling on arrival. The Fireflies were all lined up. The gloomy soldiers manning them were men of the 4th CLY. The crew required to hand over their tanks to us were completely heart-broken, having become almost attached to this steel monster as a cavalryman becomes attached to his horse. [Later] My troop leader, Lt Bryan Marshall was one of those jockeys who, with Jack Bissill had been recruited into the regiment by [Col.] Perry Harding.

CHAPTER NINE

Operation Bluecoat – 'Step on the Gas for Vire'

Alan Moorehead wrote in *Eclipse*:

> The whole plan was to keep attacking, never to let the enemy rest, to bomb him all the way to the Seine, to shell him all night, to submit him to infantry rushes day after day. We now had overwhelming fire-power and at the end of July it was in continuous operation for a hundred miles along the front. There was little enough to show on the map. Villages were won and lost by the dozen and still the front-line did not move. All the way down the Odon river to Mt Pinçon and thence to St Lô the German line bulged under an intolerable weight and still somehow it was patched up and kept together.

Monty was determined to keep up maximum pressure and Operation Bluecoat was another massive three Corps operation – practically the whole of the British Second Army was involved. VIII Corps on the right (west) would push south-east from Caumont to the east of Vire. XII Corps on the left (east) would advance to secure a bridgehead over the River Orne at Thury Harcourt. In the centre would be XXX Corps (7th Armoured Division, 43rd Wessex and 50th Northumbrian) with the main objectives of Aunay-sur-Odon and the dominating Mont Pinçon 5 miles south.

When the Skins joined the division at the end of July 1944, Jim (Snatch) Boardman wrote:

> The sabre squadrons were expecting to take over Shermans. This we thought was why we had spent those last days on the Kirkcudbright ranges. The Recce squadron had retrained with Stuarts Mk V and VI. It was a nasty shock for the squadrons to find themselves back on to Cromwells and the Recce to be issued with very dilapidated Stuarts Mk III, a vastly inferior tank to the Mk VI. To boost each troop's firepower and to give them a chance against the deadly Tiger tank armed with an 88mm gun, there was one 17 pounder Sherman per troop. The Recce Squadron had only one tank per troop and were completed with Daimler scout cars and Bren carriers. However the Sabre squadrons were quite delighted to go back to the faster Cromwells which we

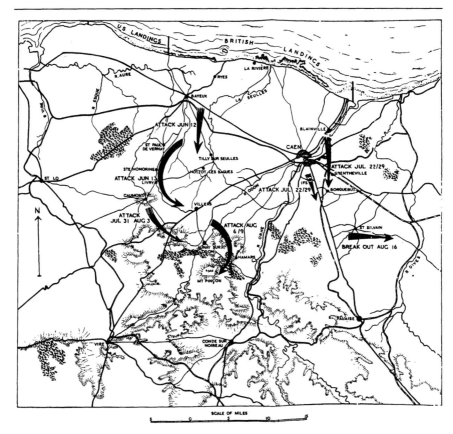

The battle centre lines of the Desert Rats in Normandy, June–August.

understood better. The Sherman had a nasty habit of catching fire and reports from the RTR indicated that they went up as soon as hit.

On the last day of July the division started to move south across 8 Corps centre line and became hopelessly tangled up with 50th Division who were also using the same centre line. Trooper Hewison, 1st RTR, noted:

Back at Ellon. Came right through Caen over Churchill bridge. Never seen such devastation in my existence – or otherwise. Practically whole city a mass of rubble – slivers of walls and lone chimneys and unbelievable standing parts of buildings. Must have been a grand place before. The hospital is only large building unscathed. Smiles everywhere for our battle scarred tanks and men!

Bill Bellamy with 8th Hussars wrote:

by mid morning on the 31st we were back on the tank tracks and headed south through La Belle Epine, St Honorine-de-Ducy, passing near the crossroads at Livry and the village of Briquessard where the Regiment had experienced so much bitter fighting earlier. We by-passed Caumont, ended our journey at La Lande, west of Aunay-sur-Odon. It had taken us twelve hours of stopping and starting to do the 12–15 miles.

The Queens Brigade moved south – 1/5th via Torteval, the outskirts of Caumont and towards Ecrigny. 1/7th Queens started at midnight and reached the Livry crossroads at dawn.

The 11th Hussars had just rejoined the division and Trooper Colin Thomson's troop spotted a small convoy of enemy vehicles – all 'soft', including a staff car, wireless truck and four transports at the bottom of a valley. The Cherry Pickers demolished the convoy. Part of the spoil was a quartermaster 'with two suitcases filled with new French bank notes. We had a big share out. Everyone received enough to ensure they did not need to draw any army pay before they were "demobbed".'

The newly joined Skins had already suffered casualties after two weeks in Normandy. Their padre John Newson, Lieutenant Rawlins and Trooper Bloom were drowned swimming off Arromanches, and two more casualties were caused by shelling the following day. They moved from Crauville, north-east of Caumont, to Cahagnes, which Jim Boardman in the Recce Squadron described as 'resembling scenes from the Somme during the First War: trees were stripped of all their leaves, cattle lay dead in the fields and

Skins held up by a minefield. POWs are on the left.

were already smelling of rotting flesh: the whole area was pitted with shell holes'. The Skins were attacked that night with fifty small anti-personnel bombs. 'We still had not fired a shot in anger and were not doing very well.'

On the first day of August 1/5th Queens were ordered from Cahagnes to pass through 43rd Wessex Division commanded by Major-General G.I. Thomas, nicknamed 'The Butcher' for his apparent disregard of casualties suffered. The Queens were to capture the high ground near Brevil from the new, fresh German 326th Infantry Division. Progress was slow in a thick morning mist through minefields covered by small arms fire. There were twenty casualties and three carriers knocked out, but prisoners were taken. At 0400 hrs on the same day, the Cherry Pickers started their recce from outside Caumont towards Aunay-sur-Odon via Robin and Jurques. On the way they confronted successfully four dummy cardboard tanks but met with mortar fire, AP shot, bombs and shelling. They captured an 88mm gun manned by a German, a Czech and three Poles!

Meanwhile the Skins were in action for the first time at the Quéry crossroads. Lieutenant Derek Philo, 'A' Squadron, noted: 'Ray Irwin commanding the leading tank was soon in trouble. A tank in the troop ran over a mine; flying shrapnel and stones struck Ray in the face and cut him badly.' Philo's tank crew spotted more mines in the centre of the road and they halted two feet short of them:

A knocked-out Cromwell: an 88mm shot has pierced the front glacis just below the identification number.

I ordered 'Driver reverse'. We then learned that the enemy gun was a very well positioned 88mm and firing at a devastating range of about a hundred yards. The shot entered the co-driver's hatch and went on through the driver's side killing Eddie Booth and Billy Hodgson instantly. The turret was jammed. We couldn't move, nor could we use the gun. We had no alternative to bailing out . . . The three turret crew almost fell out of the turret half blind and choking with the thick smoke. [Philo had thrown a smoke grenade to cover their exit.]

5th RTR meanwhile had reached Breuil and taken thirty-seven prisoners.

Lieutenant-General Bucknall, XXX Corps Commander, now demanded reasons for the apparently slow advance by the division and was told at 1520 hrs by the GOC Major-General Erskine: 'Mist not cleared until 1200. Heavy traffic on centre line. 43rd Div had not captured "Robin" objective [later taken by 1/5th Queens and 1st RTR] and finally 1/5th Queens were shelled at Cahagnes from Pt 238 and had to debus earlier than planned.'

By the evening of the 2nd 1st RTR had reached the Robin crossroads, 4 miles south of Caumont, despite thick mist, 88mms and numerous Bazooka teams.

Trooper Hewison's diary for 3rd August noted:

Coulvain. Last night we had the very bad luck to get Hobby Bullett killed. Bloody awful bad show. Tank went over mine, blew bottom in, these Cromwells no use on mines. Granny Wainwright's tank also got mined a few minutes later, no one killed though Durrant wounded. Then when they'd baled out a Jerry stonk came down and all except Hobby had shrapnel wounds. Ted Daniels got a packet in the stomach and legs. Durrant copped it again, poor bloke and Ginger Lincoln got a nasty head wound – hope he'll live. Rifle Brigade too had a few casualties. Had to stop up in the wood until midnight when the SPs [of Norfolk Yeomanry] came up to take over – glad too because Tigers were milling about somewhere in front.

1/5th Queens took twelve more casualties during the day clearing woods around Breuil. At La Rivière they took thirty-four prisoners and their CO, Lieutenant-Colonel Griffiths, was interviewed by the BBC Home Service. Bob Bellamy, 'B' Squadron 8th Hussars, wrote:

the battle was hard and progress slow . . . We were dispatched to assist the 1/7th Queens in their task of clearing some woods between Aunay and Villers-Bocage. It was a copy book operation advancing with the infantry . . . battling through the thick hedges. The danger was that we would fail to notice a German concealed in the undergrowth armed with a Panzer Faust.

The pressure to get results had started with Monty, who had told

Eisenhower: 'I have ordered Dempsey to throw all caution overboard *and to take any risks he likes and to accept any casualties* and to step on the gas for Vire.'

After two days of Bluecoat the Desert Rats were still 5 miles short of their first objective, Aunay-sur-Odon. On their right flank 11th Armoured had made great strides towards Vire. General Bucknall was now ordered by his master, General Dempsey, to, in effect, 'Get on or get out!'

On 3 August the unfortunate GOC, Major-General G.W.E.J. Erskine CB, DSO, who had commanded the division with much success since Tripoli – for eighteen months, a long time in the midst of war – was ordered to Army Command. He was replaced at 1500 hrs on 4 August by G.L. Verney, who had been brigadier of 6th Guards Tank Brigade. In the next week there were a hundred officers, 8th Army veterans, cross-posted either to other units in Normandy or back to the UK to training units. Trooper Clifford Smith, 11th Hussars, wrote: 'There was a feeling that some scapegoats had to be found for our lack of progress and hope that the new command would have better success in the direction we were taking.' Private Bill Hinde, 1/6th Queens, wrote: 'Brigadier Hinde got the chop – no relation to me, I don't think so, and General Erskine went too. It made no difference we were well down in the rifle companies.'

After a night attack 1/6th Queens had secured the high ground around Sauques, but on the morning of the 3rd – indeed throughout the day – 5th RTR were involved in a ferocious battle. Starting from Breuil their objectives were first Courcelles and then La Lande, about 2 miles west of Aunay. A heavy mist lay over the countryside as 'A' Squadron led and quickly took forty prisoners. When the ground mist lifted the entire regiment on a downward slope was in full view of the enemy. A Mk IV was dispatched, and when 'B' Squadron came through in heavy shelling the enemy counter-attacked strongly with Mk V and Mk IV tanks. 5th RTR lost six tanks during the day.

Norman Smith, 5th RTR, wrote:

We and another squadron [B and A] were now close to being annihilated. We had advanced well to the east of Aunay and were getting the worst of a tank battle with enemy Tigers and Panthers. In addition we were being heavily shelled by German artillery. By the time a mist began to come down at dusk we had lost six tanks and their crews for the price of one Panther knocked out. As light began to fade the German infantry crept up on us and knocked out more of our tanks with Panzerfaust (bazookas).

A defensive laager was handicapped by the trees around. Major Thomson, Squadron CO of 'B' was accidentally shot and badly wounded by one of his own sergeant tank commanders, so Dennis Cockbaine, the 2 i/c, ordered a general break-out when the two squadrons were reduced to twelve tanks out of the original thirty-two: 'each crew for itself' order was given. In the wild dangerous charge back another three tanks were lost. 'Right,' Norman, then nineteen years old, thought, 'if I just live to be twenty-five that will be great. I'll have had my share.' Many crews were killed or captured, thirty-nine casualties altogether that day, but one Panther was knocked out and no fewer than eleven Mk IVs knocked out or damaged.

During that day (still the 3rd) 1/6th Queens were savagely counter-attacked south of Aunay by Wehrmacht of 326th Division, supported by SPs and Nebelwerfers. The fighting went on all day and 1/6th Queens took 150 casualties including six officers, and 1/7th Queens took thirty-four casualties from accurate mortar fire. The Norfolk Yeomanry lost three of their A/Tank guns and suffered thirty-four casualties. Altogether on that black day the division sustained over 200 casualties in the fighting around Aunay, a flattened town of rubble.

On his arrival General Verney wrote:

> The 1st and 5th Tanks were no longer having a go and the Brigade Commander [Hinde] was dead tired. The Inniskillings on the other hand were a fresh regiment whose dash and enterprise set an example to others.
>
> The Rifle Brigade was in a bad way. In the Goodwood battle in July they had a very bad time and 131 Infantry Bd had had a lot of losses and their state was the worst of all.

During General Verney's first week in command there were over 120 cases of desertion in the division, indicative of poor morale caused by the division's heavy losses in battle.

For three days the Queens Brigade kept up the painful pressure around Aunay, losing men almost every hour. 8th Hussars had relieved 5th RTR east of Aunay on the 4th, but progress was slow against the lethal combination of minefields protected by A/Tank guns and Bazooka men. The Cherry Pickers met 69th Brigade of 50th Division south of Villers-Bocage, and the main armour was directed to La Poste, a couple of miles south-west of Villers-Bocage. The plan was to move south and then outflank ruined Aunay to the east, which was entered the following morning by 50th Division. The CO of the Norfolk Yeomanry A/Tank regiment, Lieutenant-Colonel W.S. Stewart, was killed on a mine and was replaced by Lieutenant-Colonel J. Goring.

1st RTR and the Skins were able to reach Bonnemaison, south-east of Aunay, as Sergeant Pat Whitmore of the Skins wrote:

> In one day we covered the countryside between Villers and Aunay. We harboured the night on the ridge at Hamars much exposed to German fire. The early dawn [of the 6th] broke into a beautiful day; Mont Pinçon to our right rising out of the early mist; in front a valley calm, untouched by the battle. The gunfire had ceased. It soon began again.

Skins dig in south of Caen.

All day we remained on the ridge as the Wessex Division was working its way up Mont Pinçon after an air-raid had reduced Aunay to rubble. A solitary church spire stood out to mark the town centre. Armoured bulldozers cleared a path through the rubble.

Private Bill Hinde of the Queens wrote:

Our objective was Mount Pinçon down the road to Villers-Bocage . . . 'Mount', it looked like a hill of Kent to us. 50 Div and 43 Div were going in with us. In one area the SS were stripped to the waist and shouting and screaming like maniacs but were stopped by Vickers machine-guns of the Northumberland Fusiliers. The Canadians had armoured turret-less tanks for their infantry [Kangaroos] to travel into action. A pity we did not have something like that. It would have saved a lot of lives.

After a massive tank, artillery and mortar assault Trooper Albert Mitchell, Norfolk Yeomanry, near Mount Pinçon saw 'a small tubby German officer in uniform and peaked cap, wearing red cross armband and a leather belt, holster and pistol come out of a nearby hedge. I grabbed my rifle, beckoned him to put his hands up and come forward. He was soon taken back [to the POW cages].'

La Valleé stood on the vital crossroads of the Aunay–Caen, Villers-Bocage–Condé roads. Here on the morning of the 6th 1/5th Queens started to move up through the pine and chestnut woods to the plateau of the 1,100 ft

Aunay-sur-Odon from the south.

Mont Pinçon feature. 1/7th Queens were caught by heavy mortar fire near La Valleé and many of their carriers were destroyed and casualties sustained.

The Cherry Pickers had reached the bridge over the Odon, the entrance to Aunay from the west, at 1430 hrs, and reported the town full of dead Germans and cattle, mines and booby traps everywhere. 1st RTR had a relatively peaceful day and Trooper Hewison's diary noted:

> Got a prisoner yesterday. He was 42, an Austrian from Vienna, married with 2 children (photo of younger girl really beautiful). Glad to get out of the war. He had umpteen small arms wounds in thighs. A decent chap – made me think really hard – this war's so bloody futile. There's ordinary blokes on each side with no desire to kill each other, yet here we are.

On the night of the 6th/7th a textbook attack by the 1/7th Queens took place, to clear the wooded areas 2,000 yards south of La Valleé towards Les Trois Maries on the plateau beyond the thick woods screening Mont Pinçon. It was clear from air photographs that the enemy would continue to fight bitterly to retain this vital hilltop, with forty guns concentrated, including 88s and 75mm SPs. A trial barrage by the FOOs of 3rd RHA (Major P. Hilton and Captain Stokes) was fired at 0230 hrs for the Queens to see where it landed. Then at 0300 hrs, to the battle cry of 'Wakey, Wakey', the Queens advanced under the box barrages fired by 3rd and 5th RHA, and all three stages of the advance went according to plan. Lieutenant-Colonel Griffiths, CO of 1/7th Queens, was pleased to record 142 prisoners taken, three 88s and a 75mm SP captured or knocked out.

The divisional sappers did a fine job clearing minefields under fire and the Norfolk Yeomanry destroyed several houses used as strongpoints. At 0700 hrs the predictable counter-attack came in and was only driven off by DFs, fired by 3rd and 5th RHA. 'Some incredibly accurate shooting' was reported. 1/7th Queens suffered twenty-seven casualties in the main attack and another sixteen during the counter-attack, and 1/5th Queens in their supporting attack towards the high ground south-west of La Valleé, suffered twenty. While this attack was in progress, a few tanks of 13/18th Hussars with the Wessex Division found a farm track up the side of Mont Pinçon and, under cover of a smokescreen, reached the top. Despite losses on the way they held their ground. It was not until the 9th that the entire ridge between Aunay and La Valleé was completely cleared and 1/7th Queens and 1st RTR stayed on their wooded hillside until they were withdrawn on the 10th.

> These 18 hour days with a guard every night plays havoc with the old energy – but somehow we seem to keep going [wrote Trooper Hewison]. The days seem an eternity cooped up in the turret all day with brief dives out for some cold corned beef and a drain off now and again. Sergeant Major got shrapnel in his foot yesterday. Mr Prouse wounded a day ago when tank he was guiding went over a mine. We've only got about 10 tanks in the squadron now so we'll have to draw out soon. Ten days in the line without a rest is no joke!

His sentiments were shared by the Cherry Pickers. Lieutenant R.N.B. Brett-Smith of 'C' Squadron noted: 'I never wish to see again this plain of Caen with its harvest ungathered, villages smashed beyond recognition, choking dust for miles and miles and a smell of general destruction beyond belief.'

3rd and 5th RHA and the Skins stayed on in action supporting 43rd Division, while the rest of the division concentrated and rested round Aunay.

The Skins fought a brisk action on 12 August supporting 5th Wiltshires of 43rd Wessex to capture the high ground at Le Jardin-la-Vardière, near Mont Pinçon. Sergeant Bob Price was now a troop sergeant in 'C' Squadron:

> Lieutenant Peter Martel was my troop leader. We were very tired after two weeks of continuous fighting and movement, long days and short nights affecting most of us. Added to the tiredness was the extreme and continuous stress . . . During the days fighting we had lost the Firefly in the troop. The enemy also lost three tanks, a Mk IV and two Panthers plus two 50mm guns which were credited to the squadron. The shooting was excellent and many German infantry were killed. Corporal Carr's tank was brewed up, and Trooper Verrell and Capt Blundell-Brown wounded.

A Panther destroyed by the Skins at Carpliquet is examined by 'Tadpole' Bridgewater (left) and Guy Glover.

Major J.M.D. Ward-Harrison was awarded the DSO for the action.

For a few days, until the 14th, mobile bath units appeared and also new uniforms for every man. Also a rest camp by the sea and Jerboa club opened in Aunay, cinemas, Ensa shows and 'Variety Calls' with George Formby cheered up, to some extent, the very bruised and weary division. Brigadier G. Webb, the chief admin. officer and an old desert hand, organized these relaxations. A Naafi bar arrived with writing/reading rooms, and boxing and football matches were organized. During these few days of rest Bill Bellamy, 8th Hussars, visited Bayeux from Briquessard, sent a fruity Camembert cheese home to his mother (it matured nicely en route), washed his clothes in neat petrol, hung them to dry in the sun and came out in a terrible rash later. General Horrocks visited: 'He came over to us as a very warm man, exuding confidence and determination but one who cared for the welfare and safety of his troops. It was the Feast of the Assumption, the 15th of August, and I attended Mass with as many Catholics as I could muster, in a cornfield.'

After his 'blighty' in England, Gordon Johnson rejoined 'C' Squadron 5th RTR as gunner in the Cromwell of the 2 i/c, Captain B.L. Butler. The wireless operator had brought out from England a kitten called 'Smokey'. 'It had been all through Normandy, didn't mind enemy shellfire or our own gun. It deserted later in Holland (sensible cat),' remembers Gordon.

Kenneth Clayton was TMSO (Technical Maintenance Officer Signals) for the division. During Bluecoat *all* the key wireless links (Corps, CRA, both brigades), using Canadian 9 sets, began to give trouble by 'speech

Skins form up for attack near Mt Pinçon.

clipping' by several seconds after being changed from 'send' to 'receive'. The sets were brand new and Kenneth had to deal with the problem. Lieutenant Colonel Tom Lusty (ADOS) pulled out all the stops to get *new* replacement rotary transformers with tighter bearings. Kenneth reported: 'Sods Law worked overtime to ensure that the ACVs (Armoured Command Vehicles) were moving as fast as possible on the narrowest lanes with German pot shots obstructing my tradesmen and myself making changes to the rotary transformers.'

Dramatic changes had now taken place. Lieutenant-General Brian Horrocks (Jorrocks), a very popular, capable Corps Commander, newly recovered from severe wounds received in North Africa, now took over command from Lieutenant-General Bucknall as GOC XXX Corps. Brigadier 'Looney' Hinde, the brave, eccentric leader of the Armoured Brigade, was replaced by Brigadier H. Mackeson from 9th Armoured Division on 10 August, and the CRA, Brigadier R. Mews, was replaced by Brigadier T. Lyon-Smith, also from 9th Armoured. On the 9th the CO of 1/5th Queens, Lieutenant-Colonel J.B. Ashworth, was wounded and replaced by Lieutenant-Colonel I.H. Freeland.

Monty's order about pushing on *regardless of casualties* during Bluecoat had certainly been heeded! During the period 1–9 August the division suffered 523 casualties, with altogether 1,000 since the end of Goodwood. 1/6th Queens rifle companies now totalled 8, 15, 40 and 55 all ranks instead of their usual 450 strength. Reinforcements soon arrived from 59th Infantry Division, which had to be broken up. But the Queens still remained under strength.

CHAPTER TEN

Break-out – 'Push On and Don't Bugger About'

General Bradley and the air forces contained and then drove back a dangerous German counter-attack, consisting of four divisions and 250 tanks, on Mortain and Domfront aimed at Avranches. Hitler replaced von Kluge with Field Marshal Walter Model, who was summoned hastily from the Russian front. On 10 August Hitler gave up his plan to hold Normandy and gave the order to 'Disengage'. On 13 August the retreat started and the remains of Panzer Lehr – 1st, 2nd, 9th and 12th Panzer – started to pull back and force their way through the gap between Falaise and Argentan.

The iron pressure intensified on the German 7th Army with Panzer Group Eberbach and Panzer Group West partly trapped inside the ring. American, British, Canadian, Polish and French divisions were pushing and prodding, backed by the full fury of war. Artillery barrages, tank and infantry attacks and, above all, non-stop RAF and USAAF bombing day and night took a frightful toll. Patton had disappeared into Brittany in a cloud of smoke, logging up a huge mileage and forcing German troops in his way to retreat and hold the ports of St Malo and Brest.

After a few days of rest post-Bluecoat, the Desert Rats, now under command of General Crocker's I Corps, and with new divisional management, set off from May-sur-Orne on 14 August for the final break-out. The centre line of some 65 miles ran due east to St Pierre-sur-Dives, 10 miles to Livarot, 11 miles north-east to Lisieux, and 25 miles north-east to Montfort on the Seine. Each of four rivers would be defended, although in the event the dashing Cherry Pickers 'found' three crossings out of four – of the Vie, Touques, Orbec and Risle. The going was now better, as the roads were straighter, the fields larger, there were fewer woods, and contours, apart from river valleys, were less extreme. The opposition was formed from the remnants of 12th SS and 21st Panzer Divisions. Their technique was to fight tough little rearguard actions with a few SPs, mortars, and minefields planted everywhere to delay progress, particularly around the frequent road blocks. Occasional tanks and 88mms would exact their toll, but usually the small battle groups would conduct a classic defence and, like thieves, vanish in the night a few miles further east to another prepared defensive line. All the bridges were blown and sappers with scissor bridges had plenty of opportunity to show their skills.

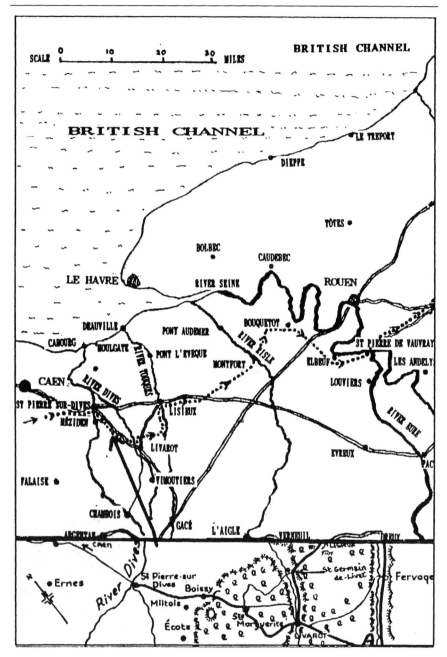

The Breakout from Normandy to the River Seine.

By 16 August the division was in place and the Cherry Pickers led the Queens Brigade through St Pierre-sur-Dives, just recently taken by 51st Highland Division.

Colin Thomson, 11th Hussars, recalls:

On August 16 we moved to Egbed-Cremesnil. The dust was so thick it was impossible to see more than a few yards. We moved over the bridge at St Pierre-sur-Dives to work up the line of the river. The village was full of burnt-out vehicles. I learned later that some of our Lancasters bombed a mixture of 51st Highland Division and the Polish Division by mistake.

The historian of the Cherry Pickers noted:

A familiar pattern to be repeated now time and time again. First a fairly rapid drive in pursuit of a retreating enemy interrupted by mines and road blocks lightly held. Then a difficult and hazardous reconnaissance to the bank of the next river in search of a bridge that might still be intact. After that a day or so of probing the rearguard defences until a broken bridge had been made passable or even an unbroken one discovered in some obscure corner: another day of waiting as the Division expanded the bridgehead after the crossings – then the process repeated. *The probable sacrifice of the leading armoured car produced the vital information for division and corps.*

The Queens Brigade initially had concentrated at the villages of Poussy-la-Campagne and St Silvaine, 10 miles south-east of Caen. About sixty reinforcements had joined 1/5th and 1/7th Queens and on 17 August 1/6th had reached Bassy and 1/7th Miltois, where prisoners were taken from 272nd Division.

On the next day 1/7th in Bois de Queunie and 1/6th in Ste Marguerite-des-Loges, were strafed by the RAF *and* USAAF. The Skins, having started at Cauvcourt, were attacked in St Pierre-sur-Dives by three Spitfires and German bombers. The RAF strafed 8th Hussars and the Norfolk Yeomanry, causing twenty casualties, despite the white star of Bethlehem on all tanks and halftracks and the firing of yellow smoke canisters, which was distinctly unpopular. Bill Bellamy's 'C' Squadron had had two Cromwells knocked out by an 88mm and his close friend, Mike Young, was killed. A nasty massacre of a local farmer's family by 12th SS had just occurred near Ste Marguerite-de-Viette. 'It did nothing to make us feel charitable towards German troops.' Trooper Hewison, 1st RTR, was now a little happier. 'People really glad to see us, waving and smiling and throwing stuff on the tank.' It was the beginning of the Liberation, except that many towns and villages had been flattened and the population dispersed.

Talking of Liberation, Bill Bellamy wrote:

We were given priority as the Regiment with C Sqn up was leading the advance after St Pierre-sur-Dives towards Livarot. We had some fun at

St Pierre itself as the 51st Highland Division were there and we always got on well together. There was a great deal of leg pulling if the tanks were held up for a minute. Once when we stopped a tiny little Jock appeared, bent under the weight of his Company wireless set, but in addition, slung across his back was a huge goose. When Goldsworth offered to relieve him of that problem he shouted back 'These F——g French hens were half the size of a good Scottish one and he'd manage.'

Brett-Smith, with the Cherry Pickers, wrote in his diary at the time:

Jory, St Pierre-sur-Dives and the Poles gabbling unintelligibly on our frequencies but fighting like lions, then Livarot (later Lisieux, Fervacques and up to the River Risle near the Forêt de Montfort). For the first time we were cracking on *and not coming back* and it was exhilarating. The guns were firing nineteen to the dozen, found it hard to keep up, let alone the Echelons. Livarot had a timely Calvados brewery and with a quiet pull of the bottle we rushed off to chase the enemy back across the Seine. He did not need much chasing. Now and again the Luftwaffe showed itself but was swamped by our excellent air support. In fact one was, as like as not, strafed by Thunderbolts and not Focke-Wulfs.

At Jory the Cherry Pickers had breakfast with the HQ of the Polish Armoured Division but lost three armoured cars clearing the town. On the 18th they captured a German lorry full of typewriters and most days their own 'guns' fired 200 rounds per day. The Pickers were highly experienced in clearing mines on *their* centre lines along the valley villages of Boissey, Mittois and Ecots. Lieutenant Chapman, aided by the Maquis/FFI, found a small bridge over the River Vie and the 8th Hussars and 1/5th Queens entered Livarot, despite 88mms and snipers. The Rifle Brigade followed in and found the little town – amazingly – undamaged. They encountered flags, flowers, wine and welcome from the FFI, and freed some Allied airmen. By 1500 hrs the 1/6th Queens had also entered the town, where a petrol-less Panther and a Tiger with damaged tracks were found.

Lieutenant Derrick Watson, 1/5th Queens, was also more optimistic: 'The infantry fighting in the "bocage" where we suffered heavy casualties from snipers, mortar fire, shellfire etc and where the Divisional Cromwell tanks were outgunned and out-armoured on ground quite unsuitable for open warfare – was about to finish.'

Trooper Colin Thomson related a bizarre incident in Livarot 'where one of our sergeants was attacked by a horde of drunken SS with swords! The platoon of Queens with us rebuffed the assault after a stiff fight!' They were twelve drugged Hitler Jugend with bayonets.

That night the enemy withdrew but the three days and the 10 mile advance had cost the division 140 casualties, many it must be admitted to Spitfires. On the 19th the town was secured despite increased 88mm

By mid-August nearly every town in Normandy was a heap of rubble.

airburst fire for much of the day. 1/7th Queens had an unhappy meeting with three Tiger tanks and their escorts, and a dozen of their men were captured in the battle. 11th Hussars to the south and east distinguished themselves, knocked out a Panther and destroyed many A/Tank guns with their little 2-pounder guns. In a violent storm they discovered at Fervaques, 7 miles to the east, an intact bridge over the River Touques, and despite mortars, shelling and Spandaus prevented the enemy 272nd Division destroying the bridge – a good effort.

Trooper Hewison with 1st RTR mentioned in his diary on 20 August:

We were 5 miles west of Livarot; air raid on A2 Echelon pretty bad, 7 trucks went up with ammo, 3 men injured inc Bill Wilson and Ray Povey. Last night *we* had the bleeding things – HE, antipersonnel and incendiary bombs all around us. Quite a few of RHQ injured and the Doc was killed. Lt Col Gibbons left us the other day – new CO [Lieutenant Colonel P.R.C. Hobart] seems alright – son [nephew] of a general [Hobo of 79 'Funnies' Div fame]. Haven't been in action with him yet. With 5 RTR leading until teatime (on the 20th) then A Sqn followed by B Sqn into Livarot – best welcome yet, cheering and waving. Post office girls – très jolis – in 1st storey windows throwing flowers down on us. Older women were weeping and throwing kisses. On Monday had quite a good morning, brewing an armoured car, a truck and a staff car.

1st RB and 5th RTR crossed the vital bridge at Fervaques and captured the cook's lorry belonging to the German garrison, which meant a hot breakfast. The RB had ensconced themselves in the local chateau, which had 5 ft walls, and they were noisily counter-attacked on the night of the 20th. RHA DF targets and their own Brownings eventually beat off the grenadiers from 21st PZ Division (a much travelled formation who had fought from Agheila, Tobruck and Alamein), and they took fifty prisoners.

'We were point tank, apart from some sharpish shelling we got right in to Fervaques without mishap,' wrote Norman Smith, 'B' Squadron 5th RTR. 'The German armour had withdrawn as we came in. My tank was engulfed by dozens of men and women climbing onto the tank. As main gunner, my line of sight was interrupted by delirious French men and women climbing on and off.' After he and Bert Diwell had finished off the tank commander's whisky (he had gone back to squadron for a briefing), a bottle of pale golden liquid Calvados was their undoing. 'I came to under a blanket in a field by the side of the tank with a headache that extended down to my boots.' Enemy opposition intensified around Fervaques particularly to the east and south-east, with road blocks, Bazooka teams and Spandaus, so the main advance went due north towards Lisieux.

During the 21st two determined counter-attacks were made on the Queens, holding Livarot. One came in from the west and the other from the east, but 1/5th Queens not only beat them off with their mortars with support from RHA, but took seventy prisoners out of the division's bag of 200 for the day. Meanwhile the sappers had replaced two blown bridges in and near Livarot, and the advance continued with 5th RTR leading.

When Rex Wingfield joined the 1/6th Queens he was told that 'in the battle for Livarot, "D" Company was over-run by the SS of Langemarck Division made up of renegade French, Belgians and Dutchmen. When we counter-attacked the SS were smashing in the heads of the wounded and prisoners with pick-axes. "D" has gone. It has never been replaced.'

Just 2 miles south of the major objective of Lisieux, north-east on the D579 road, Trooper Hewison's diary recounts:

At St Martin-de-Lieu we had a sticky time clearing the houses, not many RBs around for that job & Jerry had a bazooka gang which got Jerry German's tank, killing Corporal Mayhery, and also Sgt Bernet's 'bus' although no one was hurt. Late at night Queens and RBs supported us in clearing the houses. No. 5 Troop had brewed a German truck with HE through the windscreen. Poor blighter inside absolutely torn up. I hadn't the guts to loot the bodies – too gruesome, but Ted Watkins & Vick hadn't any scruples & got quite a haul – 1,300 francs, a gold watch, camera and binoculars, another watch and odd Ackers and loot the Huns had taken. We buried them by the roadside & stuck their paybooks on the crosses.

Liberation: Skins on the way to Lisieux.

Opposition from 12th SS Panzer Division had hardened just south of Lisieux where six Tigers were reported, as well as back down the centre line at Livarot. Sergeant Pat Whitmore with the Skins recce squadron recalled:

> We turned north towards Lisieux from Livarot to find that a screen of German troops had remained to cover the withdrawal of their divisions remaining on the coast, whose only escape was towards Rouen. Somewhere between Livarot and Lisieux we were halted, established ourselves near a crossroads in an orchard. In the silence of the (next) morning I heard 'M'sieu Tommy?' Out of a farm building came a young man. Once he established we were British, calvados was produced. Glasses were fetched and we drank to la France, de Gaulle, Churchill and the Allies . . . fortified with information of enemy gun positions and more calvados we advanced. It was a wild and deadly fire that the enemy encountered a mile or so down the road!

Bill Bellamy's 8th Hussar squadron was sent out on the 21st to patrol the main road north to Lisieux, exposed and on high ground. His troop was established with the Queens and a Gunner OP from 5th RHA in the area of St Germain-de-Livet:

> We sat in a hedgerow looking out over Lisieux some three miles away, I could see the sunlight shining on the Basilica of Ste Teresa. Built of a yellowish sandstone it dominated the town. Below it I could see dust and smoke from shells raining down into Lisieux itself. I felt a sense of

shame participating in the destruction of a town which had housed so revered a saint as Ste Teresa.

Lisieux, a town of 25,000 inhabitants, lies in the narrow valley of the Touques, overlooked by wooded hills. The Cherry Pickers had reconnoitred all the roads entering the town from the south-east and east that were blocked by Spandau and Bazooka teams. The bridge across the River Orne was, of course, blown. So 1/6th Queens tried to attack from the eastern side to cut off the enemy retreat, while 1/5th Queens and 1st RTR attacked the south-east suburbs. By 1730 hrs on 22 August all three Queens regiments were in place in the outskirts. Derrick Watson, 1/5th Queens, remembers:

> We prepared for an attack on Lisieux, the battalion now commanded by that splendid man Jock Nangle, now promoted to Lt Col. We had the support of the Inniskilling Dragoons fresh out from England and full of the traditional dash of the cavalry. The Cromwells led the way through the streets of the town firing their Besas into the houses as they went. D Coy commanded by Major Pat Henderson followed in single file on either side of the street.

Derrick, as Intelligence Officer, was carrying an armful of battalion road signs to indicate the route for the troops following him. Then the leading Cromwell was brewed up and the company commander severely wounded by a mortar bomb in the Rue d'Alençon. Orders came to withdraw from the town. At the exits were road blocks covered by Panzerfausts and Spandaus, mortars and shell fire, which caused over twenty casualties. So the tanks and Queens withdrew south for 2 miles to St Martin-de-la-Lieue to allow a medium artillery and RHA stonk on the town. This did immense damage and the next day, the 23rd, the attack resumed with the great assistance of 51st Highland moving in from the west side. 1st RTR found a way in near the great basilica on the Orbec road (D519) as Trooper Hewison noted:

> Our squadron was leading again in the push through Lisieux – it got pretty sticky inside. Jerry, the bastard, is using the cathedral as an OP & mortar position and the Queens had a pretty rough time of it. We cleared most of the town but two pockets below and above the cathedral. Had to withdraw – we were quite happy but infantry didn't care much for the sniping and mortar fire. Poor Sgt Shellcock was sniped in back of head – died almost instantly. Greensburg & Sam McCready injured through mortars in St Martin but aren't too bad.

The St Jacques area was taken despite Tigers and Panthers of 1st SS Division. The Queens had thirty-eight casualties, including three officers, in the two days of fighting. Their second attack from Pt 132 on the high ground east of the town yielded twenty-one prisoners. The Highlanders also suffered badly and Derrick Watson tried to rescue some of the wounded Jocks. Later he was awarded the Croix de Guerre for helping liberate Lisieux.

Sergeant 'Snatch' Boardman, with the Skins, was also there:

> As we drove into Lisieux the road was packed with infantrymen waiting to move forward. The 51st Highlanders were having to fight house to house, street by street and had to capture the Basilica which dominated the area . . . As we approached the forward position the constant stream of stretcher-bearing Jeeps with badly injured troops from both sides was indication of the resistance being encountered. As our troop of three vehicles came up to the Queens infantry, their young officer indicated the enemy positions. The platoon was in a single file and keeping close against a wall. I cannot remember ever feeling more pity for them than I did on that occasion. As the Bren crew went forward they became instant casualties. The Piat crew took up the leading position. The platoon was soon either dead or wounded.

There were 2,000 civilians sheltering in the vaults of the basilica. 'Snatch' was ordered by the troop leader, Jack Bissil, to get a Bren gun and try to find a way up to the top of the dome. 'Snatch' leading, they climbed the 262 (or was it 268) steps to the top and he saw a party of Germans beneath him running: 'I fired magazine after magazine at them.' Two were killed and nine surrendered. Despite the predictable counter-attack led by a Feldwebel and seventeen men, the town was virtually cleared by 1600 hrs. The Bazooka teams and A/Tank guns had been liquidated, although snipers remained in the cathedral (apparently 'Snatch' did not find them all!). It was now nasty and cold with heavy rain falling. The Skins shared their hot tea from Thermos flasks with the Queens infantry, 'who, as usual, were worse off for they had with them only one blanket apiece and their meal had not yet come up to them when darkness fell'. The enemy survivors, as usual, withdrew skilfully and stealthily during the night.

It was still pouring down on the morrow, the 24th, as the Queens concentrated 3 miles east of Lisieux where unfortunately a 'friendly' tank went up on a mine and wounded three officers of the 1/6th Queens. The Cherry Pickers drove almost unimpeded for over 20 miles – the first swan of the campaign. The Skins got a very enthusiastic welcome in Thiberville, 10 miles east on the N13. This was their first genuine French liberation – tricolours waving, wine, cider, fruit. On the way, after meeting some Canadians, Sergeant Reg Worman with the Skins recce troop was sitting low in the Ferret scout car moving at 10 mph. Approaching was a column of vehicles. The leading vehicle passed and the officer, who was obviously a German, gave Captain Robert Crockett, the recce squadron leader, a wave as he passed. Robert responded by saluting. Reg noticed there was no escort with the convoy and yelled to Robert over the intercom: 'They are bloody Germans – Sir.'

'What did you say, Worman?' asked Robert as the second vehicle passed.

'They are bloody Germans,' repeated Reg. Eventually a message was relayed back: 'Enemy column has just passed me and is heading down the road towards you.' Later eight enemy, two motorcycle combinations and a Volkswagen car were in the bag. Robert Crockett's favourite command was 'Just push on and don't bugger about', which seemed to fit most situations!

The report lines running north–south were given the radio code names of Whisky, Rum, Brandy and Gin. 'Our vehicles now looked', according to John Pilborough of the Skins, 'like the pulpit at harvest festival covered in flung flowers and fruit. Our morale soared to new heights.' Even Trooper Hewison cheered up; 'The CO was extremely pleased with the squadron's work yesterday in Lisieux and the lads say they wouldn't be surprised if the major gets the MC for the squadron. He is improving no end.'

By the afternoon St Georges-du-Vièvre, 24 miles from Lisieux, had been reached by the Skins, where Maquis gave them valuable advice. 'Snatch' Boardman in Lieurey was hugged and kissed – by men and women – and shook everybody's hand several times.

The next day the Queens followed up the 22nd Armoured Brigade towards Pont Authou on the River Risle, famous for its trout, according to General Verney. 1/5th remained at Thiberville with 1/7th Queens at Les Pillards and 1/6th Queens near St Georges-du-Vièvre. 11th Hussars met

Skins take an aperitif! Left to right: James Usher, John Ward-Harrison, Sergeant Smith.

four Mk IV tanks south of St Georges, but near the main objective of Montfort, 5 miles north, were a Tiger, 88mm and two 75mm guns. 'C Sqn 1 RTR suddenly came up against enemy infantry supported by Panzers,' wrote Trooper Hewison. 'Pretty much touch and go for a while when Bill Seward got the Panther and the M-10 (from our Norfolk Yeomanry) got the Tiger and then Jerry beat it.' And later:

> Skins in lead again until they meet opposition! Then it'll be our job. Plenty loot in one house – Jerry is slipping. Ted as usual got the best. I contented myself with a small silk table cloth which I'm using as a scarf – quite natty! Also a few knick-knacks useful on the tank – we are like a haberdashers shop now. It's queer the loot question. We are normal law-abiding citizens of the Kingdom as soldiers always have been. When an army sweats blood and guts to win a town or ground, it presumes that that is their prize – quite forgiveable really! If we who have lost men and sweated pints to get there don't pick up a thing or two, the base-wallahs will. A poor excuse, I know.

A shaky-looking wooden bridge was found a mile or so north of Pont Authou, the RAF having bombed the main bridges to stop German vehicles crossing. Sappers quickly built new bridges at Montfort and Pont Authou and the division was well across the River Risle during the 26th. The Queens had a peaceful day's advance through Montfort and the Forêt du Montfort. The Skins had several minor actions at Bonneville-Aptot where they lost carriers on mines, and near Bourneville several tanks to 88mms. 1/7th Queens moved on Bourneville and then east to Rocot. 1/5th Queens celebrated the arrival of their new CO Lieutenant-Colonel I.H. Freeland from the Royal Norfolks, who brought with him from 59th Division three officers and eighty-five ORs, by taking seventy prisoners, and also a heavy mortar platoon. There were many road blocks, often booby-trapped, and 'Holdfast', radio code name for the sappers, was in frequent demand.

Each day there were a dozen sharp little actions costing casualties. As 1st RTR moved in column east of Montfort, 'C' Squadron led up hairpin bends on the very steep salient. Trooper Hewison reported:

> Just at the top we were warned [by 11th Hussars] about an anti-tank gun and Recce troop went forward, first tank was brewed. We then put out 7 troop and ourselves and HQ on the left of the road to stonk positions whilst 5 and 8 troops cut around to the right. They had RBs with them and ran slap-bang into trouble. 5 Tp had three 'brews' – Mr Ambridge's 'bus', Sgt Bennett's and Sgt Skennet's. No one hurt though Fred Oakes and Wedger Williams had slight burns. But Vick got a packet in the head – very bad though he wasn't killed . . . But the people of Routot (2 miles west of the Seine) went pretty mad when we arrived. One girl had a camera and took umpteen photos of us – a day

to remember for them. We are due to move off to doodle-bug country. As the General said 'heedless of casualties or fatigue!' Quite like the sound of that!

'A' Squadron of the Skins near Bourneville 'put a few well placed rounds of HE into the woods and were rewarded when a further 150 Germans gave themselves up, smiling as though it were the end of a game', were 'Snatch' Boardman's comments.

It was indeed the end of a deadly game. The Seine had been reached. The Canadians were in Bernay, 9 miles south-west, and 49th Division had taken Pont Audemer, 5 miles north. The division handed over to 49th and 53rd Divisions on the 28th, having taken 980 prisoners in the ten day Breakout. On 29 August the Desert Rats became part of 12th Corps under Lieutenant-General Neil Ritchie, having had two days rest in the Montfort area. General Dempsey now offered to replace the battered Queens Brigade (each battalion on average was 10 officers and 200 men *short* of establishment) with a brigade from 59th Division that was in the process of being broken up. General Verney did not accept the offer, preferring to keep his mixture of old sweats and some newcomers:

I preferred to retain the officers and men who, though possibly few in numbers, had been so long in the Division and were so familiar with their armoured and other supporting arms, rather than to try to absorb an entirely new formation unaccustomed to the workings and organization of an Armoured Division only eight hours, probably, before what was expected to be the decisive and final operation of the campaign.

John Evans, who as 2 i/c with the South Staffordshires had won a fine DSO on 12 August at the St Benin ridge in Normandy, was posted two weeks later on the break-up of 59th Division. His diary read: 'Posted with Geoff Ball, Coy HQ and one platoon to 1/5 Queens Royal Regiment. My feelings were one of sadness having just concluded the battle for which I was awarded the DSO but delighted and excited to be joining the Desert Rats with their experience and reputation.'

It had been a tough eleven days of non-stop pursuit of highly skilful and determined troops intent on buying time for the men escaping from the terrible cauldron and killing grounds of the Falaise–Argentan pocket. The division was perhaps fortunate not to have taken part in the savage closing of the gap, when the Canadians and Poles took a terrible beating.

The Inniskillings spent three days around the Château de Groveron where John Pilborough recalled: 'In a short month we had come a long way from being green troops. With the more free and easy ways of the front line we had taken to coloured mufflers and strange dress. We knew our job better.' Additional firepower was needed for the Recce Squadron so

Corporal Strickland's carrier now mounted no less than *three* Brownings plus a Bren gun!

Perhaps 65,000 men and 115 tanks of the original fourteen infantry and ten Panzer divisions who had been fighting the savage war of attrition in Normandy for nearly three months, had escaped – an astonishing victory for Ike and Monty. Half a dozen weary, battered, but determined, battle groups of Germans had escaped across the Seine. By 25 August General Le Clerc's French division was back in Paris, and by the 30th Patton's Shermans were in Sedan and Verdun. They had had a marvellous Swan: now it was time for the Desert Rats' Great Swan.

The Great Swan – 'Cracking Around'

It seemed quite unbelievable that the stench and brutality of the bocage, the death traps of the little winding country lanes, and the river valleys were now to be left behind. The daunting prospect of the invasion of Das Reich still, however, seemed to be far in the future. The prospect of cantering briskly through northern France, Belgium and Holland, with perhaps diminished resistance, fewer 88mms, fewer Nebelwerfers and probably very few tanks – was almost appealing. The immediate plum targets were Brussels, Antwerp and Ghent, and it was the latter that was to be given to the Desert Rats (and 12th Corps under Lieutenant-General Ritchie), as their first main objective. 30 Corps with 11th and Guards Armoured Divisions were on the right flank with the glamorous objectives of Antwerp and Brussels via Amiens and Arras. On the left flank were the First Canadian Army, with the twin targets of channel port clearance and the capture of as many flying bomb sites as possible.

For the long haul ahead armour was to lead. Each tank would carry 40 gallons of petrol in cans tied on to the engine covers. Major G.S. Stevens, OC 67th Company RASC, was in charge of petrol supply. A round trip of 160 miles to the beachhead would mean drivers at the wheel for seventy-two hours, more or less non-stop. The division on the move needed seventy tankers each holding 1,000 gallons every day!

Ammo and food were of minor importance compared to the vital necessity of petrol supplies. 3rd and 5th RHA, who were each to fire 250,000 rounds of 25-pounder shells during the whole campaign, and who had averaged fifty rounds per gun per day in Normandy, now would need, for some time, minimal expenditure. To some extent fresh fruit, vegetables, milk, butter and eggs would be 'found' en route, as would beer, cider and wine!

The 8th Hussars had harboured for a few days at Bouquetot near Roufot, and Bill Bellamy recalled a lot of discussion about the war ending by the autumn, Berlin for Christmas or even, especially among the married members, home before Christmas. 'I believed that we would fetch up against the Siegfried line and that a war of attrition would be battled out there before we actually captured Germany.' He was right.

The gallant and bloodied 43rd Wessex Division, who would suffer 12,482

Crossing the River Seine.

casualties in this campaign, had smashed a major bridgehead over the River Seine in the Vernon area, 30 miles south-east of Rouen. On 29/30 August the division concentrated around Le Neubourg, south of Rouen, preparatory to crossing the Bailey bridges at Les Andelys, 15 miles north-west of Vernon, through a bridgehead established by 53rd Division.

For the time being 4th Armoured Brigade commanded by Brigadier Carver, recently CO of 1st RTR, was under the wing of the Desert Rats. Led by the Royal's armoured cars they were to take the right-hand centre line and 22nd Armoured Brigade led by the Cherry Pickers would take the left flank advance. Brett-Smith wrote '11th Hussars over the Seine at Louviers, and another traffic jam, the first for some time. And by the very beginning of Sept, we were up to the Somme and across it and in the Pas-de-Calais which made the V-Merchants think again.'

'We crossed the Seine at St Pierre-de-Vauvray on the 31st August,' wrote Bill Bellamy. 'These bridge crossings were always frustrating as delays occurred, traffic jams developed and senior officers waxed indignant if their own particular babies weren't allowed over first.' In the soaking blinding rain 3rd RHA took ten hours to cover their first 18 miles but 1st RTR seemed in happier form, as Trooper Hewison noted in his diary:

Everyone is out to watch us rumble past – babes in arms to centenarians, smiling, laughing, shouting, waving, clapping, throwing kisses, weeping, chucking dahlias and rhododendrons and all sorts of flowers on to the tanks, passing up fruit, cider, milk and lord-knows-what when we stopped for a few minutes. Jerry here is pulling out pretty fast and has only horsedrawn guns with very few trucks. Plenty of smashed up carts and vehicles on the road and many dead horses.

Mushrooms for breakfast, fields abound in 'em here. We've been feeding very well lately with eggs and tomatoes galore.

The recce squadron of the Skins who were leading 22nd Armoured Brigade found that their paths crossed the Royals and 11th Hussars many times. In the first day of the Great Swan an astonishing 72 miles had been covered despite a sharp fracas at Abancourt, cleared by the 1st RBs. Lieutenant Ben Tottenham's armoured car operator passed him up a biscuit loaded with marmalade as part of his 0530 hrs breakfast. Unfortunately in the half light he failed to notice it was embedded with wasps. Painful.

Minor engagements took place at Bazancourt and Poix but one way or another an amazing 2,200 prisoners were bagged on the 31st, and the Cherry Pickers destroyed a battery of 150mm guns.

'For the first time since the African and Italian campaigns the division was once more to be used in its most successful role,' wrote Derrick Watson, 1/5th Queens, 'the break through unhampered by pockets which could not be by-passed. The rifle companies got their lorries back and we became lorried infantry again.' As Bill Bellamy reported after liberating Gournay-en-Bray: 'It was a day in which we tasted victory.'

The 8th Hussars' objective was the capture of the bridge over the Somme

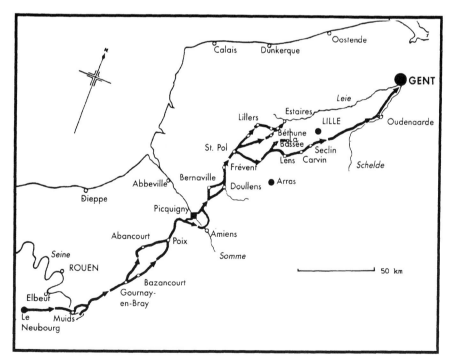

The Great Swan from the Seine to the capture of Ghent.

at Hangest-sur-Somme, 12 miles north-west of Amiens, which was about to be stormed by 11th Armoured Division. In fact just north of Poix the Cromwells of the 8th Hussars nearly confronted the Shermans of the Black Bull. Bill Bellamy's troop was racing that of Tony Venner's. The latter ran out of petrol 10 miles short and the former 2 miles short – but the bridge was blown anyway! Predictably all the bridges were blown except a lock-type gate near the village of Dreuil, a western suburb of Amiens. While the sappers of 4th Field Squadron RE, supported by the Queens, built a Bailey bridge under fire at Picquigny, 8 miles north-west of Amiens, through the night and in record time, the GOC ordered a night advance across the river.

By the night of 1 September the astonishing 'cracking around', as Monty called it, continued unabated. The Cherry Pickers had reached the Somme and were in the eastern outskirts of Abbeville.

At the little village called Nuncq [south of St Pol] the inevitable for once happened [reported Brett-Smith], and we like the rest of 2nd Army ran out of maps. We prepared to use our silk handkerchief maps and local guide books but the War Office came through just in time. It was curious to be racing through the Somme country leaving in our wake such famous and bitter names as Béthune, Arras, St Pol and Vimy. We were practically out of France, enriched by the company of a large number of Maquis who became our good and faithful friends.

So 5th RTR Cromwells very gingerly threaded their way through Molliens Vidame, followed by the Queens Brigade in pouring rain on a pitch-black moonless night. By dawn the mixed brigade was across and the bridge reluctantly condemned. On the morning of 2 September practically all the division had 'bounced' the River Somme. It was an untidy operation in that the Canadians on the left flank frequently crossed over the 7th Armoured centre lines and on occasions the 11th Armoured Division centre lines on the right had to be borrowed, temporarily. The German 15th Army was still ensconced to the west along the line Béthune, south-west to St Pol-sur-Ternoise, south-west again to Auxi-le-Château. The advance north towards Ghent was always likely to be threatened, even heavily attacked from the west and the north-west. Meanwhile 4th Armoured Brigade on the right now came under command of 11th Armoured Brigade, and 71st Infantry Brigade of 53rd Division arrived to take over left flank protection.

Major John Evans, 1/5th Queens, wrote in his diary for 2 September:

Made bridgehead over the Somme at Picquigny. 76 prisoners. No casualties. Met Mlle Georgette Cavillon who spoke English. Division going like hell. Expect to cover 250 miles this week. Mlle Cavillon was 20 years old and pretty. She was very brave and acted as interpreter and messenger between us and the Resistance sometimes in front of our lines.

Once across the Somme two lines of advance took place. 5th RTR and 1/6th Queens headed towards Bernaville, 15 miles north of the Picquigny bridge, and after brisk engagements at Domart and Berneuil they arrived north-west of Doullens by nightfall. They had taken 400 prisoners, knocked out four 105mm guns and smashed up a flying bomb site. Rather satisfying!

The second advance was made by 8th Hussars and the 1/5th Queens, who after a sharp fight at Frévent where, with the help of the FFI eighty prisoners were gathered in, pushed on towards St Pol-sur-Ternoise. Bill Bellamy wrote: 'We continued the advance at high speed in the direction of Doullens and St Pol [30 miles due north]. The battle for St Pol was a very tough one fought by B and C squadrons, whilst we (A Sqn) were used to support the Queens, fill gaps in the line or probe other areas. This very tiring process went on for two days.' At 1500 hrs the small battle group with three A/Tank guns in St Pol was bypassed and left for 1/7th Queens to deal with on the following day. Auxi-le-Château was masked (i.e. guarded but not attacked) by 1/6th Queens, while 1st RTR, 1st RB and CC Battery 5th RHA starting 25 miles south were ordered up in double quick time. They were to bypass St Pol to the west, advance due north to Tangry and Cauchy à la Tour, which they reached at midnight as Trooper Hewison recalls:

Route main road to Frévent, passing Arras 14 kms to the right, bypassed St Pol to Auchel and la Guillotine with wild welcomes. We were treated as Gods and were borne round the square amongst the multitudes shoulder high, being clawed down every few yards to be kissed and pummelled by young and old. I didn't mind the young much. Never been kissed so much in all my life . . . We got back to the tanks at 0230 am as drunk as Lords. C'est la guerre . . .

On the following day St Pol was attacked by 1/7th Queens, who in the process lost a ten-man patrol. Well-concealed guns caused problems for the 8th Hussars. 53rd Division then took over responsibility for final clearance but not before RHQ of the Skins was viciously shelled and lost fifteen men. Corporal 'Poggy' Cooper went into a wood to commune with nature and came out with eleven prisoners, having also destroyed a machine gun. As a result he was awarded the MM!

The northern advance was now through an enormous industrial maze of canals, dykes, railway embankments (all easy to defend), factories, coal mines and shafts and many small villages. Fortunately the main towns were not held in strength otherwise the infantry and armour could have been sucked into their maw and never seen again. Indeed Lillers, 5 miles north of Cauchy, was held by a small battle group where 1st RB and 1st RTR had a rough skirmish, strongly assisted by a brave Maquis group. After a few tricky hours the Skins arrived to help, having been held up at Cambrin. 'C' Squadron pushed some tanks across the La Bassée Canal, 3 miles north over a partly burnt bridge. The Rifle Brigade formed a bridgehead while the sappers put a Scissors bridge across the canal.

Information from the Maquis at Cauchy on the 3rd enabled Sergeant Meyer and 'I' Company 1st RB to stalk three German 105mm guns, drive off the crews, destroy the guns themselves and their ammo lorries, and kill a rare German officer making off in an Opel car. On the same day, during their involvement in street fighting in Lillers, 1st RB had two officer and seven rifleman casualties as the Germans filtered back into the town. That night 1st RB reached La Bassée Canal near Béthune and then went on to Mazingarbe near Lens. They took 300 prisoners in three days. In this mining region volunteers from the French and Belgian resistance movements were recruited to the colours and stayed for nearly ten more months. They included Yves Dumy (christened Ifs and Buts), Noel Paniez (Christmas Basket), Dennis Vanoystaeuen and fifteen others. Alan Parker, the RB adjutant, and the RSM were shocked at their unorthodox garments, so they were all issued with army kit and looked extremely smart. Initially they existed from company and regimental funds. They all fought well and two were awarded the Croix de Guerre, two were killed in action, and Gilbert Cleret was wounded and invalided back to England.

It was curious how many tanks of 7th and 11th Armoured ran out of petrol in a village square where *les patrons* in the *bistro* gave excellent military advice and alcoholic refreshments! Trooper Hewison, with 1st RTR, having commented on the real opposition at Lillers with SPs and A/Tank guns, found that in St Pierre-les-Auchel a minor fire in the engine delayed him, *and* a Sherman with mortar damage, *and* another Cromwell that had broken down: 'For three days we have had a bloody good time. It really is surprising the number of attractive girls there are about – a greater percentage than in England.' From his tank he conducted community singing of 'Beer Barrel Polka', 'If you were the only girl', 'Tipperary' and 'Sur le pont d'Avignon'. Sam from the Fitters happened also to be 'lost' and 'happened to see our 3 tanks from the main road'. Our 'card' attended a mass funeral of twenty-six Maquis recently killed in the street guerrilla fighting, and Simone proposed to him and asked him to stay on in St Pierre. 'I can't arraff [sic] these French,' he said. He had a girl in every 'port'. It was to be Irene in Mechelen and there had been another in Bayeux. . . .

The Maquis or FFI (Free Forces of the Interior) were on the whole most helpful, with road/route directions and guarding prisoners. Their military information, delivered in thick *patois*, was not always reliable and estimates of enemy numbers needed to be taken with a pinch of salt! The Queens were rather doubtful about a *canard* that 2,000 Germans were advancing from Béthune to counter attack. They failed to arrive! When the Skins issued German rifles and ammo picked up on the way, the FFI 'received them delightedly', reported John Pilborough, 'and grinned and nodded at our warning not to waste bullets but to make it *"Un Balle, un Boche"*.'

A supply problem was now developing that Colonel Cardiff, the AQ, had to resolve. The main petrol point was way back at Beauvais, but forecasting future requirements of petrol/ammo/food was difficult. The Germans were

'B' Squadron 1st RTR 'Baker' Cromwell tank crew, Nordewick, Belgium, September 1944. Left to right: Trooper D. Wells (turret gunner), Trooper H. Barnett (co-driver), Corporal R. Spittles (commander), Trooper Bill Bagguley (wireless operator/gun loader), Trooper Albert Garrett (driver).

defending the Lillers area with machine guns, Bazookas and Spandaus. The centre line was cut frequently and Frévent had to be recaptured. If Lens, Béthune or Ghent were to be seriously defended much more ammo and less petrol would be needed – vice versa if this was not to be the case. Major N.A. Smith, 2 i/c Division RASC, needed a precise daily brief to keep his dozens of lorries full of what was needed. Bridging materials for the canals and rivers in the region took up a lot of space, as well as time to load up.

The situation around Béthune remained confused for three days and three nights. The 11th Hussars had found two small partly destroyed bridges over the Aire Canal, which runs west–east, north of Béthune to south of La Bassée. One bridge was at Hinges, the other at Cambrin. Lillers to the west of Béthune was strongly held and 1st RTR, 1st RB and the Skins were all committed in this rather large dreary industrialized area. Béthune itself was captured by the RB, Maquis and 8th Hussars driving north from St Pol. Fortunately the GOC, General Verney, knew the region west of Lille of old, with its maze of canals crossed by wooden bridges, and asked permission (which was granted on 4 September) to move east of Lille.

1/5th Queens had caught up, and on the 4th took Givenchy and Festubert across the canal at La Bassée, taking 188 prisoners, guns and mortars from 59th Division, while 1/6th and 1/7th Queens were near Aubigny. Lieutenant Chapman of the Skins nipped into, through and out of Lille, confirming it was still full of Germans, and that La Bassée continued to be held strongly.

While 7th Armoured were moving north to Ghent, the enemy moved two fresh divisions, 59th and 712th, to the La Bassée–Béthune area in order to protect the Channel ports, and farther west (north of St Pol) 64th Infantry Division, fresh from Germany, joined the fray. Our 53rd Division and 4th Armoured Brigade kept these three Germans divisions quiet.

So for a variety of reasons, most of the division were relieved on the 5th by 53rd Division, while a small 'Ghentforce' set off on a new centre line south and south-east of Lille. Most of the Queens, 1st RTR, 1st RB and 3rd RHA stayed in reserve, surrendering their precious petrol lorries to 11th Hussars, the Skins and 5th RTR with part of 1/6th Queens.

Bill Bellamy's squadron officer mess was in the Château des Près in Sailly-Labourse, a mining village on the outskirts of Béthune, a poor area populated by ex-patriot Polish miners. He found it hard to sleep in a real bed. The 8th Hussars now had a week of enforced idleness.

CHAPTER TWELVE

Belgium and the Liberation of Ghent – 'an Incredible Welcome'

The historian of the Queens noted the 'flat country where 131 Queens Brigade had fought 4½ years before, long poplar lined road, rich farms, orchards, ugly little villages but bright with flags and excited civilians. In May 1940 1/5 and 1/6 Queens had been part of the BEF rearguard in fighting near Oudenarde.'

The recce troop of the Skins went through Lens, a scene reported by John Pilborough:

> a victory parade where the people thronged the streets, cheering every vehicle that went by. Sweeping south of Lille and Roubaix we drew clear of the drab scenery of slag heaps and crowded dwellings, factories and cheering people and at nightfall (on the 4th) crossed the Belgian frontier at Toufflers (suburbs of Roubaix). If our reception in Northern France had been enthusiastic, here it became ecstatic. The red, white and blue French flag gave place to the red, yellow and black colours of Belgium. There was hardly a house without one and most cafés and houses had several. There was dancing and music in every café, 'Tipperary' was sung, the black-out was forgotten. It was a riot.

It was a relief to get out of the drab industrial north of France – Picardy – despite the warmth of their welcome, into the more interesting Belgian Flanders. The advance was north-east, parallel to the Schelde/Escaut Canal. General Verney noted: 'except for one blown bridge at Warcoing we had a clear run through. Our reception in Belgium exceeded even the tremendous scenes we had already experienced in France. It was quite unforgettable and most inspiring.'

5th RTR under Lieutenant-Colonel Gus Holliman, moved very fast through Lens, Carvin, Sellin, Lesquin, Hem, Toufflers and Helchin, and Oudenarde was liberated early on the 5th. Their Corporal C. Calas was marched off to the Hotel de Ville to be the first of *les Anglais* to sign the post-liberation Golden Book. He made a speech in fractured French – fractured, he said, by the cognac proffered. But some of the villages around Oudenarde changed hands several times, and many Belgian civilians were shot by the Germans for hanging out their beloved Belgian flag. Next 'C' Squadron 5th RTR led for Ghent via Nazareth, and 'A' Squadron rejoined the centre line at Eke. Near Hutepot, 1½ miles from Ghent, Keith Crocker's troop were held up by a road block, infantry and an A/Tank gun.

Meanwhile at first light the Skins had crossed the bridge at Oudenarde and advanced rapidly north-east to secure the key bridges over the Schelde at Wetteren and Melle, some 20 miles north-east. The Melle bridge was blown and the one at Wetteren was raised in a vertical position. The Belgian *Brigade Blanche*, under covering fire from the Skins, swam across the Schelde and lowered the bridge. Later they were joined by 1/6th Queens to hold the vital bridgehead. At Melle Lieutenant-Colonel J.H. Mason, their CO, met Count Henri de Hemptinne of the Resistance, who provided key guides in the next few days.

Major Arthur Crickmay, 5th RTR, recalled:

I had arranged a stonk [by 5th RHA] on the road block. I remember hearing the shells exploding and also seeing the smoke, just as Ronnie Morgan came up on the air and said he was in a very difficult position. I couldn't get anything very concrete out of him (he was obviously worried about security) and so I followed him round, rather expecting him to be pinned down with Boche swarming all over his tanks. To my amazement I found him in a built up area in the middle of a crowd of some hundreds of euphoric Belgians with girls, flowers and wine in about equal proportions.

The recollections of Harry Upward of 5th RTR were:

Day break came at about 0430 and though the tanks spent the night in close leaguer we moved out at first light, getting about 3 hours sleep a night with a spell on guard as well. Night was when you refuelled and re-armed. I think a Sherman Firefly did about 1 mile to the gallon. We refuelled out of jerry cans and lived on dry rations keeping close contact with the Queens and the RB. We carried infantry on our tanks and had some Canadians as well during our advance into Belgium. On the swan up to Ghent we were going up to 100 miles a day or thereabouts, a bloody long way and it was hard to keep awake. It's hard work driving a tank across country and easy to lose a track. At night we would dig a pit and then drive the tank over it, it's dangerous to get under a tank for a kip on soft ground, for it can settle on you. Anyway we had a great reception from the Belgians, cheering, bottles of wine. My battalion of 5 Tanks took Ghent and later on we got a little plaque for it but I lost mine afterwards.

Derrick Watson with 1/5th Queens wrote:

we were told that our Armoured cars and tanks were advancing on Ghent and were urgently requiring the infantry for protection. Late on

Members of 5th RTR near Ghent. From left to right: Barker, Brady, Sergeant George Stimpson.

the evening of 4th Sept I was ordered to accompany A/Lt-Col Jack Nangle on a long drive to link up with our tanks on the outskirts of Ghent. The battalion was to follow at first light. Jack was driving and I was supposed to navigate. We came to a fork in the road and Jack said 'Which way?' Crossing my fingers I guessed the right fork and the Watson luck held. Vehicles following us about half an hour later took the left fork and ran into a solitary German tank in ambush. The leading vehicle went 'into the bag' with its crew.

Ghent was defended by a garrison of 1,000 men with some 88mm guns. The Cherry Pickers were as usual the first to enter, followed by 'A' Squadron 5th RTR. Lieutenant Ronnie Morgan and Sergeant Leonard Watkins, with their new-found Belgian friend, Alexis Janssen, found themselves at 1430 hrs on the 5th in the main square of Ghent. They had travelled through the villages of Landuit, Zevergem and Zwynaarde, guided by the Resistance. They were given an incredible welcome. Thousands of people were in the streets, milling around the tanks, all laughing, cheering and crying. The editor of *La Flandre Liberale* wrote on 6 September (translated): 'The unforgettable hour came. Each man keeps in his heart the memory of the first Tommy to be spotted. We have awaited this day for four years. Four long black years with only our patriotic faith giving us the strength to hope . . .'

Ronnie Morgan's 12th Troop was on the Boulevard Militaire. There were German patrols and road blocks still manned in the centre of town. Lieutenant Crocker's troop took a German prisoner, who suggested a large-scale surrender might be possible. Their OC 'C' Squadron, Major Arthur Crickmay, back at Hutepot received a radio message to this effect. Crickmay and Major Goodridge with 'B' Company 1/6th Queens now carried out a series of negotiations that culminated at midnight with the arrival of Brigadier H.R. Mackeson. Lieutenant-General Wilhelm Daser was about sixty years old, immaculate in his uniform, great coat with red collar, boots and spurs. He commanded the 70th Infantry Division, a defensive division formed from men invalided from the Russian front with stomach complaints (the Stomach or Whitebread Division). The problem was that of 'face', so the brigadier said he was 'almost a General'. However, negotiations broke down and the Germans retired to the north end of town and the shelling diminished. Now Lieutenant-Colonel Mason of 1/6th Queens sent his Pioneer Platoon to hold a bridge north of the town, 'A' Company east to Wetteren where 4th Field Squadron RE were engaged in fierce fighting with an SS company, and 'B' Company to Gavere to protect a bridge over the Escaut.

Gordon Johnson, 5th RTR, recalled:

The city was declared open and we drove into a welcome that would make the Coronation look like a side show. I was given a 6 month old baby to hold! Beacon the wireless operator needed to go to the toilet at St Peter's railway station. The crowd all suggested he went over to the Gents. He walked in and there was a German with his rifle. The German handed the rifle to Beacon who then handed it back whilst both carried on with their 'toilet'. The next day we were sent up to the canal to pull and close a swing bridge over the river. We were mortared a lot and finally the shelling got our crew commander. He was killed and buried at Adeghem. We found his Diary on the turret floor. One page read '11th, buried Mr Graham Parker, rather worried about it, during the Burial we were shelled and it unnerved me coupled with the strain of long hours with no sleep and little food. 12th. After breakfast I baled out, I did not tell anyone I could not stand the strain any longer and I was worried how I should fare in action again.' This man had fought in Africa, Italy and now Normandy and Belgium.

Later Lieutenant Ted Zoeftig, 5th RTR, took 300 prisoners at St Martens Latem, a western suburb. Rex Wingfield's 1/6th Queens claimed to be:

[the] first walking patrol of 17 with a 38 set into the city, undefended except for a few snipers. The Belgian resistance helped force a speedy German retreat over the canal in the north of the town. There was

dancing in the streets to the Andrews Sisters (recorded illegally from American short-wave transmissions). Later there was a colossal banquet in a large town hall, with T-shaped tables, snowy linen, silver cutlery, still wet Desert Rat signs. The Belgians cooked bully beef, tinned fruit puddings, fresh fruit, Belgian beer and wine. The cigars were marked 'Fur Deutsche Wehrmacht'. And precious saved-up English tea and talked about the Belgian Royal family. Slept for 14 hours.

Later Derrick Watson, 1/5th Queens, describes two incidents that took place in Ghent:

The Germans fired 2 shells into the city which started a small fire and cleared the streets like magic. I found myself alone in the Central square in charge of Tac HQ where the signaller, Peter Knight, operating the 19 set was trying to trace the whereabouts of the leading rifle companies. The leading company commander (a lugubrious 6 footer, nicknamed Tiny) reported back 'If the RHA aren't firing, we're being shelled. I hear they're having a dance at BHQ.'

Derrick then visited the forward Queens lining the banks of the many canals: 'Each and every one had been taken into the families living there – eating and drinking and in some cases doing the washing up! A sight for sore eyes.' Later that day:

Lt Col Jack Nangle [Derrick's CO] had been approached by the White Brigade asking for a British officer to go and accept the surrender of a German company which would not surrender to the Belgians. I was given a Bren gun carrier and with Lt Ted Sarginson (6 months junior to me and considerably younger) my 'Battle Group' set off. We located the German company busily chatting in groups in a busy shopping centre – going in and out of the cafés – some of them with rifles slung over their shoulders – some having 'piled arms' in the centre of the road. We roared up to them in the carrier with Ted behind his Bren gun on its tripod. Some of the Germans turned their heads briefly; otherwise they showed no interest in us! Ted gave me various bits of advice. 'Tell them to lay down their arms – tell them to surrender – shall I fire at them?' etc. I was extremely annoyed at being ignored (Didn't they know we are at war?) so strode over to the nearest group and rather irritably asked 'Does anyone here speak English?'
    'Yes.'
    (Even more irritably) 'Do you want to surrender?'
    'We won't surrender until our officer gives us the order.'
    'Where are the officers?'

1/5th Queens help to liberate Ghent, 5 September 1944.

'They're having a conference.'

After a long wait an ober-lieutenant appeared, formed up the men, marched them off behind the Queens carrier.

At Brigade HQ Derrick said: 'You're always asking us to knock off the odd Boche – I've brought you seventy of them.'

Major John Evans wrote: '1/5th Queens made a triumphal entry with crowds lining the streets, cheering, throwing up flowers and bottles of wine etc. After nearly three months of pretty hard going and hardly seeing a civilian it was heady stuff and it was necessary to keep rigid control of the troops who were being kissed and cuddled as we slowly moved forward.' His Belgian guide was Gustave van Bocxstaele, an artist and language professor who was made an unpaid lieutenant and put on the ration strength. John now 'took over command of "B" Coy as Major Scott-Joint was suffering from melancholia. "Even the dogs go mad down here." He was a casualty of war and the trouble was that the company were in a state of low morale.'

We were beginning to run short of everything [recalls Albert Mitchell, Norfolk Yeo]. We held a conference and one lost Northumberland Fusiliers Brengun carrier fitted with a Vickers machine gun joined us. We decided to take Ghent and Stop! In we went, crowds everywhere. The odd sniper shooting. We halted in Boulevard Beguinage. Soon the Germans cut us off. We were there for about 8 days until relieved by the Polish Brigade.

'C' Squadron of the Cherry Pickers in the Zwijnaarde suburb of Ghent, 5 September 1944.

Meanwhile 11th Hussars had been fighting and holding Deinze, 10 miles south-west of Ghent, where seven important roads intersected from Courtrai, Tielt and Ghent. For two days, during which they had several spirited actions, they captured twenty horsed weapons, a paymaster, knocked out an 88mm gun and took 400 prisoners. The divisional centre line was being crossed constantly by small German forces moving from the west to the east. To stop this happening divisional sappers were ordered to blow up the vital bridge at Deinze that the Cherry Pickers had been so zealously defending. What a crazy war!

Within two days the barracks back at Oudenarde were filled with over 2,000 prisoners, many from 70th Infantry Division with negligible casualties to the Desert Rats. John Pilborough of the Skins remembers that Sergeant Andrews of the Recce Squadron brought back a German horsed transport section captured intact with their horses. Their colonel rode on the Honey tank while 200 prisoners followed behind. The Skins were also involved in the vicious counter-attack on the Wetteren bridge. 'Our A1 Echelon was at the time of the attack ready with the daily supplies occupying the station yard near the bridge.' When the SS launched their attack 'The echelon drivers quickly joined forces with the 4 Field Sqn REs who had been detailed to look after the vital bridge. Between them they held it until C Sqn of the Skins and the 1/6 Queens arrived. Fierce fighting took place in the houses and gardens around the bridge but 22 SS were

The first British troops, 67 RASC, to liberate Hebeaux, near Roubaix, 6 September 1944. Sergeant Rick Hall is second soldier from the right.

killed and 60 taken prisoner.' SSM K. Clayton of the Skins won the MM for his tommy gun actions, but the real heroes were the sapper defenders with Corporals Crutchley and Stuckfield and Lieutenant Turpin doing yeoman work.

Later on the night of 6 September 1/7th Queens, coming up to join the fray from the south where they had been guarding the long centre lines, fought a heavy action at Eine, just north-west of Oudenarde, killing and wounding 100 Germans. Lucky Trooper D.R. Bamford, 'C' Squadron 11th Hussars, was captured at Eine on the 5th, then freed by the Belgian resistance. The Germans retook the village and slaughtered sixty men, women and children. Bamford was captured again and freed on the 6th by the Queens.

Although on 7 September the Glasgow Highlanders of 15th Scottish Division relieved 1/7th Queens at Oudenarde, another five days passed before the final clearance of the factory areas around Ghent. Also on the 7th the Skins' Cromwells patrolling round Ghent captured a horsed cavalry regiment. During the capture of Ghent almost 10,000 prisoners were taken, many handed over to the White Brigade for 'safe keeping', all for a total loss of a hundred casualties, mainly Queens, 5th RTR and the Cherry Pickers.

St Niklaas, an important town 20 miles east of Ghent and north-west of Mechelen, was taken on the 9th by a combined force of 11th Hussars, who had moved from Zele, 1st RB, 44th RTR (from 4th Armoured Brigade) and 1/7th Queens. After a wild reception Lieutenant-Colonel Griffiths, CO of the Queens, was made a Freeman of the city.

Major Derrick Watson leading the procession after the liberation of Ghent ceremony, 6 September 1944.

The Skins now withdrew to the Wetteren area for a couple of days, then to Mechelen for a complete rest and refitment. HQ Squadron was housed in the St Joseph seminary. 'Leave out the spirit of liberation, the cognac and the mademoiselles, and Mechelen', remembers John Pilborough, 'will still remain in our memory for another thing – ice cream, masterpieces decked with cherries and laced with syrup. It was worth the 300 miles we had come for those alone.' And Derrick Watson wrote: 'After 10 days in the Ghent area, all good things come to an end. So in due course we had an emotional farewell and marched off to continue the war. There was much cheering from the citizens and some weeping from the young women, two of whom ran beside their loved ones.' Ghent was a notable battle honour for the Desert Rats. J.P. Marchal's *Gent – Sept '44*, published by Uitgave J. Verbeke, gives a most colourful description of the town's liberation.

CHAPTER THIRTEEN

Unsung Heroes

The sappers of 4th Field Squadron had fended off the Waffen SS attack on the Wetteren bridge most courageously, but the CRE, Lieutenant-Colonel A.D. Hunter, had many other problems. Frantic reconnaissance of all the river and canal bridges, nearly all demolished, involved intricate calculations about bridging materials, scissor bridges and explosives to try to clear up the damaged bridges. The REME workshops under Colonel J.D. Berryman had continual problems rather different from those in Normandy. The Cromwell tanks, halftracks and carriers had now covered nearly 300 miles, and their tracks needed much attention. Captain Charles Maple, CO of the Skins REME detachment, wrote:

> What marvels of logistics were performed by B and A2 Echelons to keep the Regiment moving. It is remembered as a blurred kaleidoscope of dust, night expeditions to steal spares and the relics of a stricken army. Most tank crews loathed the outcome of a lost tank which resulted in relegation to the Forward Delivery Squadron which was responsible for the issue of a replacement vehicle. The crew might be posted to another regiment. No 'Skin' worth his salt was going to suffer that! The silly rule was that if a tank required more than *four* hours work by a fitter it would be sent to the rear for repair. There was no rear in the fast, daily moves during the break-out. Any tank which had to be temporarily abandoned was *rendered thief-proof to the infantry* by lightly welding its hatches. Those who served in the echelons were certainly the heroes of this phase.

Major Stevens, 67th Company RASC, was responsible for petrol supplies to the division, and even using twenty lorries from the grounded 15th LAA Regiment could not produce supplies for *all* of the division's vehicles. And Major L.J. Aspland was CO of 58th Company RASC responsible for ammo and food supplies to the Queens Brigade, who had fifty vehicles.

Many RASC convoys were under threat, even ambushed, on their long centre line back to the bridgehead or the Beauvais petrol dump. One platoon of 67th Company RASC logged up 462,000 miles, or 14,000 miles per vehicle, during the campaign.

Colonel A.C. Lusty, i/c RAOC workshops, had less work and responsibility now that the enormous tank and other armoured vehicle 'casualties' in Normandy had thankfully decreased. They sent spare parts up as required, formed dumps of 'crocks' for eventual repair and helped clear the lengthening centre line roads with bulldozers.

There was no time or need on the Great Swan to lay signal telephone lines, since static positions were now rare, but Lieutenant-Colonel G.S. Knox, i/c Divisional Signals, was proud that the hundreds of 21, 19 and 38 radio sets rarely failed to work, despite the distances between for instance, 11th Hussars and Divisional HQ.

It was unusual for anyone to praise the Corps of Military Police whose 100 Provost Red Caps were responsible under APM Major E.P. Wedlake for law and order, prisoner of war 'cages' or the equivalent and, above all, for marking the many centre lines with the Arrow number of each individual unit. They also kept a severe eye out for looting and desertion – always a minor problem in every army.

Casualties since Normandy were fortunately at a low level and Colonel L.R.H. Keatinge, the ADMS (in place of Colonel E.C. Eccles) used civilian hospitals in Oudenarde and Ghent for both Desert Rat and Wehrmacht wounded soldiers. Major K. Borland was in charge of 29th Field Dressing station and his prompt and efficient medical care was much admired.

Although every infantryman and tank crew carried medical kits, often with chloroform and morphine as well as bandages, the regimental Aid Post and RAMC team carried out serious operations, including amputation. But they needed to get the badly wounded casualties back to a hospital as quickly as possible.

If there is such a thing as glamour in war, it is usually accorded to the cavalry regiments, rarely to the RTR, PBI and RHA and extremely rarely to the support services, without whom the division could not continue the combat!

CHAPTER FOURTEEN

Left Flanking: Operation Market Garden – September/October

For a week after the liberation of Ghent the division was in the main out of action around Malines, until 16 September. The Polish Armoured Division had now taken over control of the centre of Ghent. Fuel was short and many units were living off captured German rations – tinned stew, tinned Limburg cheese and black bread, supplemented by a good deal of local milk, cheese and fruit. Chickens and ducks often found their way into the divisional cuisine. Leave visits were made to Malines and Brussels, where the charm of the ladies and the thriving Black Market were frequently noted.

Tom Ritson, 3rd RHA, wrote home:

> We have just had a remarkable two days. The regiment was detached and sent [to Antwerp] to support the infantry [of 11th Armoured Division] who were trying to clear it against quite strong German counter-attacks coming from the northern suburbs over a canal. We were located in a big hotel pretty well right on the canal. So Colonel Norman and I got an observation post on the hotel roof and we went up to it in the elevator! At one time I phoned down for some drinks and sure enough they came in double quick time. I even went down to the main rooms and had a drink and a dance with a pretty Belgian girl before going back up to the OP. It's a funny war (sometimes).

The 8th Hussars had stayed south near Béthune until 10 September. Corporal Alan Howard wrote home to his brother Fred: 'The FFI are armed with all sorts of weapons, old French arms, captured or stolen German arms, hand grenades, bottles, anything in fact and their enthusiasm and real hatred of the Germans amazes the unenthusiastic British soldier . . . I discover why the French always prefer wine – their beer is terrible.' Bill Bellamy noticed 'the roads were straight, cobbled and had a terrific camber which made driving tanks very difficult . . . We became ready targets for girls of all ages to kiss, but in common with most of the others, I soon found that as you were unable to be selective it was best to duck.' On the 15th Bill's Cromwell was on the Albert Canal overlooking the small town of

Herenthals. The tank was driven right up to the top of the 40-ft embankment: 'At that moment all hell was let loose and the tank juddered under the impact of shells striking the front glacis plate and the turret. Although I had my head out of the turret top I was unable to see the [20mm multi-barrelled Oerlikon] gun. We reversed out as fast as possible firing the machine guns.' His Cromwell, christened 'Abbot of Chantry', had been penetrated by several shells to the extent of 2 in. He had been issued with an *un-armoured training* tank made of soft steel, lighter and therefore quicker!

The great and daring Operation Market Garden started on the 17th with three airborne divisions dropping on Arnhem, Nijmegen and near 's Hertogenbosch. For two days the division watched myriad Dakotas, Stirlings, Albermarles and glider-tugs crammed with paratroopers swooping and wheeling like great birds over Eindhoven towards Arnhem dropping their precious, doomed cargo. Bill Bellamy said: 'They looked so small and vulnerable. The towing aircraft seemed fairly steady but many of the gliders were yawing up and down behind them.'

The Queens Brigade were back in the line on the 18th to 20th near Herenthals on the Canal de Jonction, 20 miles east of Antwerp. Patrol clashes, shelling and mortaring took their toll, with forty-eight casualties, but snipers of 1/7th Queens had some good autumn shooting from a factory overlooking the canal and claimed twenty 'hits'.

When 1st RTR arrived at the Dutch frontier Reg Spittles was with 'B' Squadron:

Three 'tankies' of 'B' Squadron 1st RTR, near Brugge, Belgium, 1944. Left to right: Reg Spittles, Jack Mitchell, Sergeant Taffy Ellis.

Suddenly a man scrambled up the side of our Cromwell and proceeded to embrace me with a great deal of emotion and tears. I gathered from the way he spoke we had most likely arrived in 'Holland'. I asked him (in English of course) 'You are *Dutch?*' Now comes the misunderstanding. 'Nay, Nay, Hollander, Hollander, nix *deutsch.*' He had a great panic on because he thought I thought he was a *German*, anyway I pacified him with some Bully Beef and biscuits and he gave me a rare 2½ Guilders coin which he had kept to give to the first Allied soldier he met to show his gratitude.

5th RTR were loaned temporarily to 15th Scottish Division, who together with 'I' Company 1st RB and the Skins crossed the Dutch frontier at Hoogiend into 'a country of dreary sand-dunes, sparse fir trees, a waste of flat open plain scarred by deep black dykes'. Then they too were sent off to support 53rd Welch Division in the area south of the Meuse/Escaut Canal. This lasted for three days before they were moved to the south-west of Eindhoven, and joined 71st Infantry Brigade of 51st Highland Division to capture Middlebeers. Against SS troops armed with Bazookas and mortars, Lieutenant Henry Woods recalled 'it became a house-to-house battle', and Sergeant Bob Price remembers: 'While the fighting was at its height a white flag was waved and an SS man came forward, asked for a MO to assist with a difficult child-birth taking place in the house they were defending. All fighting ceased and recommenced when the child was born.' The village battle lasted for two days!

Brigadier H.J.B. Cracroft had now arrived to command 22nd Armoured Brigade. He would have been glad to read this excerpt from the diary of Lieutenant Heinz Krueger, 2nd Company 1036 Panzer Grenadier Regiment: '20 Sep. We had a heavy day yesterday. There were 11 NCOs and 112 missing from the Company. We were attacked and fought our way back through Tommy positions all in one day! In the end I had saved 2 sergeants and 10 men. Today we have been resting. Who knows where we shall go.'

History does not relate what the old Africa hands had to say about autumn in Holland after the arid, dusty heat of the desert. 8th Hussars moved north from Geel on 23 September and Bill Bellamy relates: 'The heavens opened. We trundled our way through the bleak flat afforested heath lands near to Mol and Lommel, reaching Eindhoven in the late morning. If the drive had been miserable the ensuing wait was worse. We harboured at Heeze, just inside Holland, the rain drenched us and we sat in silent dripping misery. Not a happy day.' Still he was presented with a filched wireless set from the huge Phillips factory. 'I have never seen quite such a scene, pouring rain, lorries of all shapes and sizes drawn up onto the verges, dejected sodden drivers, irate Military Police trying to get the fighting troops through and bunches of civilians waving and cheering, despite the weather.'

On the 24th the rest of the division moved south of Eindhoven to protect the left flank and centre lines of the extended 43rd Wessex Division, both straining every nerve to link up with the airborne division dropping zones. Indeed their first objective was to retake and reopen the 20-mile centre line between Eindhoven and the Zuis Willemsvaart bridge at Veghel. In three days of drenching rain 'Snatch' Boardman of the Skins reported:

the regiment was now under command of the Queens Brigade. The road was packed with vehicles nose to tail unable to move forward or back, but the Military Police once again played a wonderful role in sorting it all out. By 0700 hrs (on the 25th) we reached the main square in St Oedenrode where we met a very angry Corps Commander, Lt-Gen Brian Horrocks who was desperately trying to get forward to join his own TAC HQ.

Along the centre line a troop of 11th Hussars had been fired at by an 88mm gun hidden behind a bend in the road. Shortly afterwards Sergeant Bob Price recalled: 'a troop of Shermans arrived on their way up to the Guards Division as replacements. When told of the gun around the corner they said they would deal with it. They motored round the bend one behind the other. There were three bangs and three Shermans were knocked out, a sharp lesson against such recklessness.' 'C' Squadron of the Skins was fired upon by the US 506th Paratroop Battalion who were apparently 'feeling kinda lonesome having been dropped into the blue'. For several days as American K rations had *not* been dropped, the kindly Skins dished out meat and veg for breakfast. 1st RTR had their problems at Nulands Vinkel where a Cromwell and 2 Honeys were brewed up by Bazookas, but a savage attack on the 26th on Heesch cost the enemy 250 casualties. The RHA did well that day.

A few days later Rex Wingfield, 1/6th Queens, met the Dorsets of 43rd Wessex retreating from the Arnhem pocket. 'A shuffling column of men came down the road. We rushed to greet them. We shook their hands. They were dirty faces, grimy, unshaven. God! Those eyes! Glazed, ever moving, twitching, not seeing, staring south, ever south. We lit cigarettes and passed them out.' John Evans, 1/5th Queens, wrote: 'we did succeed in relieving some American paratroopers at Veghel. They were commanded by a namesake Captain Evans and had just been eating dinner with a table and spotless linen tablecloth. Our faces must have been a picture.'

One account of the desperate little actions to keep the centre lines open between Eindhoven and the River Maas to the north was given by Rex Wingfield:

Next morning one reg. of tanks and an Inf Bn was left to hold our gains. The rest of us mounted on Cromwells turned back to clear the roads. We soon found the targets of last night's firing – ten gutted

RASC lorries, one blasted to fragments. That had been the ammo truck. Two hundred yards further down the road was a roadblock of logs. By it lay another burnt lorry and four blackened bodies. A clatter of tracer bounced and sang off the tank as a Spandau opened fire from the roadblock. Cordite fumes blasted from our tank gun into our faces. A sixpounder shell hit right in the middle of the logs. The beams sailed upwards. A fieldgrey rag doll jerked high into the air. We burst through, firing Stens and heaving grenades into the back of the smoking roadblock. The performance was repeated three times in four miles and then we pulled into the relief column. Each morning we had to clear the roads in front and behind before we could move on. Guards Armoured tried to smash through beyond Nijmegen to Arnhem to reach the poor devils. Only one road could be used as the surrounding land was either too soft or under water. One road they had. That road was zeroed exactly by 88s. As soon as a tank poked its snout beyond a building, it was hit. We tried to use the ground on the lee side of the embanked road. The tanks bogged down and churned themselves into a hopeless mess.

On the 26th the 8th Hussars moved from St Oedenrode towards Olland.

We crossed a small bridge over a drainage dyke, fanned out again, broke through a hedge, almost in line and found ourselves in the middle of the German positions. Of the group of four 88mm guns which were in the centre of the adjacent field [remembers Bill Bellamy], two were still in an anti-aircraft attitude pointing to the sky, but like the others were traversing on to us. Instinctively we all fired our 75mm guns and machine guns. I fired the smoke canisters on the side of the turret and ordered everyone back through the hedge at maximum speed. The odds were too great, there were Germans everywhere and as we shot through the hedge we were accompanied by 88mm shells, small arms fire and anything else that they could find to throw at us.

Unfortunately they had to act like steeple-chasers and jump the drainage dyke at 30 mph. Some days later they returned and measured the width – 21 ft! Bill and the Hussars spent the next five days in the area of St Oedenrode, with leave and visits to the Jerboa club in Eindhoven, hot baths and a cinema. They met the troops of 101st US Airborne, who were avid collectors of Luger pistols.

By this time Derrick Watson had been promoted from IO (Lieutenant) to captain and adjutant of 1/5th Queens, and three weeks later he became a major and CO of 'A' Company. Fifteen months earlier he had been a platoon commander in the same company during the Battle of Alamein. 'Needless to say there were very few survivors of the battle still with the Coy but one joyful reunion with CSM Sniffy Parker with whom I shared a slit trench after advancing 2,000 yards across the January and February minefield at Alamein.' Derrick was carrying out a recce at Veghel:

I met a small American parachuter sitting on the edge of a slit trench with his automatic rifle across his knees. He had landed three days previously, had not washed, shaved or eaten very much since landing. They advanced up the road every night and withdrew to the woods before first light. That night A Coy of the Queens shared their blankets in slit trenches with the men of the 101st Airborne. Perhaps that's why we got Marshall Aid.

As adjutant, Derrick welcomed forty reinforcements from England, none with battle experience and some with only six months service in the Army. Major Vincent Lilley, a regular, also joined, as did no less than eight Canloan officers. Rex Wingfield, with 1/6th Queens, was told on his arrival as a replacement:

Everybody looks after everybody else. Your life and *our* lives depend on that. The platoon is one unit, one family. You new lads will have to fit in with us. Each of you will be paired off with a chap who's been around. He'll show you the ropes. Some mobs shove replacements straight into the line. We don't. We can't protect you all the time. You must learn fast. No stealing. So lay off your mates in the rifle platoons.

The salient between St Oedenrode and Veghel, north-east of Eindhoven, was protected by the Queens Brigade and the armour pushed out in dreary conditions, 5th RTR west towards Dinmer and Heeswijk and the Skins and 1st RTR north towards Nistelrode. It rained for much of September and most of October, the tracks and roads were covered in mud and it was cold to boot.

Trooper Hewison's diary commented on the 1st RTR activity:

Sep 28 In Veghel. Jerry is fairly strong on this side of the corridor with Spandau, mortars and heavier artillery including 88s. One B Sqn tank's knocked out by a bazooka, the commander killed. Yankee paratroopers still maintaining patrols in this locality. [But two days later] Had a nasty day, ran into all sorts of stuff – small arms, sniping, bazookas, spandaus, 88 and 105s. Lost 3 tanks brewed. Sgt Smith's, Johnny Wooder was alright, operators Pete Eccles killed, Shep and Sgt Smith moderately wounded with blast & shrapnel. 2nd tank had to get it, had three killed – turret people. Driver and George Travis brought it back to Echelon. 3rd Tank – Capt. Stephens with two simultaneous 105mm or heavier on front and rear. Micky Perrin killed, Jock Brady and the rest baled out and tank immediately brewed, Jock with burns and blast wounds, others Okay. Bags of MGs firing all day and brassing up with HE. [On 31st] refugees came past this morning very early – pitiful sight with very small children and old folks with a few of their chattels and blankets carried off in all kinds of contrivances.

For the period 28 September to 21 October the division held the line from Veghel to the Maas and north of Oss, a front of 14 miles. Patrols on both sides, supported by Brens and Stens or Spandaus and Schmeissers, took their daily toll. From 28 to 31 September the division had seventy-five casualties and in the first twenty-two days of October another 162. Artillery support on a small scale was frequently required. At Geffen on the 11th, when the Germans mounted a battalion attack at night, several hundred low-grade prisoners and deserters were caught and sent back down the centre line to the cages. Snipers on both sides made life unpleasant. A rotund, laconic Dutchman called 'Tom of Lith' was the boss of the active hundred members of the Dutch resistance. The 1st RB defended Geffen, and its church was a notable RHA observation post. The Rifle Brigade also defended the small industrial town of Oss with help from the 11th Hussars, and again its tower was a useful OP for the gunners. Maren village was attacked on the 5th, 7th and 20th by SS and Kriegmarines, who burned thirty houses but were seen off by 11th Hussars.

On 2 October Brigadier Pepper, CO Queens Brigade, left to take command of the School of Infantry at Barnard Castle and was replaced by Brigadier W.R. Cox from 50th Division, and on the 16th, after only three weeks in the saddle, Brigadier Cracroft had to go to hospital and was replaced as CO 22nd Armoured Brigade by Brigadier A.D.R. Wingfield from the 10th Hussars.

Corporal Reg Spittles, a Cromwell commander with 'B' Squadron 1st RTR, who had served with 2nd Northants Yeomanry in Normandy before they were taken out of the line and merged with their sister regiment, was wounded on 4 October helping keep open the centre line. With a section of the Queens in deep ditches on either side of the road, Reg checked out a large farm. 'This resulted in a nice bowl of fresh fruit and cream for the crew from the farmer and his wife and a bonus of 7 prisoners hiding in the cellar.' But a hamlet 600 yards ahead was obviously held and Reg's solitary tank and the Queens were stonked by accurate air burst that caused casualties, so the infantry withdrew. Reg's troop leader told him on the radio that he was 'the fly in the ointment' causing enemy reaction and to stay where he was. 'I was sitting there with my flaps open but keeping low in case of snipers when suddenly a fuselage of grenades came on and over the tank, several into the turret, nothing for it to bale-out.' Four of the crew including Reg received shrapnel wounds. They managed to stagger back to the RAP. Later Reg and his unwounded co-driver volunteered to go back with the troop's Sherman Firefly to recover his tank with its damaged electricals. Eventually the REME rewired it but Reg was sent back to hospital.

Gordon Johnson, 5th RTR, recalls how one very cold night the tank was parked in a village and the crew moved into a nearby house to sleep. In the morning he went out with the operator: 'We found a number of contraceptives frozen to the engine covers. We had stopped outside the local Bordello!'

Lieutenant Peter Kiddle with the Skins, wrote:

> That evening [11 October] under new orders, Martin Fitzgerald rattled his troop into Geffen. This large village unoccupied by day was held by a platoon of the Rifle Brigade plus a troop of tanks at night . . . Martin held two O-groups and the most extensive set of artillery DF tasks were issued and marked up together with their code names. The radio net to Regiment was endlessly checked. The quiet warm October night became a chattering, booming, flashing pandemonium due to my tank's guns, plus those of the Rifle Brigade, the 'burp' of Spandaus and the undivided attention of the 3 RHA 25-pdrs. The church tower stood in the path of some of the DF rounds. Small flames now flickered in the undergrowth ahead of us . . . glimpses of German helmets milling about near the RB positions. Two Panzerfaust bazookas hit the road, one damaging the tank track. [Later] Martin the RB platoon commander and I walked the perimeter of the infantry positions. The area was strewn with scores of German dead lying singly and in heaps just as they had fallen . . . A massive debt of gratitude to our splendid and ubiquitous gunners of 3 Royal Horse Artillery.

The Cherry Pickers spent this dreary period of three weeks based on Oss, backed up by a troop of Norfolk Yeomanry A/Tank guns. Het Wilt on the left and Ravenstein on the right were 13 miles apart. They slept in private houses or small farms, took shower baths with *hot* water in the local canning factory, played football, attended dances, went duck shooting. Their knowledge of the Dutch language increased dramatically but textile production in the town flagged as the girls liked talking to the 'Red-headed boys'. The Burgomeister was not amused. 1st RTR's diarist reported on the 14th: 'Regiment taking it in turn to watch sector at Geffen with the Skins – 4 days and 4 days out. No active patrols, just observation. In Oss the number of girls in jug for collaboration and fraternization with Jerry is colossal.' Trooper Hewison's girl was called Reik, 'hasn't been round yesterday', and he carried out a thriving barter business involving Yankee pants, officers' raincoats, towels and packets of fags. The Queens held the line with their south flank Zuidwillems Vaart Canal and the line Veghel/Everse/Middelrode and Laar. Derrick Watson was promoted to major when the CO of 'A' Company was killed by a shell. His CO was Lieutenant-Colonel Ian Freeland, 'a fine soldier from a family of soldiers. Both his father and his grandfather had been generals and his brother was another Lt-Colonel.' Bill Bellamy wrote:

We were facing the German 'Stomach' division of low medical category soldiers. Despite their handicaps they fought extremely well . . . The enemy were not very aggressive. The most aggressive person in the area was the heavily decorated commanding officer of the 1/5th Queens. He ran a series of the most bloodthirsty exercises in the deserted village of Dinther, designed to train his men *and us* in the not-so-gentle art of house to house fighting. The whole exercise was done at the double and his shouts of 'Grenades through downstairs windows – Sten through the door. Door down – Grenade top of stairs – Rooms right and left. Sten through the ceilings – Up the stairs – Grenades through doors – etc' still ring in my ears. He was a tonic and we blessed his foresight during the fighting which lay ahead.

Rex Wingfield and his mates of 1/6th Queens went to see *Champagne Charlie* and *Henry V* in the garrison theatre and talked to the Africa Star veterans mourning the sands of Knightsbridge, Alamein, Mareth line and Tunis. 'Rommel's dead. He was a cunning bastard'; they toasted his memory. But Rex's 'A' Company with its Canloan CO was down to 120 men. Since D-Day, up to 1 October, the division had suffered 2,801 casualties, compared with 11th Armoured and Guards Armoured losses of 3,825 and 3,385 men.

CHAPTER FIFTEEN

Operations Alan and Don – Late October – *'der Moffe Aweg'*

Western Holland was still held by the enemy and fierce fighting was taking place in Walcheren, Beveland and Southern Zeeland. Antwerp was therefore not yet opened up to shipping. The salient at Nijmegen, so hard won by 43rd Wessex, Guards Armoured and the gallant paratroopers, still held. But hastily assembled German battle groups – cooks, flak and grounded Luftwaffe, the deaf, the 'stomachs' and other invalids, with a leavening of bitter young SS – fought savagely to keep the British 2nd Army away from the Siegfried line. Tanks were confined to miserable dirt tracks commanded by A/Tank guns and Panzerfaust teams, and everywhere there were minefields. Uffizier Droste wrote home to his brother on 17 October:

> During the last few days my A/Tank gun has done good work. In one half hour I destroyed four tanks and after that I went after the infantry with HE shells. Of course I didn't have to wait long for retaliation. Fighter bomber attacks and the usual artillery fire, luckily none of my crew was hit although a hit destroyed the gun. I haven't got my gun any more. I have been made platoon commander. I think I'll get the Iron Cross 1st Class.

During October the main enemy battle groups encountered were named after their commanding officers: Gramse, Bloch, Dietrich and Hermann. In November they were Menzel and Grasmehl (of 7th Parachute Division), Brehmer (of 180th Division) and Hübner (of 344th Division).

The Peel country fields were waterlogged and surrounded by dykes, so slit trenches were a soaking wet misery. It was soggy, cold, the nights were lengthening, and anyone who fought in Holland during the winter of 1944–5 will remember it forever. Added to which the cruel V1 and V2 rockets were still raining down on London, southern England and Antwerp.

Operation Alan had been planned by XII Corps as a four-divisional attack to take Tilburg. 51st Highland Division were to break through the enemy divisions (712th and 59th) south of the Zuid Willemsvaart as far as the rivers and canals running north and south through 's Hertogenbosch. 15th

Scottish would attack from Best towards Tilburg and then 7th Armoured would pass through 51st and 15th Divisions to clear the wooded country between Tilburg and 's Hertogenbosch, and then move westwards between the Wilhelmina Canal and the River Maas. Finally 53rd Welch Division would attack 's Hertogenbosch, clear the town and push on towards the Aftwateringskanal and the River Maas.

The Queens Brigade, backed by 8th Hussars and 1st RTR had as objectives, Loon-op-Zand, Udenhout and Oisterwijk. Quite separately 5th RTR and the Skins were lent to back up the 53rd Welch Division. D-Day was 19 October, but for the division the advance started on the 22nd. Behind a formidable artillery barrage the Queens advanced across 'schu' and 'teller' minefields and elaborately dug and tunnelled village defence posts. 1/7th Queens took a day and a half to capture Middelrode, taking 130 prisoners but losing forty casualties in the process. 1/5th Queens encountered large minefields east of Laar, which they captured at 1430 hrs, and then went on to take Doornhoek by 1700 hrs. The supporting flails and fire-breathing Churchill Crocodiles loaned from 79th Armoured Division were a great success and twenty-one prisoners were taken at a cost of twelve casualties. On the right flank 1/6th Queens also did well, taking sixty-four prisoners and securing the important roads round Deelsburg, east of Doornhoek.

Lance-Corporal Jimmy Kay with 1/7th Queens, wrote:

Our attack started at 0600 hrs but while it was still dark I was struck down by a shell splinter and knew no more until I woke in a Brussels hospital some *six* days later. The shell had smashed my 'tin-hat' and made a large dent in the back of my skull. I was eventually flown home in a Dakota and landed up in a hospital in Cardiff and then to the Royal United in Bath.

His silver trumpet was lost but turned up two years later!

'A' Squadron 8th Hussars was supporting 1/5th Queens, as Bill Bellamy reported:

We were to advance with three Troops up, Frank Saxby on the right, Tony Hind in the centre and my troop on the left. Our objective was the small hamlet of Doornhoek. The heathland with pine woods was divided up by sandy tracks where mines could be laid easily and remain unseen. The going in the small boggy fields was wet and treacherous. At 0700 hrs Tony, Frank and I huddled together in the lee of Tony's tank talking, laughing and smoking endless cigarettes until the order to move came. [Later] There was a continual flurry of small arms fire and some mortar bombs but nothing to suggest anti-tank guns. We halted just over the track, located the machine guns. They, coupled with snipers, were in three thatched houses 200 yards to my front. The shots were uncomfortably close pinging off the armour plate. Three flail tanks of the Westminster Dragoons appeared through the hedge about 300 yards to my right. They advanced majestically towards the cottages, their chains flailing the ground ahead so as to explode any mines. The three tank commanders were standing up in their turrets directing the operation, unaware of so much small arms fire in their vicinity. Two of the tank commanders were shot dead and all three of the tanks turned and disappeared back into the woods.

Bill's tank was hit by Schmeisser fire but his troop fired shells and machine gunned the three cottages. 'Bill Pritchard came on the B set shouting "look out! Your tank is on fire". I looked back over the engine covers and saw all our bedding blazing, the spare battery was on its side, one petrol jerrican had fallen over and was spewing out petrol.' Bill threw a smoke grenade out to provide cover, leapt down to remove the burning impedimenta risking MG and sniper fire, looked down and saw the right-hand tank track was actually resting on the edge of a Teller mine! That was his first adventure of the day. The main enemy positions were on the edge of Doornhoek. Trooper Chamberlain by mistake drove the tank into a dyke containing 3 ft of water, in full view of the Germans. 'Chamberlain and Goldsworthy told me they were both sitting up to their arses in freezing cold water and I replied that that was their fault!' When Bill Bellamy saw the Queens' company commander near the bridge, he scrambled down from his tank to tell him what the situation was with the Skins troop. The commander in his Bren gun carrier slowed down slightly and said 'What the bloody hell are you doing here?' drove straight across the bridge and disappeared into the mist. Soon up came the ARV (Armoured Recovery Vehicle) with the ever-smiling Trooper Sharpe and the Welch Sergeant Davidson, the squadron fitter sergeant. 'Swimming now are we, Sir?' But better luck was in store. A German loot wagon had been captured, which was piled high with Dutch bank notes, household goods, blankets and linen. Bill still has a beautiful linen tablecloth, hand embroidered with flowers and motifs! The captured bottled foodstuffs included chicken in jelly, runner beans, and red and black currants. 'Our troop mess became a popular RV for the rest of the squadron.' Bill was awarded an immediate MC for his part in the Doornhoek battle.

Meanwhile the Skins had been lent to support 160th Infantry Brigade, of 53rd Welch Division, in their attack across flat open common, low thin hedges, scrubby cover and the usual deep, wide dykes. Nuland and Kruisstraat were the two objectives. On a two-battalion front 'A' Squadron was with 2nd Manchesters on the right, 'C' Squadron with 4th Welch on the left and 'B' Squadron was in reserve with the 6th Royal Welch Fusiliers. Flails and AVREs helped clear the minefields, and Crocodile flame throwers helped the attack into Nuland which was taken by 0845 hrs. Under heavy shell fire, Spandaus and 88s, by 1330 hrs they were into Kruisstraat. Despite tanks getting bogged down it was a completely successful operation. Lieutenant Henry Woods, 'C' Squadron, wrote about the attack on Nulands, which was strongly held:

1st troop on the right and the Crocodile troops were soon bogged in soft ground, then they extricated themselves and ran into a minefield, breaking tank tracks. 3rd Troop on the left came under intense fire from mortar and machine guns, sited in the village and the woodlands to the left front. Two more tanks became bogged, Lt Ackroyd was wounded by mortar fragments, and 3rd Troop had a tank knocked out by an 88mm.

The village was taken and two 88mm guns destroyed.

On the next day, the 23rd, the Manchesters, 'A' Squadron Skins and the Crocs fought their way into Bruggen by 1000 hrs, then north of the railway, and by nightfall had taken 300 prisoners and had reached Rosemalen. On their left 'C' Squadron and the Welch Regiment were in Molenbroek by 1700 hrs having knocked out two 75mm SPs. That night the East Lancs worked their way from Rosemalen into 's Hertogenbosch and at dawn on the 24th called for tank support. Major Gibson, CO 'A' Squadron, decided on a charge *along* the railway line embankment as the lesser of various evils (dykes, minefields and 88mm guns). They thundered along the narrow railway lines where one tank lost a track, joined up with the East Lancs, pushed into the north of town and seized the only undamaged bridge over the Zuidwillems Canal.

Sergeants Carr and Albert Morris gave their account:

The long straight railway line leading into 's Hertogenbosch was raised and provided a perfect silhouette for any anti-tank gunners. Smoke

'B' Squadron, 1st RTR, 's Hertogenbosch, 1944.

was to be fired to prevent observation from the dyke where we expected fire. The Sherman Firefly commanded by Albert Morris led the troop. Progress was agonisingly slow and demanded expert driving to keep the tank straddled across the lines. I urged the driver to speed up but he assured me that he was already standing on the accelerator.

Lieutenant Peter Walworth lost one tank to an 88mm gun, and the following day (24th) he was again 'brewed up' by an SP on the far side of the town's main canal. Sergeant Sydney Swift met an old friend from the North-West Indian frontier days, now commanding a Flail tank. He was with the squadron who helped the East Lancs storm the lock gates of the vital town canal and get a bridgehead across.

But back on the 23rd to the main divisional attack when 1/5th Queens took Berlicum, cleared Vreden-Daal and patrolled to Beekveld, taking thirty prisoners. 1/7th Queens advanced on Heeswijk but poor 'B' Company was now so depleted they had to be disbanded and merged with the other companies, and 1st RB took over their sector. 1/6th Queens with 1st RTR advanced steadily taking ninety-three prisoners, as Trooper Hewison recorded in his diary:

From Heesch to Berlicum to 's Hertogenbosch losing 3 casualties from mortar fire and Besa blowback. Had 3 tanks bogged, deadly ground, ditches and marshy. In the asset line we got 21 POW, one 88mm and our objective. Bags of brassing up all around – especially Besa. POWs just shot their officer who wanted to continue the fight. Dirty bastards! However they got wounded by their *own* mortars. We have 'Himmler' Stephens as OC for the present – a deadly bloke all round. Hasn't much idea, gets on your nerves with his eternal asking for repetitions.

The 8th Hussars, having spent two days near Doornhoek and Middlerode, moved on the 24th to Schijndel. Their next objective was Oosterhout – an attack due west in the opposite direction to the Siegfried line! In the event they crossed the river at Esch and 'arrived in Udenhout which had been captured by 1st RTR after a fierce struggle. Houses were blazing everywhere and it was obvious that the German infantry had needed to be driven out of each farm and building. We leaguered for the night near a gutted farmhouse,' recollects Bill Bellamy. 'The Dutch used the phrase "Alles Kaput, der kinder sind im keller, der moffe aweg". "Everything is destroyed, the kids are safe in the cellar and the bloody Germans have gone!"' The 1/6th Queens were now esconced in the outskirts of Kloosterhoek in a sanatorium, and officially Operation Alan was over and Operation Don was to follow on almost immediately. The plan was to advance and take Loon-op-Zand due north of Tilburg.

As the key bridge at Esch over the River Aa was blown and under heavy fire, the division was moved to Dinther to cross a new sapper bridge over the Zuid Willemsvaart Canal. After much to-ing and fro-ing the Queens

1/5th Queens in Berlicum. Left to right: Captain John Franklin, Lieutenant Doug Sadler, Major John Evans (in front), Lieutenant Arthur Traplin, van Boekstaele (interpreter).

Brigade crossed the Esch bridge on the evening of the 26th in support of the armour. Some progress was made the next day by 1/5th Queens and 1st RTR to Udenhout, where eighty prisoners were taken, and by the 8th Hussars and 1/7th Queens towards Loon, which was strongly defended. But the progress was considered to be too slow. Brigadier Wingfield went back to Divisional HQ. 'I found the Corps Commander, General Ritchie, ranting at poor Gerry Verney.' Everyone was tetchy and bad tempered. Wingfield noted on the 27th: 'Saw a green pennant near road, RHQ 8th Hussars with nearly all the officers having breakfast with their CO sitting at its head with a green and gold side cap perched on his head. When I recovered from this Crimean tableau, I blew my top. I asked the CO what the hell he thought he was doing here when I expected him to be in the outskirts of Loop-op-Zand.' His reply was that the 11th Hussars just down the road were held up. 'If the armoured cars could not get off the road, the tanks of the 8th Hussars bloody well could and would do so *at once* even if they sank submerged in the polders. The Irish doves flew out of their dovecote pretty quick.' Bill Bellamy's squadron was married up with 1/7th Queens and on the brow of a hill east of the main Tilburg-Loon road he remembers:

As Alan Howard fired [towards the village] there was a brilliant flash from the bushes and simultaneously an incredible roar and a whooshing noise seemed to envelop us. The shot came from a German

Tac HQ 22 Armoured Brigade: Brigadier Wingfield and his staff.

77mm A/Tank gun. It went diagonally from left to right across the front of my glacis plate, missing us by inches, then struck the ground at the front of Bill Pritchard's tank, passed straight under it, emerged at the rear and ricocheted over Alan Howard's turret before disappearing noisily into the rear areas.

They promptly knocked out the impudent SP. Meanwhile the Skins were in trouble. In thick woods and confused tracks the fourth Recce Troop tank was struck by two Bazookas – Sergeant Tom Wagstaff, Trooper Sid Parr, Ginger Percival and Trooper 'Nipper' Daley were killed, and a sniper badly wounded Corporal Bob Edwards, while 'B' Squadron lost two tanks. Later eight men were buried in the Uden cemetery, including poor Sergeant Bowley, who was accidentally killed by another Skins 77mm gun. Tilburg was captured by 15th Scottish on the evening of the 27th and the attack was switched to the north. Dongen was to be the objective of the Skins and RB and the final attack on Loon-op-Zand would be by 1/7th Queens plus 8th Hussars, reinforced by 1/5th Queens.

In the sandhills of Loon-op-Zand, far from the sea we had an interesting battle [recalled John Evans, 1/5th Queens]. Platoon Commander Doug Sadler was sent forward with a fighting patrol. The objective a ride – codename 'Blue'. He had to send codeword 'Red' and 'White' on his set as he reached certain map references en route – which he did but we never received the Blue signal! The patrol had been captured, but L/Cpl Bailey survived despite a heavy artillery stonk and Doug Sadler returned safely – after the war.

It was the turn of 1/7th Queens to attack the Kasteel south-east of Loon, mopping up in woods, clearing trenches with grenades. It was a hard fight and four guns and thirty-five POWs were taken for the loss of twenty-two casualties. Later on the attack was called off to allow 1st Gordons from 51st Highland Division to come in from the east to finish the job. Bill Bellamy with 8th Hussars reported:

We were delayed by very heavy and accurate shelling which made life especially difficult for the Queens. There was a lot of firing from machine guns but the mortar fire was intense, much bursting in the treetops. I left Alan Howard as point tank on the left hand side of the road. Bill Pritchard drew up to him on the right – thus we were able to bring all three tanks' fire to bear on the houses and the crossroads ahead.

Bill needed, urgently, to attend to a very personal matter, jumped out of his tank 'and before the delighted eyes of a company of the Queens undressed to allow nature to take its course, to good-humoured advice, realistic grunts and groans and a barrage of raspberries.' Despite their protests his troop was ordered back:

suddenly we heard the skirl of bagpipes. To our astonishment, two companies of the Gordon Highlanders appeared in extended order and marched across the meadows towards the main road. Behind them was their Piper, followed by their Colonel with a walking stick and presumably the Adjutant, other HQ staff, behind them a further company in extended order. There were mortar bombs dropping and the casualties were picked up by their stretcher bearers. They disappeared into the trees to our left. I felt I had been watching a battle in the Peninsular War.

The battle continued briskly on the next day, the 29th, with 5th RTR and 1/6th Queens taking Zandkant with nineteen POWs, and 1/5th Queens attacking the road running west of Loon taking thirty-four POWs and losing a dozen casualties. But the main attack on Loon, even though supported by two RHA regiments plus four medium regiments, alas failed. John Pilborough of the Skins described it:

The enemy was in possession of a belt of woodland which could *only* be approached over a wide stretch of open marshy ground. 'C' Squadron carrying Rifle Brigade infantry on their tanks, attempted a frontal attack on this wood. The artillery put down a preparatory barrage but moving across the open ground, two tanks became hopelessly bogged, two were knocked out by mines and another by a 75mm anti-tank gun. The RB's came under Spandau fire from the wood and the attack was completely broken up. 'C' Squadron withdrew to re-group. [Later] 'A' Company 1st RB went in on foot from the flank supported by the tanks and cleared the wood, taking 40 prisoners and the regiment then advanced without opposition towards Dongen, which was later taken by 8 Hussars and 1/5 Queens to the best welcome in Holland.

The final day of operation, the 30th, began with 1st RTR and 1/5th Queens starting from Vaart, heading for Oosterhout. Major F.D. Pile MC, of 'A' Squadron, remembered that 'at the capture of Oosterhout, SSM McKee's troop excelled themselves by capturing in half an hour a group of A/Tank guns and enemy infantry'. Peter Roach, 1st RTR, wrote:

My fear gauge was registering nil and I was feeling thoroughly aggressive. There were Germans running in many directions so we helped them on their way with the Browning MG. Some men ran into a house so we put a few rounds of HE in after them. We were all reduced to the level of primaeval animals running their quarry down, so thin is our veneer of civilisation.

John Evans, 1/5th Queens, had two good stories:

Near Ittervoort we took up a ghastly position on flat ground overlooked by a flat-roofed factory. We couldn't move in daylight, stayed in limited slit trenches all day. We were grateful for this because we asked for Typhoons with their terrifying rockets to take out the factory. We cheered as they arrived but the radio operator who was sharing my slit trench said 'You'd think they were diving straight at us, Sir, wouldn't you?' I said 'They bloody well are!' Five minutes of explosions, columns of dust, noise and the smell of cordite . . . The CO told me later that the RAF had reported they had wiped out a party of Germans . . .

Near Zandfort the RHA FOO brought down fire on a concrete pillbox. 'When we eventually took it, it was scarred but inside a kettle was boiling on the stove and on the table was a hurriedly written note reading "Well done, boys. The way to Berlin is long and strong. Lieut. Kessenich L62282 G LGP Minster."'

The ten days of these two operations had cost the division over a hundred casualties, mainly in the Queens, and twenty-two tanks were lost. However, 900 prisoners had been taken, at least 800 casualties inflicted on the enemy, eight SPs and twelve A/Tank guns had been knocked out or destroyed. The conditions were very difficult for the armour with heavily wooded country, poor tracks, embanked roads, and dykes and polder waiting to bog Cromwells. It was basically an infantry, but not a lorried infantry, series of small bitter engagements. Rex Wingfield described some of the prisoners taken:

> This lot were a rabble, a couple of Mongolians, ex-Russians who were used as stooges and general dogsbodies by each Wehrmacht platoon, a more contemptible shower, but one 12 year old Hitler Jugend from Langemark division, skinny, blubbered and writhed when captured . . . The dangerous lad had a Schmeisser machine pistol, a Lüger pistol, 3 potato masher grenades and a wicked paratroop knife. The culprit received a damned good spanking and was sent off to a POW cage.

However wretched the prisoners appeared to be on surrender, they had been perfectly capable of laying mines, firing Spandaus, Bazookas, even anti-tank guns.

The division deserved its ten day rest, mainly billeted in warm Dutch houses. Divisional HQ pitched up in some comfort in Tilburg, the day after its liberation by 15th Scottish. At a dance in the town hall on 2 November, sponsored by the Lord Mayor and Mayoress, Colonel 'Cuthie' Goulburn, CO 8th Hussars, danced with the prettiest girls in the room. At the same time 1st RB on the Maas at the fortress town of Geertruidenberg were under mortar fire fending off enemy patrols. The four squadrons of the Cherry Pickers and 8th Hussars, with concerts and football marches had their 'feet under the table' in Dongen.

Brigadier A.D.R. Wingfield DSO, MC, wrote of his first impressions on assuming command of the 22nd Armoured Brigade:

> Teddy Swetenham, CO of the Skins, was an Etonian friend a year younger, 1 RTR and 5 RTR commanded by Pat Hobart [nephew of the famous 'Hobo' who formed 11th Armoured and now commanded the 'Funnies', 79th Armoured Division] and Gus Holliman both several years younger than myself. Gus was to be killed later on. Victor Paley, CO 1st Rifle Brigade was several years my senior as was 'Cuthie' Goulburn CO 8th Hussars. The 131 Queens Brigade commanded by a nice light Infantry man called Cox, the Div Artillery is under Brigadier 'Tiger' Lyon-Smith. The 5 RHA are with my Brigade, I knew Lt Col Freddie Moore in Cairo. The Brigade Major Joe Leaver soon to be replaced by Toby Farnell-Watson, also RTR. Bob Lipkin was DAQMG and Pat Fitzgerald commanded the signal squadron. Nice to have two Irish cavalry regiments.

CHAPTER SIXTEEN

Watch on the Maas in East Brabant and Limburg

For ten relatively peaceful weeks, until the middle of January, the division was almost entirely motionless, initially guarding the west bank of the River Maas and later the east bank. Only two or three small actions of any consequence took place, although patrolling took place both night and day and there was frequent RHA support, which was returned by shelling and mortaring from across the river. It was a sodden autumn with flooded fields and dykes, disintegrating roads and tracks, which kept the sappers busy. Then followed a winter that was severe and cold, with snow lying on the ground.

The Skins spent November in clean, comfortable, warm billets at Opoeteren, 20 miles north of Maastricht. John Pilborough in *First in, Last out* describes their activities:

> In the Recce troop we got rid of the carriers, instead had three 'sawn-offs'. All new Brownings were mounted to depress and fire within a yard of the tank side. We never again lost a vehicle to a 'Geyser with a bazooka' as Corporal Proudlove called them. As a change from the everlasting tinned food, such articles as flour and rice, fresh meat and vegetables were issued. The regiment took over a café in Mechelen and was running it as a short leave centre, in a bustling city with a good shopping centre.

The Belgians were extremely friendly and hospitable and leave to Brussels was very popular. Peter Roach, 1st RTR, noted: 'It was gay and sleeping in a bed and having a bath were luxuries which I enjoyed to the full. Beer was plentiful and there were lots of pretty girls to look at . . . We did practically nothing for five weeks, I became thoroughly discontented. I desperately wanted to see the end of the war.' Bill Bellamy, 8th Hussars, wrote: 'We arrived in Maesyeck on Nov. 11th – Armistice Day. It was not a very exciting town in which to be billeted, although we made the best of it. I personally never felt very welcome there. Our squadron Officers Mess was up in a café on the main street.'

The Cherry Pickers were watching a 3-mile stretch of river front between Maesyck and Ophovem along the Wessem Canal in unattractive country with minefields everywhere. Radio was rarely used and signallers ran out

Panheel Lock.

field telephones to the forward OPs manned by RHA FOOs. Everyone was issued with the new zoot suits, which had tricky zips but were warm and nearly waterproof.

The Queens were initially near Waalwijk and Vrijhoeve Capelle, but moved to Elshoot, Haarsteg and Vlijmen, having been first relieved by the Royal Netherlands Brigade and then by the Canadians on 9 November. Next they moved to new positions facing east and north, 1/7th Queens at Kessenich, 1/6th Queens at Thorn and 1/5th Queens facing north at Ittervoort. Private Wingfield wrote later: '3 weeks same slit trenches, bored & strained with constant patrols.'

On 13 November 53rd Welch Division were to make an attack east across the Wessem Canal, and the Desert Rats were ordered to make a diversionary attack to secure the large Panheel Lock, with undamaged gates at the south-east end of the canal. Any sudden alteration of the water level in the canals would disorganize the Welch attacks to the north dependent on pontoon bridges. This task – and it proved to be a very difficult one – was given to 1/7th Queens backed up by a squadron of 8th Hussar Cromwells. Under a heavy artillery stonk on all known targets, Major D.C. Sleneck, CO 'D' Company with 'A' Company in reserve attacked at 1615 hrs in pouring rain and was met with heavy artillery and MG fire. As Bill Bellamy reported: 'Panheel Lock lay between the villages of Thorn and Wessem about five miles north of Maeseyck. The canal was between high banks and the enemy were well entrenched there with a good field of fire. It was wet country, horrible for tanks.'

Most of the Queens were soon pinned down by heavy fire and three times the successive company commanders became casualties. Lieutenant D. Wilkinson-Cox, who had just joined his platoon from REME and had never been in action before, and Sergeant Allen performed nobly. Eventually the gates were examined by a sapper officer and pronounced OK. But 1/7th Queens took thirty-seven casualties including seven officers in three-quarters of an hour. The objective was reached but at an appalling cost. There were rumours that 21st Army Group had been told that the Queens Brigade was punch drunk and should be withdrawn from the line!

Nick Nice was 2 i/c 'B' Company 1/6th Queens at Thorn when they were ordered to stir things up and make a *silent* night attack on the small village of Wessem. 'All went well until we reached the canal when we found that Jerry had opened the sluice gates and flooded the area, the only apparent way over the canal was by a very large blown tree – "bloody monkeys on active service" – booby traps had been laid among the branches.' But the village was taken more or less peacefully. Coy HQ was set up in a comfortable house, with loo and running water marked 'OC and 2 i/c only.' The Canloan company commander Major Lilley decided to go on leave. In his absence Queens snipers so provoked the opposition's patrols that:

> Jerry sent over a dirty great concentration which landed smack on the 3-tonner (with 4 days rations and stores), on our beloved shit-house (with running water). Talk about chaos and confusion, our signaller wounded, his 19 set u/s, the Major's bed and (quality) greatcoat riddled with shell splinters. Next day Major Lilley returned and carefully, slowly and awfully he told us in unadulterated lowest of the Canadian low [language] exactly what he thought of a 2 i/c who had reduced *his* Coy within 48 hours to a complete and utter shambles.

On another occasion the Queens Brigade HQ at Neeritter was rudely stonked by twenty shells, which upset the occupants of the handsome Kasteel.

Brigadier W.R. Cox, CO of the Queens Brigade, now moved to command 69th Infantry Brigade and was replaced by Brigadier J.M.K. Spurling from 50th Division. There was also another significant change of Top Brass. Major General Verney moved on 22 November to command 6th Armoured Division in Italy. He was succeeded by Major-General L.O. Lyne DSO, who in Normandy had commanded first the 59th Infantry Division until it was broken up in August, then 50th Northumbrian Division, which now reverted to a training division in the UK, and now, third time lucky, the Desert Rats for the final lap through the Siegfried line into Germany.

The Cherry Pickers, often dismounted, carried out the role of 'Military Government' as each troop leader assumed duties of local 'commandant'

Monty inspects 1st RTR in Holland, winter 1944.

reigning over the Dutch or Belgian farms and villages within the boundaries of the defence zone allotted. Detachments of Dutch Resistance, and a company of Belgian Fusiliers came under command – light on the trigger, profligate with ammo expended, but 'fire-eaters'!

Field Marshal Montgomery carried out an investiture at Bree on the 29th. The Cherry Picker CO, Lieutenant-Colonel Wainman, was awarded the DSO, and MCs and MMs were given to many brave young leaders, alas many posthumously.

The division was now told about Python and Lilop. All men who had served overseas for five years could be returned to the UK (Python), or, if they volunteered to return, have extended leave (Lilop, Leave in lieu of Python). As a result many of the Queens, RHA, RTR, 8th and 11th Hussars, extremely experienced officers and men, now left the Desert Rats and returned home. A hundred men each of 1/6th and 1/7th Queens returned to the UK to 50th Division (Training), and the remainder were transferred to fill gaps in the 1/5th Queens. So on 30 November the Queens moved back to the villages of Rothem, Eelen and Neeroeteren, 4 miles west of Maesyck, and were addressed by the new GOC, who had once commanded the sister unit of 169th Queens Brigade. There were sad farewell messages from 3rd RHA, 8th Hussars and the Northumberland Fusiliers. Captain A.F. Perdue, platoon commander of 1/6th Queens, related how, on 3 December:

the Battalion convoy led by the carrier platoon crossed the start line [on the way back to Ypres for disbandment]. There to our surprise lined up to the right and left of the track exit were the guns of the 3 RHA. Their gun barrels were elevated to an angle of 60 degrees so as to form a triumphal arch. As we made our way through this guard of honour the gunners on either side cheered and applauded a brave but battered lorried Infantry Bn whom they had accompanied and protected all the way from North Africa.

They drove off via Brussels and Oudenarde to billets in Ypres and Poperinghe; thence to embarkation on 14 December at Ostende, and finally to Helmsley and Yeadon in Yorkshire. There they trained large numbers of RASC and AA men as infantry. Lieutenant Colonel W.D. Griffiths and J.H. Mason held moving farewell parades. The Queens Brigade had fought with BEF in 1940, at Alamein and Salerno and were some of the earliest troops in Normandy. But the rumours proved true. Peter Knight, a signaller at TAC HQ, 1/5th Queens, wrote: 'Both 1/6 Queens and 1/7 Queens were no longer considered a fighting force because of casualties but the break up still came as a very big shock.'

Rex Wingfield remembers how the news of their disbandment reached him at Thorn, and the Brigadier gave every man fifty fags, and on the way back on the N19 to Bourg Leopold they sang 'Fred Karno's Army', 'Keillies Jam', and 'Or would you rather be a fish?' Near the Menin Gates in Ypres was the new Cloth Hall used as the regimental cookhouse. The RSM came in followed by a tearful Belgian civilian. 'Which of you bastards flogged this man a TCV [Troop Carrying Vehicle]?' Several of 1/6th and 1/7th Queens then joined the 1st Herefords and 3rd Monmouthshires of 11th Armoured Division. 'Naturally we think 7th AD is the best. The 11th is next. It must be pretty good to have captured Antwerp. Wherever you go don't ever forget 131 Brigade and 1/6th Queens. Good luck lads. Fall 'em out, Sar' Major.' The two new arrivals were the 2nd Devonshires, commanded by Lieutenant-Colonel P.H.W. Brind, and 9th Durham Light Infantry, CO Lieutenant-Colonel H.J. Mogg (now Field Marshal). Both infantry battalions came from 50th Northumbrian Division and joined at 1630 hrs on 31 November at Dilsen in Belgium. They now had the new role of lorried infantry, reshuffled their transport and had an incoming draft of 200 men each.

When I returned in Nov 1944 from being wounded during Market Garden [wrote Ronald Mallabar, HQ Company, 9th DLI] 50 Div had gone and 9 DLI was part of 7 AD. I was doing an interesting job as a Regimental Signaller for which I had been trained. By this time the 9th Battalion had become my whole life and everything else seemed unreal. When I was away from the battalion, even in hospital, I fretted to be back. I missed hearing a Geordie voice calling out 'How way, me bonny lads, get forward. Your mates are up there.'

Many of the newcomers were eighteen-year-olds known as 'six-weekers', the length of their initial infantry training course. Training was in fact still taken very seriously at this late stage in the war. At Quatre Bras, near Brussels, the Cherry Pickers sent 300 men to the training school under Major A.V.C. Robarts: leading and probing the advance in lightskinned armoured cars is not for the fainthearted nor for the careless! Many refresher courses were held in all the armoured regiments – gunnery, tactics, maintenance and radio signals.

11th Hussars garrisoned Roosteren and Gebroek and 1st RB guarded the deserted villages of Holtum and Nieustadt. 'At Nieustadt in freezing weather tank engines had to be started up frequently during the night,' wrote Christopher Milner, 1st RB, 'very helpful to German patrols. "A" Company HQ was in a cellar on the side of the town square facing the Boche – a shell enters, bounces on stairs and kills Corporal Kelly and wounds the CO Eric Sergeant in the head and I then took command of "A" Company.' Lieutenant Brett-Smith described Gebroek as 'more sinister than Roosteren, a knot of mined and semi-ruined houses and farms knocked about by shellfire and without a sign of human habitation. Nothing was alive here, all crumbling and rotting away as the wind and the rain did their destructive work.' The Rifle Brigade was holding a 3,000-yard front from Nieustadt on the right, a large village near the deep, fast flowing Vloed Beek, which had 30-ft banks, then the main road from Maastricht and Sittard northwards to Holtum on the left. Colonel Paley, their CO, wrote:

It was a long and rather exasperating month. We had not really got enough men to hold the villages *and* put out as many patrols as we would have liked. The Germans were very active at night and had dug tunnels into the banks of the Vloed Beek making themselves practically impervious to shelling. The 5 RHA strictly enforced the ten-for-one retaliation rule for defensive fire stonks. Before Christmas we were regaled with a good assortment of propaganda pamphlets from the enemy artillery. Bn HQ was in the large village of Born in pretty good comfort!

Bill Bellamy was not particularly happy.

It was bitterly cold and the snow began as we arrived. To my initial horror I was told that our [8th Hussars] role was to be that of infantry and our tanks were to remain in the rear area. We then all went out in squadron transport to the village of Gebroek where I was allocated a few semi-demolished houses on the forward edge of the village, shown where the enemy were and told to set up a defensive position. A young officer from 1st RB told us about infantry patrols, standing patrols, siting Bren guns on fixed lines. 500 yards away, in and around Bakenhoven was a German Parachute regiment and they were very tough indeed.

Loading ammunition into a dug-in Cromwell tank, Holland, December 1944.

Then Bill in rapid succession had a severe attack of sinusitis and virus infection, went to hospital, was presented with the MC by Colonel 'Cuthie' Goulburn, recovered, went back to Grevenbicht and was posted to a mine clearance course at the Divisional Battle School in Brussels. There 'life centred around the Officers Club in the Rue de la Loi, sited in the old British Embassy, "Le Jockey Club", a night spot in the Ave. Louise and the "Eye" Club for the Guards Officers in the Bd. Anspach.'

Captain Bobby Wolfson, who had served with 4th RHA in the desert and Italy, was crossposted back to the UK, and arrived unannounced in Brussels to look for a proper job. He found an officer wearing the Jerboa sign, and said: 'Take me to your leader.' On the morrow the CRA told him: 'An officer of 3 RHA skating on a Dutch canal fell in, drowned. Wolfson, *you* take his place.' So Bobby joined 3rd RHA as troop commander of the famous Java troop in place of Gordon Dale who had been nicknamed 'Swee' Pea' as in the Popeye cartoon!

Norman Smith, 5th RTR and Joe, his mate, had leave passes to Brussels, and stayed at a little hotel near the Gare du Nord:

We had both acquired new battledresses so we were comparatively respectable. We had quite a lot of money considering the level of a trooper's pay as we had not drawn any cash since D-Day. We had a delightful leisurely and comfortable meal in a splendid place in the Rue Neuve. One or two British Army brass-hats came in, looked surprised to see Joe and me sitting there. I noticed a Brigadier looking at the Desert Rat on our arm flashes but he did not send a brandy over to our table!

Later they settled in a jolly little café/brothel near the Gare du Nord called 'Café Mimosa'. 'The madame was a kind motherly figure . . .'

'I was appalled by the class distinction which prevailed between the officers and the "other ranks",' noted Mallabar of the 9 DLI. 'For example no matter what the situation, there *has* to be an "Officers Mess" be it only a barn or a corner of a wrecked building. I was always amazed at the way in which the officers whisky and gin rations managed to reach our front line positions.' Life is, of course, rarely fair. Divisional HQ was at Limbricht with only an exiguous minefield between them and the enemy 3,000 yards away. Eventually they changed places with 5th RTR, who were in reserve at Geleen.

On 7 December the division, part of XII Corps, moved east across the Maas to relieve the Guards Armoured – on a new front about 7 miles long between Maesyck and Sittard. 131st Brigade (now alas, no longer called the Queens Brigade) were on the right and south of the line at Millen and Tuddern. The newly joined 9th DLI occupied ground in three countries – Rifle companies in Germany, 'A' Echelon at Sittard in Holland, 'B' Echelon at Dilsen in Belgium. 1/5th Queens along the small Vloed Beek Canal, in the village of Wehr, sent their patrols out in white camouflage suits, but lost men to the enemy minefields hidden in the winter snow. The dykes were frozen hard, which made patrolling easier but more dangerous. 'It was Sod's law, of course, that this winter was one of the coldest that even the Dutch could remember,' recalls Norman Smith, 5th RTR. He wore an army vest, an American cotton shirt, an army sweater and an American leather cotton-lined aircrew jacket: 'We looked and felt a bit like penguins in all this with our revolvers belted on the outside of the new canvas tank-suits with zip fasteners and clip-on hoods. We had a choice of army woollen gloves or tank issue unlined gauntlet gloves. They came in one size – bunch of bananas size. There were a number of cases of frost-bite.'

On 21 December the Skins moved back to Munster Geleen, a small mining town, and their Cromwells were painted white. The Ardennes counter-offensive had produced many stories of Germans dressed in Yankee uniform scudding behind the line and Lieutenant Duckworth of the recce party saw a jeep-load of genuine Americans arrested! The recce troop was turned, temporarily, into a mobile mortar section and went off to the front to learn their new trade from the 9th DLI. Both RHA regiments were kept quite busy with minor stonks and firing 'propaganda' leaflet targets. Nothing serious! Hurricane lamps were left burning in tank turrets all night and engines of *all* vehicles had to be run every two hours to prevent freezing. The oil on machine guns froze and had to be removed.

Much thought and military planning was given to Christmas. The divisional concert party, of West End standard, wrote their own music and plays, designed sets, scenery and costumes, and their Christmas pantomime had a long run at Sittard. The Skins produced a regimental revue by Lieutenants Peter Duckworth and Ben Tottenham, and their 'Western Brothers'

The Desert Rats Christmas card, 1944.

monologue, 'It's frightfully 5 DG' was praised. John Pilborough, Tony Price and Bob Sawtell wrote their own monologue, 'Push On, Recce, Push On.' The Durham Light Infantry reported dances, socials, first class Christmas fare, a Christmas tree and the regimental band playing on church parades. 3rd RHA dug in just outside Sittard in the snow, but an adjacent monastery provided a large hall and the monks were most co-operative. A regimental competition for the best song, with short leave in Brussels as prizes, was won by Major Jack Tirrel (who had earned more MMs and MCs than anyone else in the division). Wines were imported from Belgium and pretty girls from Holland, but the regiment was in action on both 25 and 26 December.

Lieutenant-Colonel P.R.C. Hobart ensured that 1st RTR at Neeroteren had plenty of rum to go with their pork and the officers played the sergeants in the traditional football match.

> Our platoon officer in I Company 1 RB was Lt Gerald Lascelles [recalled Harry Hopkins on his return after being wounded in Normandy], who apart from being related to the Royal Family, was also a pianist with a leaning towards jazz. When I joined 15 Platoon it was in a café in Belgium. The men were sitting around listening to someone dressed in a flying jacket playing the piano. He said 'Welcome, I am your platoon officer, I hope you like music.' Unofficially it appeared that whenever we entered a village or town the batman's job was to find a piano!

> Trooper B.L. Roberts, 'B' Squadron 1st RTR, came from Northampton and had worked at Barratts shoe factory. He was billeted with the family Ehlen – Mum, Dad and four children – in Braeksittard. In a nearby German village he found the local cobbler's shop and liberated half soles, heels, bit, hammer and rivets and mended the Ehlen family shoes. His fame grew as 'Robart was a schoonermaker'.

Every unit in the division reported that local dances were usually a disaster area. Inevitably the local pastor, who probably had German relations, banned or discouraged the local girls in his congregation from 'fraternizing' with the enemy. In a way it was rather funny, since strict 'non-frat' orders were shortly to be inflicted on the whole of BEF/BLA/BAOR troops!

Bill Bellamy, back from Brussels, found his troop in its infantry role supporting the 1st RB near Holtum. On Christmas Day he visited the abandoned dark and gloomy church and had a strange encounter: 'When the person appeared I was stunned to see a young German officer in his long grey greatcoat and peaked cap. For a brief second we both looked at each other in horror, suddenly he flung himself down the stairwell and escaped back to the German lines.'

The Cherry Pickers' Christmas fare was the ubiquitous pork, tinned turkey, mince pies, Christmas pudding, cake, fruit, plenty of fags, two bottles of beer per man plus local fowl, hare or geese. But Clifford Smith wrote: 'The Germans launched an attack on Gebroek village on Christmas night driving 'D' Squadron & RHA FOO out, but they left the next day after being extensively shelled.' It was a rude little battle involving thirty Germans, a stonk of twenty-five 88mm shells and much Spandau fire. Several Hussar vehicles and the RHA Cromwells were lost. 1/5th Queens in Wehr alternated their companies in the line and took over the local Gasthof. Mr Frank Gillard, BBC correspondent, spent Christmas with them and introduced Corporal Pass of 'D' Company into Monty's Christmas broadcast, which was just before the King's speech. Sadly Pass, a veteran of Greece, Crete and the Middle East, was killed later before Hamburg. Derrick Watson wrote: 'Those of us with a sense of history felt it was fitting that our Christmas was being spent on German soil. John Gordon of the Sunday Express visited our front line and then asked "Where are the Germans?" "Over there, presumably", I answered, pointing across the level countryside. He seemed disappointed.' But boisterous singing of 'Heilige Nacht' floated across the frost-bound no-man's land and the RHA were ordered to disturb the revelry by night – and did so. 'On Christmas Eve,' wrote Private Verdon Besley, 1/5th Queens, 'my friend David Butcher from Bath and I were in a forward look-out post. We were both feeling a little homesick and I remember saying that the same stars above were shining at home.'

CHAPTER SEVENTEEN

January and Operation Blackcock

The cold New Year's Day found the Desert Rats still holding a defensive line, patrolling and stonking, watching V1s and V2s and the new jet-propelled aircraft. When 8th Hussars and 1st RB had retaken Gebroek after the Boxing Day fracas, Bill Bellamy noted:

> We stayed there for four weeks, celebrated the New Year well and then woke up to witness the tremendous air effort which the Luftwaffe mounted at that time. We watched the dog fights going on above us. Later in the day we were astonished to see large numbers of V1 bombs on their way to Antwerp. 'A' troop on our left deflected one which sailed joyfully back towards the Reich. We all cheered at that.

The Luftwaffe had in fact caught every aerodrome and their defences napping, and the RAF lost scores of planes on the ground. The Divisional 15th LAA came into their own and their Bofors guns claimed at least nine victims.

The savage German armoured attacks in the Ardennes were eventually contained. Monty ordered 11th Armoured to act as longstop on the Meuse guarding several key towns, where they had a number of brisk actions. And the RAF and USAAF eventually turned defeat into victory. Lucky troopers and riflemen, including Clifford Smith, 11th Hussars, gained UK leave: 'I was lucky enough to be drawn out for the second batch at the beginning of January.' Rex Wingfield went on a three day 'Intelligence' course at 131st Brigade HQ, 'compass work, map reading, OP work, field telephone working, interpretation of aerial strip photography, recognition of enemy uniforms and insignia, captured pay book data, and learning basic German phrases'. He and his mates gave a birthday party for ten-year-old Gerda in their billet house at Capelle – coffee beans for the adults, not seen or tasted for four years, little bars of toilet soap, chocolate bars, a box of boiled sweets, gloves and a Blighty knitted scarf for the little girl.

> The Rifle Brigade were resting for a few days from 3rd Jan in the mining village of Geleen [wrote Lieutenant-Colonel Paley] and the RMO, Capt Carpenter, who had been with us since the end of the

Tunisian campaign caused a good deal of ribald comment by putting the Regimental Aid Post next door to the leading town brothel – possibly rather a shrewd move as it precluded any rifleman from patronising it! . . . David Clive went to Rheims on a successful expedition to bring back champagne for a big *divisional* officers' party.

Back on the front line, on the 9th, a raiding party of 9th DLI advancing towards Isenbruch took heavy casualties in a snowstorm, as Ronald Mallabar relates: 'I took part in an abortive night raid by A Coy at a village called Isenbruch in deep snow. Talk was that it was to snatch some German prisoners from a house. During the creeping artillery barrage shells fell short and the Durhams had to jump into a dyke six feet deep, six feet wide, half full of water.' On the other side were minefields covered by the falling snow. 'Immediately men were being killed or wounded or losing their legs. Within a few minutes we had suffered so many casualties that we were obliged to give up and withdraw without ever seeing a German.' The next day 1/5th Queens were relieved by 2nd Devons and went back to Geleen to prepare for Operation Blackcock.

XII Corps was given the task of clearing 176th and 183rd German Infantry Divisions, which had dug-in SPs and 88mms, from a triangle formed by the rivers Roer, Wurm and Maas – an advance of 12 miles in a north-east direction. The Desert Rats were on the left flank with 131st Brigade attacking northwards to secure Echt, Schilberg and Susteren. Then the plan was for 22nd Armoured Brigade to break through northwards to Montfort and St Odilienburg. If the ground remained frozen the operation was possible, but if a thaw turned deep ditches, canals and water meadows into a quagmire then it would be extremely difficult. Much of 52nd Lowland Division was under command – their 155th Infantry Brigade plus 8th Armoured Brigade.

The first task on 13 January was the capture of Bakenhoven, a small village on the west side of the Vloed Beek stream. 1/5th Queens 'D' Company did this after Lothians and Border Yeomanry flail tanks had cleared the minefields in the way, and after a heavy RHA barrage.

The extrovert Canloan Major C.V. Lilley commanded 'D' Company, which repulsed a determined counter-attack by white-suited German infantry. This caused seventeen casualties but twenty-seven enemy dead were counted on the frozen ground. Now thick freezing fog descended on the battlefield and D-Day was set for dawn of 16 January. The Durhams crossed the 20-ft Vloed Beek at 0730 hrs using carefully made ladders. By 1030 hrs a bridge had been captured over the second dyke in front of Dieteren and many prisoners taken.

Derrick Watson wrote:

Rather apologetically my CO (Lt Col Freeland) told me that my first orders as a company commander would come from the 9th DLI to

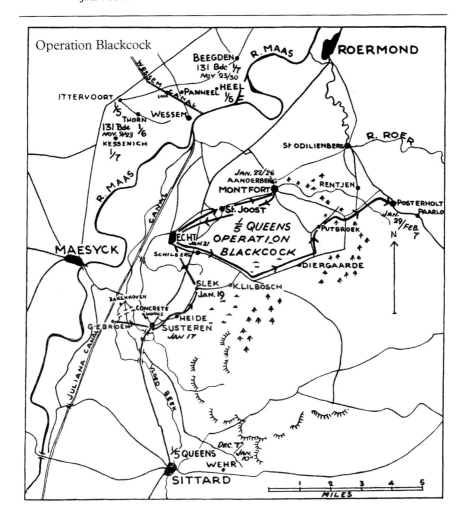

whom I was detached under command. We were to advance across two water obstacles [over the Vloed Beek] carrying sections of capok bridging, then towards a main road [Sittard to Roermond]. I was given a map and an incomprehensible aerial photograph. So we set off at last light – in the distance there was continual mortar fire, Very lights, Spandaus firing on fixed lines.

They reached their first objective, the derelict buildings of a concrete works, safely. Derrick Watson was next ordered by Lieutenant-Colonel Freeland to take his company to join up with 'C' Company under Major Lilley, who had been supporting the tanks and the Rifle Brigade near Millerode. 'Contact had been lost. With a heavy heart I ordered the Sgt Major to fall the men in on the road – they had spent a cold night – no sleep, no food or drink for more than 12 hours. Was it too much to ask? I had a dreadful thought – suppose they refused to follow me? As we marched off the men behind me spontaneously burst into song!' After a mile or so they reached the next village, 'a scene of devastation which silenced the singing. The houses in the main street had been shelled to ruins.' Some wounded 'C' Company told him where to find Major Lilley and 'he greeted me with a broad grin and said "This rum has kept me going for the last 36 hours."'

To get armoured vehicles across the Vloed Beek, 621st Field Squadron RE bulldozed a causeway under fire in thick fog and smoke, and Churchill tanks laid fasces and 'scissor' bridges across. They were protected by 'I' Company 1st RB who had to deal with two enemy patrols with their sniffer dogs.

At 0200 hrs on the 17th 1/5th Queens attacked Susteren from the west in the pitch dark and in thick mud. It was impossible to get the 6-pounder A/Tank guns across the dykes. A counter-attack was driven off by Brens and 3rd RHA stonks just after a foggy dawn.

'B' Company under Major John Evans moved forward at 0400 hrs and got within 30 yards of the outskirts of Susteren, 2 miles from the German border.

We heard a guttural shout and a single shot was fired [wrote Evans]. We then adopted our usual tactic of rushing in screaming and shouting, firing from the hip. We ran through the forward part of the town taking about 37 prisoners and not suffering a single casualty . . . At dawn we discovered three enemy tanks in the town. There were no 6-pounder A/Tank guns. Our own tanks had failed to reach us because of the dykes, drainage ditches and soft ground. There followed some desperate fighting with the tanks demolishing corner street properties on top of our men. Corporal Dolly knocked the track off one tank with a Piat for which he later received the Military Medal. I fired my captured Schmeisser – two short bursts at two tank commanders in their open turrets. It was obvious we were in for a long day and would suffer many casualties.

The acting CO, Major Jack Nangle, arranged that the Corps Artillery would shell the village to try to knock out the tanks. During the shelling and counter-shelling Evans was badly wounded and Lieutenant Stone was killed. It was a shambles but the company held its position in spite of thirty-nine casualties, including all the officers, but twenty-nine Queens were taken prisoner. Against that forty enemy prisoners were taken and at least that amount killed. 'Less than 40 men survived that day. Captain John Franklyn and all the platoon commanders were killed.' John Evans was the only officer to survive, although with two sets of wounds including the eventual amputation of his left arm. The war artist Bryan de Guingeau had two pages of illustrations of the Susteren battle in the *Illustrated London News* of 17 February 1945.

'B' Squadron 1st RTR finally managed to cross the Beek and come to the assistance of the surivors of 'B' Company, and in the mopping up next day took another seventy-seven prisoners. Peter Roach describes 1st RTR's start to Operation Blackcock:

We moved off [from Stadtbroek near Sittard on the 16th] on ice-covered roads and in a thick fog which held up the attack and gave us time to whitewash our tanks as some sort of camouflage. With the daylight [on the 17th] came a thaw which though slight turned the tracks to quagmire. Slowly we made our way forward but the main advance down the centre got bogged down. All through the late afternoon we sat near a stream which the engineers and Pioneer Corps were trying to bridge under constant mortar and shell fire.

In the Susteren battle 1st RTR lost seven tanks to Bazooka teams and A/Tank guns.

Despite the savage Susteren battle, the 11th Hussars had put a patrol into Oud Roosteren, which was later captured by 6th KOSB under command from 52nd Lowland Division. Lieutenant Alan Parks, with 'C' Squadron 1st RTR, wrote: 'My orders were to take my troop and capture the small village of Heide, just NE of Susteren, across a railway line as 'A' and 'B' Sqns were moving north to Echt and Schilberg.' Later 'C' Squadron 1st RTR with the 2nd Devons and flame-throwing Crocodile Churchill tanks, pushed north to capture Ophoven and the western sector of Echt, taking 100 prisoners. The historian of the Devons described the operation:

In thaw and thick fog at 1630 hrs on Jan 17th, the dyke bridges came under heavy shellfire which delayed the tanks. When they got across our carriers had to be hitched to them. In the snow, slush, sniping, across minefields and despite MG and 75mm fire the two columns moved off. Each column consisted of a mobile screen of two troops of 1 RTR tanks, a section of bren gun carriers, a section of assault Pioneers, then 2 more troops of tanks, our infantry company in [armoured] Kangaroos, a section of Norfolk Yeomanry SP A/Tk guns, a section of 3 in mortars, a 6 pdr A/Tk section, a RE recce party and the RHA FOO. Major Overton took D Coy on the left route towards Echt, and Major Howard took C Coy on the right towards Schilberg. In the villages Nazi slogans were painted on the walls, 'We will never capitulate.'

'Snatch' Boardman wrote in *Tracks in Europe*: '1 RTR pushed into Echt and soon met heavy resistance from well-placed A/Tk guns and bazooka men. They lost a number of tanks. The Skins were to pass through Echt and supported by 1/5 Queens, to capture and hold Montfort.' The Germans had several SPs and A/Tk guns in Echt and Schilberg, a mile to the east. But by

1st RTR and Devons take Schilberg.

dawn on the 18th the 2nd Devons and 1st RTR occupied Echt and Hingen, a mile to the north-east. Despite losing tanks to SPs they linked up with the rest of 1st RTR to take Schilberg.

Alan Parks, a troop leader with 1st RTR, remembered: 'After Echt and Schilberg had been captured we moved on towards Posterholt which dominated the River Roer [north-east 7 miles]. From a tank man's point of view it was not a great battle but the closeness of the country offered protection to the enemy and this exercised one's judgement and tactics.'

A rapid thaw caused the fragile roads behind to collapse and bomb craters and minefields delayed consolidation and follow up, but nevertheless the next battle, for St Joost, started on the 20th. The experienced Group Hübner with three companies of parachutists, plus a number of SPs and A/Tank guns, held the town and a bitter encounter now took place. The plan was for 'I' Company 1st RB under Major Peter Luke, a squadron of the 8th Hussars Cromwells commanded by Major Henry Huth, and a troop of Crocodile flamethrowers to take the town. Some riflemen wore rabbit skins stitched to their battledress for extra warmth. It was house to house fighting with Sten guns and hand grenades against Spandau and 'potato-mashers'. After a delayed start at 1500 hrs 500 yards had been gained, but the RB quickly took twenty-six casualties, in the process killing twenty enemy and taking sixty prisoners. A Crocodile went up on a mine and two Honeys were knocked out. Two of Lieutenant Peter Apsey's platoon tell their tales. Corporal Cable:

We went round the back of the house and found 6 Germans, 3 of them in single slit trenches, and the other 3 in a concrete silo with a bazooka. The first 3 fired at us with rifles at 10 yards range, so we nipped back, lobbed a grenade over the wall, blew the first Jerry up and saw the other 2 join the main party in the silo. There was a handcart between us and the silo, so we couldn't get a direct line on them. I placed 2 men with a Piat armed through a little window and told them to blow up the cart and fired twice: the first shot missed but made the Germans pile out of the silo. One of our men winged one of them at 30 yards range with a pistol and the rest of the boys got him properly and also the remaining 4.

Corporal Smith added:

The crowd in the left hand house were believed to have a Bazooka but when we rushed it we found 7 of them in the cellar all mixed up with the civilians. We couldn't throw grenades under the circumstances so we loudly threatened to chuck 'em and out they came. Then our sergeant went round the front of the house, was shot in the back and killed by an officer. Then I went upstairs and from there I could see him clearly and put him out with a rifle shot.

The Rifle Brigade dealt with each house separately, taking twenty-five prisoners. A party of eight paratroopers of Regiment Hübner drove ahead of them, women with babies in their arms, to make sure of a safe surrender.

By now it was dark except for the light thrown by the flames of the burning houses set on fire by the flamethrowers and phosporous grenades. It was now the turn of the Durhams. Major Willie Anderson's 'C' Company had moved through Hingen across the Krom Beek, disappeared from view and, as their radios packed in or were destroyed, *were never seen or heard of again.* Eventually thirty survivors straggled in to report very heavy shelling with sections and platoons being killed or captured piecemeal even *before* they reached the outskirts of St Joost. At dawn on the 21st 'B' Company, with a tank in support, tried to rescue the remains of 'C' Company. The RB were driven back 150 yards in street fighting and six hard-won houses were given up, while 'B' Company met bitter resistance and were withdrawn. Under a new plan 'A' and 'D' Companies with 'A' leading, plus two squadrons of 8th Hussars and two troops of Crocodile flame throwers were to advance straight up the centre of St Joost. Major Sam Macartney, CO 'A' Company, was quickly killed and his company pinned down, so 'D' Company tried to work round the left flank – but the Crocodiles could not follow and that advance too came to a standstill. Bill Bellamy, 8th Hussars, reported:

> Meanwhile the battle in St Joost itself became fiercer and fiercer. It was a desperate struggle between first class British Troops and one of the toughest of the German Parachute Regiments – Hübners. Early on the morning of the 21st another attack was mounted on St Joost. Once again 'B' Squadron under Wingate Charlton fought with great gallantry in support of the infantry. Thick fog reduced visibility to less than 100 yards. Richard Anstey and Douglas Ramf were ordered to take their two troops, retrace the route of the previous day and find a way round St Joost to outflank it from the east. I was sent to the bridge in Hingen to act as a forward wireless link if needed. The tanks clattered off into the dense fog and all went well for some minutes. Then I heard Richard shout over the wireless 'Two SPs to our front – engaging', and at the same time I heard the crack of three shots from tank guns, followed by a series of shots, then silence. [Two of Richard's and one of Douglas's tanks had been knocked out by three Mark IV 75mm SP guns.] I had an extraordinary view of St Joost and could see and hear the noise of the battle. It sounded and looked to be terrifying, flames, smoke, continuous machine gun and rifle fire, the crack of tank guns and the whistle and crump of artillery shells.

The three lost tanks were recovered the next day, as well as a Sherman Firefly from the cellar of a farmhouse!

By nightfall the DLIs fourth attack, 'D' Company plus Crocodiles, 8th Hussars tanks and 'A' Company 1st RB, had taken the gutted little town. Hübner later admitted that one of his companies had been destroyed, another almost so.

Although sixty prisoners and three SPs were captured, the losses to the Durhams and RB had been heavy. Most of the several hundred German troops killed were inside the houses or down in their cellars. It was a savage and bitter battle in which Lieutenant-Colonel C.A. Holliman DSO, CO 5th RTR and a Desert War veteran, was killed. The Durhams licked their wounds and stayed around Posterholt on the River Roer, temporarily under command of US XVI Corps. In deep mud they were bombarded by rocket shells which left craters 10 ft wide and 5 ft deep! There they stayed until 21 February, when they retired to Weert in Holland for their first rest since landing in Normandy in the previous June.

But Operation Blackcock still had some way to go, as there were four more defended villages north-east of Echt/Schilburg that had to be cleared – Montfort, Aandenberg nearby, Paarlo and St Odilienberg.

Harry Hopkins wrote:

> I later joined 'I' Coy and in December we were issued with snow suits which helped against the 26 degrees of frost that we were

experiencing near Sittard. Our main job was to cover the main road from Maastricht northwards to Roermond and Nijmegen. The line was fairly static, with patrols and artillery shoots, with the 5th RHA enforcing the ten-for-one retaliation rule. After a short rest and refit at Geleen we moved up for operation 'Blackcock'. Our task was to break through northwards to Montfort and St Odilienberg. On 16th January we moved out to protect the Churchill tank bridge layers and dealt with two patrols, thus enabling the bridging to be completed before dawn. A further seventeen prisoners were taken by ten o'clock. Schilberg and Echt were taken by 131st Brigade but owing to a sharp thaw they had not reached St Joost. This was left to 'I' Company supported by the 8th Hussars and flame throwers. Owing to a delay in the arrival of the flame throwers the attack didn't start until three o'clock. By this time the enemy had brought down a heavy concentration of fire and 'I' Company suffered some casualties. Seven prisoners were taken – no ordinary prisoners, but members of the Parachute Regiment Hubner, than whom no German troops were tougher. What was more ominous was that the village was held by a Battalion, supported by self propelled guns. One flame thrower went up on a mine and two light tanks were knocked out. 15 platoon (of which my section was part) made fair progress in bitter house to house fighting. By now it was dark, except for the light thrown up by the burning houses. As we advanced towards a farm house we came under fire from a German tank which resulted in the end of my section, with Freddie Blackall killed and some, including myself, being wounded. We were taken back to the centre of the village on the back of a bren carrier. Some of the houses were still occupied by the Germans and snipers opened fire at the carrier but luckily they missed. I understand that forty three paratroopers were taken prisoner and more than twenty killed in what was described as 'a triumph over conditions of ground and climate as well as over German paratroopers in their most stubborn mood'. No single action had been more successful than that of 'I' Company at St Joost and the operation did much to revive the reputation of the 7th Armoured Division.

Now it was the turn of the Skins, who were ordered to pass through Echt and, supported by 1/5th Queens, to capture and hold Montfort, which had been heavily bombed by the RAF. But 'C' Company 1st RB commanded by Dawson Bates reached Aandenburg just north of Montfort, where they spent a hectic twenty-four hours until relieved first by the Queens, then by the Devons. Corporal 'Snatch' Boardman of the Skins wrote of this action: 'Many bridges were found to have been destroyed but since they spanned narrow gaps they were replaced by scissor bridges though this slowed the pace. The Recce squadron was ordered to relieve 8th Hussars at a stream half a mile from Montfort.'

It was late afternoon on 22 January when the bridge was finally in position and 4th Troop 'B' Squadron crossed. Supported by 'C' Company 1st RB they moved forward to capture Aandenberg. Montfort presented an eerie sight after the heavy RAF bombardment, with the light from the burning houses and the reflection off low cloud of the searchlights, nicknamed 'Monty's Moonlight'. The troop edged forward and into a desperate battle with the German paratroopers, with the crackle of small arms fire, shouting and the crash of mortar bombs. At 2200 hrs the 1/5th Queens arrived on 'C' Squadron tanks and joined the all night battle. The leading tank was struck by a Bazooka and caught fire, killing Barry Goulding, Larry Fison and Jimmy Read. The troop leader, Roger de Grey, and Corporal Starr were wounded. Syd Swift mourned his men with this poem:

> A Tree looked on with sorrowing sigh
> As with heavy hearts we carried them by,
> Grieving, we laid them down to rest
> Three flowers of youth, who had given their best.

In the morning, on the 23rd, 5th RTR and 2nd Devons finally cleared Montfort, arriving from the wooded western sector, with the Skins, 1/5th Queens and 1st RB moving down from the northern suburbs. Under the ruins lay 270 Dutch civilians killed by the bombing. It had been a two-day battle to clear Aandenberg and Montfort. Even the wood-clearing on the 25th cost 1/5th Queens a further sixteen casualties.

The Skins spent 24–26 January mopping up around Montfort, which was occupied by 1st RB. On the 26th the final advance to clear the Maas-Roer 'Sittard' triangle continued. To the right, with the objective of Posterhout, a village 5 miles east, went 1st RTR and 1/5th Queens. In the centre, heading north to take St Odilienberg, were the Skins and 2nd Devons. On the left (west) 8th Hussars supported 1st Commando Brigade to take Linne. Our new 'friends', 1st Commando Brigade, together with 5th RTR, carried out some combined patrols along the Maas near Linne, Heide and 'Bell' island from 25–28 January, in which Lance Corporal Harden RAMC won the VC.

Norman Smith, 5th RTR, returning from UK leave noted: 'The Big Freeze came to an end in the first week of February. The Commandos did a good mopping up job and the Maas was crossed by infantry in little boats (some men, incredibly, swimming in the icy water to get the wounded back). A big barrage was put down [on 24 January] while they got the interlinking Bailey bridges across the river for our tanks to go over.' This was in the operation against 'Bell' island on the far bank of the Maas.

Lieutenant Hugh Craig-Harvey of the Skins related his experience during the battle for St Odilienberg:

A set piece attack by two troops of 'C' Sqn. I commanded First Troop and Henry Woods Fourth Troop plus two companies of the Devons,

Flail and Crocodile flame throwers from the Lothians & Border Horse. Since the Americans were expecting to take over the area the following day – and since this was the only serious battle being fought that day (the 26th) a great number of senior British *and American* officers came to watch . . . We had been issued with aerial photographs. Why I was not sure, because the village only had two streets and was bounded on the east side by the River Roer.

Three tanks of First Troop went up on mines and in a five hour battle Craig-Harvey was blown up four times, but he and his crew survived to finish the day on their feet, still attacking the enemy. He was awarded an immediate MC for his bravery. Henry Wood's troop encountered a road full of the dreaded Schu-mines hidden under snow, which were cleared while enemy mortars and machine guns from across the River Roer made life unpleasant. On the 27th 'A' Company 1st RB arrived to round up prisoners from the cellars and to clear even more minefields.

Meanwhile to the east 1/5th Queens and 1st RTR moved on briskly, and on the same day Posterhout had been secured. By the 29th the Queens had occupied Paarlo and Holst, south of Posterhout. The Queens were involved in a sharp action at Paarlo. When on the night of the 29th/30th 'A' Company was sharply counter-attacked by 50 enemy in assault boats backed by shelling and mortaring, Derrick Watson wrote: 'The ground was frozen hard so we abandoned the idea of digging in, so Lt Max Baker, a Canloan officer with 8 platoon, occupied a large 4 storey house in the main street overlooking the river.' And Verdon Besley recalls: 'Late in the evening there was a sudden barrage and then a terrific bang upstairs and two men were brought down blinded by a bazooka. Corporal Dennis took them to the cellar for safety.' Verdon was then carrying out a spirited battle from the top of the stairs dodging bullets and grenades, retaliating with both while Dennis did the same from the cellar. Rescue was at hand by a Czech officer known better as Robert Maxwell, who with Derrick Watson and Corporal John Melmoth relieved the beleaguered garrison. The RHA and 1st RTR tanks in support gave the retreating Germans a noisy send-off. The Queens received seven casualties, took ten prisoners and caused many 'hostile' casualties. In March Monty presented MCs to the two Maxies (Baker and Maxwell) for their part in the Paarlo fracas. On the next day, 31 January, the remaining bridge over the Roer at Vlodrop, south of Roermond, was blown up and Operation Blackcock came to an end – fifteen days and nights of constant fighting against a determined foe, with horrible weather and minefields everywhere.

Amongst the many unsung heroes of the awful Blackcock campaign were, of course, the sappers, who cleared minefields and built or rebuilt bridges, usually under fire. The 'Funnies', who were segments of Hobart's 79th Armoured Division, produced flame throwers and tank flails for beating a path through minefields, also carriers of fasces for bridging anti-tank ditches and scissors bridges. The Commando forces were now given new objectives and worked closely, usually in small Commando brigades with 7th and 11th Armoured Divisions, where their controlled ferocity was particularly helpful in creating river and canal bridgeheads during the campaign to come.

The GOC of 12th Corps, Lieutenant-General Ritchie, wrote to Major-General Lyne, GOC the Desert Rats:

> I cannot tell you how I admire the really dogged and fine qualities the Division has displayed throughout Blackcock. Yours was a most important role for unless you created the breach, the operations could not have developed as well as they did. The Division did many really good things in this operation but none which I admire more than the determined fighting spirit displayed by both armour and infantry.

And General Lyne's own message to the troops on 6 February was: '. . . recent successful offensive operations. We have destroyed one German division, badly mauled a crack paratroop battlegroup and gained all our objectives. The enemy fought hard and this coupled with the very severe weather conditions called for the highest fighting qualities.'

As Major Hastings, the Rifle Brigade historian, wrote: 'The success of "Blackcock" did much to revive the reputation of the 7th Armoured Division.'

CHAPTER EIGHTEEN

The Lull Before the Storm

For the next two months the division was not called upon to act in any really offensive spirit. They did not take part in the appalling bitter battles to clear the Reichwald forests and penetrate the Siegfried line and throw the German armies back to the Rhine from the Maas.

The Cherry Pickers had spent many dreary, cold, wet weeks in and around Dutch and Belgian farmhouses and hamlets. This is Lieutenant Brett-Smith's description of Moerdijk in early February 1945. It had a world famous bridge, road and railway side by side, a mile long, a great engineering feat, which had been blown up by the retreating Germans at the end of 1944:

Moerdijk was an exception even here, for it was nothing more than a shambles, with not one house untouched by fire, shot or bomb. The only signs of life were the cats – rangy, furtive animals who would suddenly streak across the street from one ruin to another. Of the German occupation there was little enough sign – a destroyed SP on the main street, an AA gun near the convent, and one grave – a rough affair with four empty shell-cases to mark the corners and the usual scrap of paper in a bottle, the cross made by nailing two bits of packing case together. From the tower of the convent you could see as far as the fine church of Dordrecht on a clear day, and all the village spires and windmills and red-roofed hamlets in between stood out in a vivid and colourful landscape when the sun was shining. On the far bank there were a number of white pillboxes manned by the enemy who sometimes got over-confident and sunned themselves on the grass nearby or watched their rations and ammunition coming up in little carts. Occasionally we registered a direct hit on these pillboxes but they were too strongly built to yield to our small mortar-bombs. Still it no doubt shook all the occupants and may have done some harm to the careless ones. But the chief memory of Moerdijk remains the dead village itself – the upturned piano in a front garden, riddled with bullet holes, the grave grey statue of St Francis of Assisi behind the convent gazing unseeingly at a pile of empty bully-tins, an old Ford car lurching on its rims in a charred garage, its tyres nothing but grey ashes. Moerdijk was strangely reminiscent of the villages in Normandy: there was the same smell of death, the same incongruous but terrible destruction.

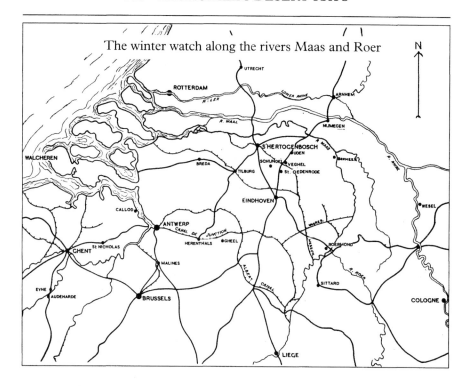

The winter watch along the rivers Maas and Roer

Lance Corporal Wingfield and the rest of 1/5th Queens were briefed by their brigadier on 6 February: 'This Reichswald Forest will be a tough nut to crack . . . a game preserve owned by Uncle Hermann Goering . . . watch out for the bloody gamekeepers.'

For three weeks in February the division stayed along the Maas and Roer, engaged in patrolling activities. The 1/5th Queens were initially in the Paarlo area, then with 1st RTR in barracks at Maesyck, a pleasant, grey, cobbled Belgian town with hospitable inhabitants, but were back in the line on 13–21 February at Rentjen and St Odilienberg. The Skins were in reserve at Schilberg for three weeks. The mining baths in Geleen were much in demand and the arrival of an APTC sergeant failed to daunt them! Bill Bellamy and the 8th Hussars were also in Schilberg. 'To my acute dismay Colonel "Cuthie" left us and Desmond FitzPatrick, a Royal Hussar, was appointed CO. We all had total confidence in our old Colonel, delighted he won an immediate DSO for his courage and handling of the recent battle, we hated the idea of losing him.' 'B' Squadron crossed into Germany at Waldfeucht and then back to Grevenbicht near Maesyck – repainting, refitting and re-organizing.

On 21 February the whole division was relieved by 8th US Armoured Division, moved a few miles north to Bree and came under direct command of Lieutenant-General Anderson of XVIth US Corps. The 9th DLI were in

Monty inspecting 3rd RHA in Holland, February 1945.

Weert (Holland), east of Bree, and the Skins in Optoeteren, near Bree.
Leave was granted liberally to Eindhoven, Mechelen, Brussels and the UK.
Inter-unit and inter-brigade football competitions were quickly organized, as
was boxing, skating, hockey and duck shooting (the RB paid £10 for
shotguns engraved with pretty pictures).

Monty came to a theatre in Weert at 1000 hrs on 5 March to present
decorations for Blackcock campaigns. Bill Bellamy received his MC for the
St Joost battle: 'He spoke to everyone . . . I was very impressed. He ensured
that each one of us was photographed as the ceremony took place and later
posed with us for a group photograph. I am sure it meant a lot to all the

Major Dennis Cockbaine, Squadron Commander 5th RTR, near Zomeren.

recipients and it certainly had an effect on me.' The 1/5th Queens had the largest contingent in the division. Major H.J. Nangle received a bar to his DSO, MCs were given to Major C.V. Lilley, Lieutenant Max Baker and 2nd Lieutenant Robert Maxwell; Lance Corporal Dennis received the DCM and Corporal Dolly the MM. The Queens regimental band came out from England and the guard of honour was under Captain N.A.H. Marsden.

The next move on 6 March was to the barren neighbourhood of Zomeren in Holland and twenty-five new Cromwells straight from England arrived for 22nd Armoured Brigade as replacements for tanks with a high mileage. The 11th Armoured had been issued with new Comets.

Major General 'Lou' Lyne assembled all officers and NCOs in a cinema in Bree and gave details in outline of Operation Plunder. 'It would not be easy,' he said, 'every German house was built with a cellar capable of defence. The new King Tiger was reported to be bigger and better than the ordinary Tiger.' The Skins were amused when a Lulworth Gunnery School sergeant talked to their recce squadron and asked them *not* to shoot up, but *capture* any King Tiger tank they encountered. 'Snatch' Boardman celebrated his twenty-first birthday in Eindhoven and reported that the

1st RB near Zomeren. The group includes Silvester, Benjamin, Hurst, Watts, Riggs, Ward and Corporal Boulton.

recce squadron billets in the Sommeren *convent* were comfortable! During the week of 11–18 March the Cherry Pickers, still manning positions along the Maas, reported their 'Linecrosser' bulletin. 'B' Squadron collected 318 civilians, twenty-four escaped allied POWs and five enemy deserters. 'C' Squadron on one night picked up three NCOs and nine men from a disgruntled German regiment who said their CO had not visited them for twelve days. They also rescued Lance-Corporal R.H. Garner DCM, captured at Tobruk $4^{1}/_{2}$ years before. But the best haul was from 'D' Squadron, who rescued two distinguished Arnhem escapees – Brigadier Hackett, ex-8th Hussars, the wounded brigade commander, and the chief medical officer of 1st Airborne Division. On 18 March the 11th Hussars were relieved by the Household Cavalry. Total casualties in the handover were three bottles of gin.

A secret document quoting the main complaints of the Wehrmacht and presumably PZ and SS as at March 1945 listed the following:

1. The lack of air support despite the reiterated promises by the Luftwaffe.
2. The lack of artillery support.

3. Shortage of rations in the front line.
4. Behaviour of officers, leaving NCOs to do their jobs and robbing the men of their comforts.
5. Lack of regular mail when in the line.
6. In some cases lack of weapons.
7. Dissatisfaction of specialist personnel (sappers, Luftwaffe, Recce) being used as infantry.
8. Drafting into SS infantry of personnel who had *never* volunteered for that Corps. (They had a nasty habit of fighting to the death.)

And so to Operation Plunder.

CHAPTER NINETEEN

Crossing the Rhine – Operation Plunder

Given the appalling losses of the last nine months and the deaths in action of so many fine desert veterans, it was surprising that morale for the last dangerous lap, the invasion of the Reich, was so high. 1st RTR's bards had invented, perhaps not their marching song, but certainly a saucy, martial refrain sung to the tune of Strauss's 'Tales from the Vienna Woods':

> Tanks, Tanks, Tanks in line
> Sweeping on towards the Rhine
> The First, the Fifth, the Skins and Guns
> We're out to bugger up the Huns!
> Cromwells, Shermans, Fireflies too
> A floating punch to see us through
> The Engineers with Scorpions
> And a troop of Bofors, half a dozen loafers
> And the Navy nice and wavy.
> RAF umbrella, nothing could be sweller
> Deutschland, here we come.

Perhaps it was too much for 'S' Squadron to bring in the Cherry Pickers, 8th Hussars and the hardworking Rifle Brigade! Anyway it expressed belligerent intent!

And not to be outdone the 1/5th Queens had *their* marching song, to the tune of the Afrika Corps' own 'Lili Marlene':

> Bags of Nebelwerfers, bags of 88
> Six barrelled mortars and Spandaus – all over the place
> When up came the Queens in TCVs
> They're quite at ease
> The smoking buggers
> We'll stuff the Herman Goering's
> As we did the Ninetieth Light.

Not to be outdone Corporal Joe Treadwall, A1 Echelon Skins, burst into verse at the 'Crossing of the Rhine':

Oudenarde and Ramillies
and bloody Malplaquet
Will your stalwarts ride amongst us
as we cross the Rhine today?

Salamanca and Vittoria
and bleak Sevastopol
Your foes are now our allies
Do you find that rather droll?

While the division had been recuperating post-Blackcock around Heeze, 100 miles west of the Rhine, great events had been taking place. General Patton's Third Army in the south had made immense progress and the vital bridge over the Rhine at Remagen seized. Further north in three weeks of bitter fighting in wretched conditions, the Reichswald and outer defences of the Siegfried line had been taken by Horrocks's XXX Corps and Crerar's Canadians, with General Simpson's 9th US Army coming up from the south.

The conditions during Blackcock – mines, more mines and mud – had been bad enough, but clearing the Reichswald and the Hochwald were probably even worse. General Eisenhower wrote to the Canadian General Crerar: 'Probably no assault in this war has been conducted in more appalling conditions of terrain than was that one.' The Canadians won two VCs, XXX Corps had 15,634 casualties, took 16,800 prisoners and enemy casualties were 75,000. The battle of the Rhineland was over and the western bank had been made secure. Now it was time for the armoured divisions to plunge their knives into the very heart of Germany.

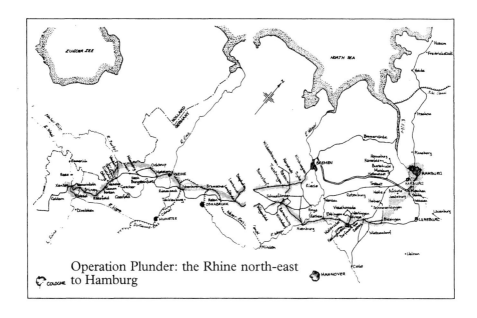

Operation Plunder: the Rhine north-east to Hamburg

Operation Plunder was the code name for the immensely detailed plan for the British 2nd Army to cross the Rhine and invade Germany. 7th Armoured Division was to be the reserve of 12th Corps, with 15th Scottish Division undertaking a crossing at Xanten, and the Commando Brigade was to land at Wesel. 52nd Lowland and 53rd Welch Divisions plus 4th Armoured Brigade were also part of 12th Corps. General Neil Ritchie had outlined the divisional centre lines, which were to be Bremen via Borken, Stadtlohn, Ahaus and Rheine. The advance, initially east, then north, was planned to cut the communications of the German parachute armies.

The 11th Hussars after a long and frustrating winter, were now to lead the advance out of the bridgehead, followed first by a battlegroup of Skins, with 9th DLI in Kangaroo armoured carriers, plus 'A' Company 1st RB, 'K' Battery RHA, 4th Forward Squadron RE and Lothian and Border flails.

But the first units in action on the night of 23–4 March, were the two RHA regiments who were thundering barrages across to support the Commando landing at Wesel, as Bobby Wolfson, 3rd RHA, recalls: 'This was the final regimental deployment and fireplan of the war and is depicted in a painting by David Sheppard. He visited the site to obtain the maximum detail and accuracy. I myself was manning an OP on the top bank of the Rhine – the Bomber Command 1,000 ton raid on Wesel was utterly terrifying and we could not visualise anyone surviving such an onslaught.' On the morning of the 24th the division witnessed the amazing airborne armada of 6th British Airborne and 17th US Airborne jumping out on a front 5 miles wide and *only* 2 miles east of Wesel, to seize the vital river crossings over the Rivers Ijssel and Lippe. The Arnhem lesson had been learned the hard way!

By the 24th the Commandos had almost captured Wesel, the 15th Scottish had a bridgehead at Bislich and were halfway to link up at Wesel. 6th Airborne had suffered nearly 30 per cent casualties but had captured the Hamminkeln bridge, 2 miles beyond Wesel. 7th Armoured left Weert on the 25th and on the 27th concentrated north of Geldern, 12 miles from the Rhine in the midst of immense traffic jams.

Lieutenant Brett-Smith, 11th Hussars, wrote:

March 24th from Heijthuizen. We stood in silent admiration watching the Dakotas and Hamilcars taking the first lift calmly and steadily towards Germany. It was an inspiring and magnificent sight on this lovely March morning and as the planes flew on in perfect formation their wings glinting silver in the sun every now and again, impervious to the 88s and 125mm bursting around them, it seemed to us on the ground that in like manner, nothing on earth would stand in our path either.

Signaller Henry Lewis, 1/5th Queens, who came from Czechoslovakia, could speak German and knew 2nd Lieutenant Robert Maxwell well, recalled the river crossing at Xanten: 'Three days after the Airborne troops had landed on the far side, we could still see some of the boys who had not made it, hung suspended from the trees by their parachutes.' John Pilborough with the Skins recce troop, recalls: 'At mid-day on the 27th we crossed the Rhine about 300 yards wide and turned east reaching the road running out of Wesel. There were many signs of the recent fighting, abandoned equipment, broken gliders and unburied Germans in some quantity. Once more the houses had hung out the flags to greet us but this time they were the white flags of surrender.' And the Skins' historian wrote: 'To this dreary scene of ruin a spurious air of gaiety was added by the brightly coloured silks of the parachutes which had floated down with the Airborne troops and their equipment now lay about the countryside like the scattered remains of a gigantic carnival. Coloured silk scarfs – the brighter the better – became instantly popular.' It took the Skins battle group all day to get through the villages of Bidlach, Hamminkeln and Brunen.

Captain Charles Pence was the first of the 9th DLI to reach the far bank of the Rhine, followed by their CO, and IO, Captain Bill Bailey, on a motorbike. The 1/5th Queens, now paired with 5th RTR, had benefited from their weeks out of the line resting and training. They were *over* strength in numbers (the first time since D+3) and in a high state of efficiency and morale.

The 1st RB were in their element. On the 28th they drove out of their bridgehead with 'their' armoured regiments – 'I' Company with 5th RTR, 'A' Company with the Skins, 'C' Company with 1st RTR – and began the apparently ceaseless process of clearing woods and villages. Major Hastings, the RB historian, noted that each operation 'demanded a rapid appreciation and a fire plan [usually involving a battery of RHA 25-pounders] followed by an energetic assault by the motor platoons supported by tanks. Casualties were light compared to those of the enemy. It was the loss of individual leaders that was hard to bear, the harder at this stage in the war.' Peter Apsey, Mike Robinson and Peter Mitchell were killed later in the dozens of sharp little actions. It was the 11th Hussars who found the miserable farm tracks and wooded hills serious handicaps to the free movement of their armoured cars. It was soon clear that if in Normandy the chief hazards of war were 88mm, Tiger tanks and Minnewurfers, in Holland the widespread minefields, in the heartland of Germany it was to be the cheap, throwaway, deadly Bazooka, which took its toll in close range fighting.

Brigadier Dudley Clarke wrote this vivid description of the irruption into the Fatherland by our armour in his history of the 11th Hussars:

> 11H would 'motor' on until they ran into resistance on a scale they could not overcome. Then two simultaneous movements would develop. The armoured cars advancing by way of tracks on either side of the main road would 'tap out' to look for an alternative way round. The Skins close behind would go into action to destroy the enemy in front. A really determined stand would bring deployment of 22 AB and if that were not sufficient the full might and wrath of the whole of

A brief stop for a 5th RTR crew on the break-out from the Rhine crossing. Left to right: Trooper Post (driver), Lieutenant 'Raggy-Tash' Wilson (commander), Norman Smith (wireless operator/gun loader), Trooper Leach (co-driver/machine gunner), Lance-Corporal Hewitt (main gunner).

the Armoured Division (with supporting artillery) would descend. However savage and determined the resistance of the Germans there was always superior strength to overwhelm it. Sooner or later the town or river bank they were defending would fall under the ever-increasing pressure and then the advance of the British armour would continue, leaving behind it shabby crowds of unshaven dirty and demoralised soldiers of the dying German Army to go trailing towards the prison camps.

One was tempted to wonder whether the British army, and people, would have resisted so fiercely for so long if the boot had been on the other foot. Every day there was a small but significant loss to the division of killed and wounded, usually the young leaders. Mines, Bazooka teams, mortar fire, snipers, the occasional 88 or SP gun and, in particular, the bloody-minded house to house clearance of the many hamlets and villages – these all took their dread toll.

From the 28th there were three advance centre lines. 1st RTR went east to Heiden, then north to Ramsdorf. On the left 5th RTR were directed on

Borken, north of the main Raesfeld-Brunen road, while in the centre the Skins and Durhams were directed north of Raesfeld to tackle Borken from the south. Progress was slow due to extraordinarily bad going on poor tracks through thick woods containing parachutists with Panzerfausts and small arms. Brunen, 4½ miles beyond Hamminkeln, was defended by Spandaus, Bazookas and SP guns, and the bridge was blocked by bomb rubble. 'A' Company 9th DLI under Major Stephen Terrell occupied the village and laid an ambush. Believe it or not, Terrell acted as traffic policeman in the centre of the village and directed enemy traffic into his *own* ambush and netted twenty prisoners, including a German field cashier who had 80,000 Deutschmarks with him.

The next village of Raesfeld, 3½ miles from Brunen, was defended by SP guns covering the blown bridge, and on the morning of the 28th 'A' Company 1st RB captured it, taking thirty prisoners from 2nd Parachute Corps. Gemen, 10 miles from the bridgehead, was cleared by the Durhams on the night of the 28th/29th.

Syd Swift, now with a new Sherman Firefly, was leading 'B' Squadron Skins' advance, and wrote:

We were held up momentarily in the small village of Gemen. I have good reason to remember that village. I saw a pig eating a dead German by the roadside. We stopped near some farm buildings and I had a chance to take a hurried look inside. At once I had a feeling about the place. 'Jerries in here' I thought [anyone who fought the Germans at close quarters knew, like bloodhounds, the strange smell of their front line troops. Perhaps they said the same thing about 'Tommies'.] We had developed a nose for them. A platoon of 1/5th Queens came forward, searching buildings, and I told the commander of my suspicions. Sure enough, they emerged some ten minutes later with a batch of German prisoners which included a highranking officer.

The Cherry Pickers had probed the defences of Borken, 20 miles north-east of Wesel, where two armoured cars were knocked out and six casualties were suffered, including Trooper J.F. Hastings who was killed. He had served with the regiment from Palestine to Africa and Italy. The centre of Borken was a shambles – the RAF had left their calling cards and when 5th RTR arrived at nightfall fifty enemy dead were counted and ninety prisoners were already in the bag. Sergeant Bob Price with 'C' Squadron, Skins, wrote: 'It was lovely weather. Apart from a bullet in the heel of one boot (my own fault for nipping out of the tank to collect some parachute material for my wife), being missed by an A/Tk gun and being shot up by a light, quick-firing AA gun and being soft with a prisoner, it had not been a bad day – sunny and warm.'

On the 29th the Skins had a brisk engagement at Weseke, 5 miles beyond Gemen, against four carefully hidden SP guns, but the Durhams dismounted from their Kangaroos and, backed by 'K' Battery RHA, captured or destroyed the SPs.

The Queens and 5th RTR fought against 33rd Panzer Grenadiers at Südlohn, took thirty prisoners and knocked out two 88mms. The RAF bomb craters caused immense lunar desolation but of course held up the advance for hours while ways round were sought. 4th Field Squadron RE were kept hard at work filling in craters, improving the roads and sandy tracks to bear 35-ton tanks. 'C' Squadron of the Skins had a tricky advance around Südlohn over 400 yards of a narrow single line railway track, along the slippery rails without losing a single track. It took two hours of hard work aided by crowbars and much bad language!

The small town of Stadtlohn, 4 miles north of Südlohn, was a harder task. Devastated by RAF bombing, it was still garrisoned by two battalions of 857th Grenadier regiment, just arrived back from Holland, who put up a bitter resistance. 'Snatch' Boardman of the Skins reported:

C Sqn continued their advance in darkness towards Stadtlohn where the Rifle Brigade were held up and without tank support. Fourth Troop shelled the first few houses at a range of 600 yards. Second Troop went to join them and sat with them all night on the edge of the town which was well alight. Mickey Tate recounting the night's watch, said 'The place was full of Germans but it didn't matter because they were all dead.' It was just getting light when 'B' Sqn and the Durhams arrived to clear the town, house by house. Tate's Germans weren't *that* dead.

'A' Company 9th DLI had a sticky time; a flimsy wooden bridge was captured by Lieutenant McNally's platoon, but the 2 i/c, Major Cramsie, was shot in the leg by a sniper. And 'A' Company 1st RB under Christopher Milner had a particularly successful action. Their lone night attack on Stadtlohn was described by Christopher Milner:

Skins try to cross canal by railway bridge but throw tank tracks or become bogged down, so our carriers find a wooden bridge across. We must not lose contact so I get two motor platoons across and proceed in dark, slowly in high gear. First carrier driver is killed, but the carrier spins completely round and we proceed with Panzerfaust German held firmly on front of my carrier. We get into Stadtlohn in time to prevent wired-up trees being blown across the road and clear some houses during the night. The RHA gunner OP is the only support but get him to lob occasional shells into town and line up all carriers and – more bluff – to cover the two platoon attack with Brownings firing tracer.

Everyone had a go in Stadtlohn and on the 30th 1/5th Queens spent the day mopping up. Three hundred dead German soldiers were counted among the rubble. The wobbly bridge survived long enough for 1st RTR and the Queens to get across while the sappers put a Bailey over the stream. During the taking of Stadtlohn Peter Bickersteth, No. 4 Platoon 'A' Company 1st RB, celebrated his twenty-first birthday (29/30 March). After a night attack, 'sometime in the early hours a real fire fight started as Germans started to recover and re-occupy Town'. He briefed a major from the Durhams at the top of the town's church tower, came down and was presented with a bottle of champagne by his company commander, Chris Milner. 'To our surprise and delight the mail came up – bloody good, especially as large package slightly squashed proved to be Birthday Cake from Mother. We all ate it and drank champagne from tin mugs.' Most officers in his company had nicknames. The OC was 'the Guv', 2 i/c 'the Egg', 1 Platoon 'the Little one', 2 Platoon 'Lanky', 3 Platoon 'Uncle George' and 4 Platoon 'The Skipper'.

Two other centre line activities were not quite so painful or dramatic.

On the left flank 8th Hussars took over from 5th RTR west of Borken and moved towards Oding, 5 miles south-west of Stadtlohn, which they reached on the 31st. Enemy SPs and Bazookamen claimed four Hussar tanks but 1st RB and the Devons cleared the woods on the way to Oding. 33rd Panzer Grenadier 'Ersatz' Battalion put up a good fight with 88s and SPs despite their name, perhaps indicating they were 'Odds and Sods'.

The right-hand centre line of 1st RTR and 1st RB had taken Heidon, 3 miles east of Raesfeld, even though an ammo dump blew up and fired the village. Thence they continued towards Gescher via Ramsdorf, 5 miles from Rasefeld, where three more RTR tanks were knocked out. Major F.D. Pile MC, CO 'A' Squadron, has described 1st RTR's progress:

On March 30 advance out of Stadtlohn into a thick wood where the two leading tanks, Lt Simmonds, Sgt Johnstone were bazooked and brewed. Trooper Justice was killed, Lt Simmons wounded and four men captured. The rest of the squadron brought under considerable shellfire. A night attack was now planned with much misgivings on Ahaus ten miles away. So at 0115 hrs on 31st with Sgt Johnson leading and every gun firing, the squadron 'set sail' at 50 yard intervals between tanks – for Ahaus. Although over 20 Bazookas were fired, not a single casualty. Ahaus captured in under an hour from time we left Stadtlohn and 70 enemy prisoners taken [1/5th Queens mopped up and Major Derrick Watson was wounded in an accident]. But Capt 'Freezer' Frost of 'C' Sqn was killed that night on a parallel route. Next towards Heek, ten miles ahead. 'A' Sqn now reduced to 7 tanks, as many were bogged down in soft ground. Moving down the CL we discovered 2 armoured cars and a Honey tank brewed up by an A/Tk gun which covered the crossing over a flooded stream running across our front [on the way at Wullen 1/5th Queens over-ran several mortar-teams and a SP]. 'C' Sqn on the right were also held up. But Lt Bob MacGregor DCM, MM, a man of immense courage, skill and as far as fighting was concerned, cunning, led the advance, searched the stream up and down until he eventually managed to find a way over. On crossing he found himself in the middle of a small network of enemy positions and was under intense fire from all sides. Moving from cover to cover using smoke, he eventually got himself on a hill which commanded all the enemy positions from their rear. He proceeded to knock out an A/Tk gun, machine guns, mortars and many enemy infantrymen till the opposition silenced. He died in an accident two weeks later.

On their arrival in Heek in pitch darkness 1st RTR and the Queens took the bridges and captured 182 prisoners. This was another little German town that had been demolished by the RAF. Brett-Smith, 11th Hussars, wrote: '1st Tanks had made a real cavalry charge in the night from Stadtlohn to Ahaus and got through hordes of bazookamen with amazingly light casualties. A terrific show and they were played out when we reached them in Ahaus.' During the night the RHA regiments stonked Ahaus, which in addition to RAF bomb craters, was heavily mined and booby-trapped. 'I' Company 1st RB had a fierce battle between Ahaus and Ochtrupp, where Mike Robinson was killed by a mine and Corporal Coward fought a gallant action on his own after being wounded in the throat. Peter Mitchell's platoon and a troop of 5th RTR took on about four hundred paratroopers in some houses and drove them into a wood, causing a hundred casualties.

Another night advance under a bright moon was also being made by 5th RTR and the Devons on 30th/31st. This was to take Vreden, (north-west of Stadtlohn), Ottenstein and Wessum. Lieutenant Ted Zoeftig was leading the advance in a Firefly and was Bazooka'd in the outskirts of Vreden: 'Then a massive vibration of thick, light and dark grey lines. I feel very heavy and find that I am being pressed down to the bottom of the turret. I feel as if I'm swimming under water. In strange slow motion I start to move up. No one is near me. The tank seems to be pointing up in the air. A high pitched whistle persists in my ears.' Several Devons and RTR were killed, while Ted was captured but escaped four days later. Ottenstein was reached at last light on the 31st and the Devons took about fifty prisoners, but the opposition was much stronger around Wessum and this held up the advance.

April Fool's Day was just that for the Cherry Pickers. 'C' Squadron were in a schloss near Heek and their breakfast of eggs and bacon was rudely disturbed by 150 Germans, so they had to abandon all their cooking kit on the battlefield. Their 'little friends', the 1/5th Queens, cleared the place, took 119 prisoners, and 'B' Squadron salvaged 'C's mess tins for them!

Bobby Wolfson, 3rd RHA, told the tale of 'tough unruly Gunner Jones, who espied a jeweller's shop relatively unscathed in a small German village. He persuaded the owners that a strong German counter-attack was imminent and advised them to return to their cellars for safety. The haul was two watches per head per wrist for that RHA troop.'

On a lighter theme, Captain H.M. Stevens MC, 1st RTR, produced this doggerel:

> I'm a rambler, I'm a gambler, I'm a long way from home
> If you don't like me, just leave me alone
> Johnnie Dingwall's our Fuehrer
> Pat Hobart's Sieg Heil
> And if I'm not Bazooka'd, I'll live till I die.

The Cherry Pickers seemed to be having an eventful day. At Metelen, north-east of Ahaus, Lance-Corporal Garner DCM, who had been a POW for four years in Italy, now drove his Dingo straight into a group of Wehrmacht. Two Bazooka men fired at a range of 10 yards, missed and forced the car into a ditch, but Garner and companions escaped to fight another day. And Sergeant Berry's troop on the edges of Rheine, 15 miles north-east of Metelen, had five near misses from a 75mm A/Tank gun, sheltered behind a house and waited for the main vanguard of the Skins to turn up. The house turned out to be an inn, well stocked with beer. The advance was now going very fast, as Brett-Smith wrote in his diary:

On the 11th Hussars' first swan on a beautiful sunny day we streamed towards Rheine. On the faces of most of the civilians was a look of blank wonder and incredulity, for to them it did not seem possible that there were so many tanks, guns and cars in the world, for by this time the whole column was almost nose to tail. Scores of wounded Germans, some with an arm missing, some one-legged, others with bandages over their heads, limped and hopped to the roadside from the hospitals we passed, most of them silent and grim, a few excited and a few sneering. In the narrow streets of Neuenkirchen the rumble and rattle of the tanks and the explosive coughing and banging of their exhausts, sounded unearthly and forbidding: a group of Luftwaffe pilots, with either no aircraft or no fuel left stared sourly out of a café, and a stream of awed townspeople hurried down the steps of the church and back to their houses for it was Sunday and a service had just finished.

Colonel Wainman, as was his wont, discarded 'used' maps from his Dingo – a gesture to indicate that there was no going back! Brett-Smith also tells how 11th Hussars used to telephone up the next village ahead and demand from the cowed operators information about troops in the region:

It was surprising how eager they were to help finish the war and on the whole their information was good.
    We soon got used to the bands of freed prisoners and slave workers whom we now began to meet daily – the khaki-clad French and

Belgians, the Russians in their tattered green-dyed rags, the Poles, the Yugoslavs. Some of them were too weakened and apathetic seemingly to realise the occasion of their liberation and would pass us on the road, shambling along with torn and flapping puttees, their wretched clothes coated with mud and a few miserable and touching possessions slung across their bowed backs. Others, though equally filthy and ragged, still had managed to keep their pride and courage intact and wave and laugh as we passed.

The 1/5th Queens with 1st RTR pushed 20 miles north-east towards Rheine on 1 April, harboured at Metelen and took eighty prisoners. They found their Kangaroos dirty, noisy and uncomfortable, albeit safer, when driving on long journeys. By now the division had advanced an astonishing 120 miles into the heartland of Germany within a week. On their right was 11th Armoured Division heading towards Osnabrück, and amazingly in this three-horse race the 6th Airborne, recovered from their costly drop east of the Rhine, with commandeered and makeshift transport (steamrollers were popular) were, almost, level pegging. 'Snatch' Boardman, Skins, wrote:

Our centre line was to be Ahaus, Heek, Metelen, Wetteringen, Neuenkirken and Rheine. There was plenty of resistance but the German population in general had suffered more than enough and most houses displayed white surrender flags from their windows. We had expected some form of resistance movement and sabotage attempts on our supply lines but there was nothing of the sort. Lack of sleep was becoming our main problem . . . [Later] My troop was given the task of checking a road parallel to the main centre line, leading into Rheine. The leading tank struck a mine, the driver Bill Whitcombe was slumped in his seat desperately wounded, he was placed on a stretcher on a carrier to be taken back to the RAP. The carrier struck a mine and the crew became casualties and Bill was killed instantly. It was a gruesome business. He had been in the Recce Squadron for a long time.

The Skins linked up with 11th Armoured Division on the eastern flank.

On the 2nd the DLI penetrated into Rheine to find the bridges blown and the far bank of the Dortmund–Ems Canal held in strength, while the Queens were combing the woods round Metelen.

CHAPTER TWENTY

The Battle for the Ibbenbüren Ridge

The Führer would have been proud of the Hitler Youth Hannover Cadet school and their highly skilled instructors, who now made a last ditch stand which gave Britain's two finest armoured divisions very bloody noses. The first barrier was the Dortmund–Ems Canal, which ran south-east from Rheine. The second was a most formidable natural hilly defensive line of dense woods, the Teutoburger Wald, an escarpment 25 miles long and a mile wide on a south-east vector some 10 miles south-west of Osnabrück.

The town of Ibbenbüren at the north-west end of the Teutoburger Wald was one of the objectives of the 7th Armoured. Originally the enemy had two companies in the area but they were continually reinforced until by 2 April there were seven! The DLI historian wrote:

> Many of them were instructors, first class soldiers, even better shots, worked in small and scattered parties difficult to pin down for artillery targets. Many tank commanders and platoon sergeants were picked off by snipers. Tanks had to demolish a building and then bury the defenders. One German warrant officer badly wounded, was buried up to his neck in debris; on being dug out was asked when he thought the war was going to end. 'When we win' came the defiant reply.

The 3rd Monmouthshire Battalion with the 11th Armoured suffered very heavy casualties. Corporal E.T. Chapman won a VC, but the losses were so heavy that the gallant Mons who had 1,100 casualties in ten months of fighting, including 267 killed, were withdrawn from the line and took no further part in the campaign. The 1st Herefords lost sixty casualties around Birgte, including twenty killed on 1 April. Tony Crankshaw, 'D' Squadron 11th Hussars, wrote: 'The cadets and their instructors had all the latest weapons at their disposal on their own training ground, the ridge gave perfect observation and the wood gave them concealment. They were the biggest lot of thugs that ever stepped and try as we could, they would not rug up till killed where they stood.'

On 3 April 22nd Armoured Brigade moved into reserve south of Rheine, as the 52nd Division followed up. And 131st Infantry Brigade now in the Riesenbeck area, 8 miles east of Rheine, prepared to move through the existing 11th Armoured bridgehead at Birgte and then advance three miles north-east to capture Ibbenbüren. This road centre lay in a valley on the far side of the Teutoberger Wald.

The plan was for 2nd Devons to attack and clear the wooded ridge from the left flank opposite the Birgte bridgehead while 9th DLI and the Skins pushed through and along the main road to Ibbenbüren. So backed by a heavy RHA barrage and mortar fire the Devons passed through 1st Herefords at the Birgte bridgehead to help rescue a company of 3rd Monmouthshires cut off on the hill, and recapture several British unmanned A/Tank guns in front of the bridgehead. Lieutenant Coates led a sortie to man them and give supporting fire to the Mons. A joint effort with 11th Armoured Division followed, and within 1½ hours they had captured 200 prisoners, killed 50 Germans and liberated 150 Mons who had been surrounded, without a single Devon casualty. Major-General 'Lou' Lyne called it 'a brilliant performance', and Robert Davey, a platoon commander said: 'When the company went in we followed our own creeping barrage and when we got to the heights we had to winkle out the cadets who were well dug-in. They had been badly shelled but they were really tough.'

But for the Durhams and the Skins it was a different matter. Sergeant Bob Price recalled:

Ibbenbüren remains in my mind as the most horrible experience a tank troop leader could undergo while supporting infantry. It was so frustrating for us and so demoralising for the PBI. As far as military tactics go, it emphasised that you could so easily be seen and heard when on the move. My troop was sent forward to assist 'A' Sqn who were losing tank commanders rapidly. My squadron leader Major John Ward-Harrison finished his orders to us with the words 'For God's sake be careful. Do what you can.' I did account for five snipers whom I spotted through the thick swirling smoke. We may have killed or injured others since we fired at every possible point where they might be located. We used both our main gun and the Besa machine guns . . . The infantry casualties mounted. Our troop fired smoke and sprayed the area. We loaded all the casualties on to the tanks and withdrew feeling we had achieved very little.

At last light on the 3rd it was a stalemate. The Devons were relieved by 7/9th Royal Scots of 155th Brigade (52nd Division). And the next day, the 4th, the Skins were held up by bogs and farmhouse defences. 'C' Squadron arrived to help a DLI company attack factory buildings outside Ibbenbüren but fighting went on all day, and troop leaders Fitzgerald and Elkins were shot by snipers. 1/5th Queens and 8th Hussars put in a flank attack north-east of Ibbenbüren, and 'B' Company lost ten casualties including their IO, Lieutenant Trewby, killed by a shell. The fanatical resistance went on with deadly enemy sniping and the elderly cadets (often aged over forty) remained in the blazing ruins before they themselves were burnt in the holocaust. The Durhams took thirty prisoners and killed many more but the terrible Wagnerian battles continued as the flames lit up the night sky – Götterdammerung indeed.

John Pilborough of the Skins wrote: 'While we waited for the relieving force to come up, we made a big meal and watched the 7.2 artillery shelling the power-house in Ibbenbüren.' Very heavy guns were needed to finish off the Hanoverian cadet force.

On 4 April both armoured divisions were ordered to disengage and to bypass the opposition. It took another two days for 52nd and 53rd Infantry Divisions to subdue the heroic middle-aged cadets who had seen off the 7th and 11th Armoured Divisions.

CHAPTER TWENTY-ONE

Hot Pursuit

After the desperate slogging battle for Ibbenbüren it was quite unbelievable that by last light on 4 April the division had had a clear run of 50 miles.

By crossing the 11th Armoured bridge over the Osnabrück Canal at Halen, thence on their centre line, 5th RTR seized a bridge intact over the Ems–Weser Canal 18 miles north-east of Osnabrück. The 2nd Devons with 1st RTR guarded the bridges and centre line behind, and the Cherry Pickers met their friends and rivals, the Inns of Court from 11th Armoured Division, at Venne. Colonel A.A.G. Bingley, CO of our 'legal' friends, had been adjutant of 11th Hussars previously. By nightfall the Skins had caught up with the division and harboured between Diepholz, guarded by 5th RTR, and Sulingen. On the 5th the Cherry Pickers 'C' Squadron near Diepholz spotted four dangerous-looking 88mm guns guarding an airfield. Having just lost a White scout car with all its crew to an 88mm, they asked the PBI for help to take this battery apart. It turned out that they were *dummies*. The PBI were only slightly sarcastic and agreed they were *good* dummies! At Lembruch, 7 miles south of Diepholz, four genuine 88mm guns were encountered and 1st RTR and 'T' Company 1st RB, backed up by 'G' Battery 5th RHA, knocked them all out.

5th RTR now had a new CO, Lieutenant-Colonel A.R. Leakey. Perhaps to greet him, the Luftwaffe sent a dozen new jet fighters and Focke-Wulfs to strafe the centre line. They rudely disturbed General Lyne and bombed the Queens and 11th Hussars RHQ, where the only victims were two German POW. Sergeant Berry's K guns of the 11th Hussars knocked down a Messerschmitt 109. 5th RTR were in Wagenfeld by the evening, having killed or captured eighty enemy and destroyed seven guns.

One of our sergeant tank commanders, George Stimpson, certainly had his share of 22-carat Hollywood stuff. George was an old Desert Rat, smallish, dark and neat [wrote Trooper Norman Smith 5th RTR]. George's troop had cleared a nest of bazooka men from a farm. He and his lap-gunner burst into the farmhouse with their sten guns. The kitchen was laid for breakfast with coffee and boiled eggs on the table. The farmer and his wife vociferously denied that the bazooka men were in the house but George and mate searched the house. Upstairs in a large bedroom they found three beds with each apparently containing four teenage girls. 'Raus' shouts George, brandishing his sten gun to the girls and lines them up against one wall.

Sergeant George Stimpson, 5th RTR.

'How can we be sure' said the lap gunner 'that one of them isn't a bloke?' George signalled the girls to lift up their nightdresses, which they did. George said it was one of the prettiest sights he had ever seen.

On the 6th the 1/5th Queens linked up with 5th RTR at undefended Diepholz and moved off towards Sulingen to chaperone 8th Hussars. Bill Bellamy, on return from leave to attend the funeral of his mother, who had been killed by a V2 rocket in London, now joined the recce troop. 'Most of the soldiers in it were middle Europeans, White Russians, Roumanians, Hungarians etc. all of whom had good reason to hate the Germans and all of them were very tough indeed.' 1/5th Queens also had some German linguists, such as Lieutenant Robert Maxwell.

Another notable night advance took place on the 5th/6th when the Devons and 'A' Squadron 1st RTR covered no less than 40 miles to reach Hoya on the River Weser. The bridge, of course, was blown, but a small battle group of 'C' Company Devons carrier platoon, plus 3 in mortars and 6-pounder A/Tank guns, crossed on a ferry 6 miles upstream and captured forty prisoners.

The Skins had had to motor 62 miles from Ibbenbüren to catch up with the division via Venne and Diepholz to Barver, between Diepholz and Sulingen.

In the first two days of the 'Hot Pursuit' 450 prisoners had been taken and as many more killed, for relatively few casualties.

Looting became a bit of a pastime [wrote Gordon Johnson, 5th RTR]. I remember a call over the radio saying some Germans with a white flag wished to surrender. Major Cuckmay ordered them to recheck and back came the reply 'Cancel last message. Enemy is a Rifle Brigade chap with a white goose over his shoulder'. Plenty of Lugers and watches from prisoners. I still wear one of the watches every day. I took a lot of Lugers to Antwerp on leave and sold them to Americans at £7 each.

The 5th RTR continued their 'German swan', on the 5th advancing 20 miles to Wagenfeld and Diepholz. Norman Smith wrote:

we ran into anti-tank guns south of Diepholz at Lembruch, where we were also strafed and bombed by a dozen Focke-Wulf aircraft. We tried to shoot them up with our turret top Brens and Brownings without success. By the evening we had got into Wagenfeld having killed some 30 enemy and taken 50 prisoners and were more than pleased to have knocked out four 88mm, one 75mm and two 20mm guns at a cost of two of our men wounded.

On the 7th the Skins and 9th DLI had a fierce scrap in Bassum and took forty-nine prisoners, but Lieutenant Ingleton was killed. 'Snatch' Boardman, with Recce Troop Skins, wrote: 'between Bassum and Twistringen a freak shot fired by an A/Tk gun at a leading tank in "A" Sqn struck the road and the ricochet hit the turret of a tank well down the column killing Lt Walworth who had served so magnificently in 's Hertogenbosch'. On the same day Lieutenant W. Newton, 5th RTR, was killed by treachery when he accepted a German's surrender and was promptly shot by another. 8th Hussars and the Queens took the lead, captured Emtinghausen, 4 miles from the River Weser, and tried to rush the bridge defended by six SPs. When it was blown they went north on the Bremen road to occupy Riede, which was undefended.

The divisional plan of advance was changed as it was clear that all river crossings would be more strongly defended now and it might be possible to prevent First Parachute Army from reaching Bremen by advancing due west. 22nd Armoured Brigade were to move from the area east of Verden towards the south of Bremen, while 131st Infantry Brigade secured Bassum and Twistringen. The latter town was Catholic and the inhabitants had been ill-treated under Nazi rule. There was a large hospital crammed with German wounded, where Sergeant Bob Price of the Skins won a MM. His troop were first in, dominated the main exits and took many prisoners.

Some rather funny things happened on the 8th. 'Snatch' Boardman found a bridge: 'I could see two sets of fins protruding from two enormous holes in the road. They must have been at least 1,000 lb bombs or rockets.' 'Holdfast' sappers were quickly summoned up and a very young RE sergeant came bounding along in his Scout car. He 'walked unconcernedly on to the bridge, kicked some rubbish off the road, went down the bank,

'A' Company 1st RB officers at Bassum. Left to right: Christopher Milner (commander), Peter Bickersteth, Colin James, George Burder.

reappeared on the bridge again and crossed to the other side. At last he emerged, stood on the bridge and shouted "OK". We were full of admiration, quite certain he deserved the VC.' Later an RHA FOO came up in his Cromwell and asked if there was anything he could do. 'We looked round, when a German staff car suddenly appeared crossing the open field from right to left. "There you are," we said, "have a go at that." He quickly traversed his six pounder on to the car and fired. The shot went well over the top . . . The bag was four high ranking German officers, complete with maps and documents and a case of cognac. We received a pat on the back for that.' 'C' Squadron of the Cherry Pickers searched a wood near Bassum for prisoners. One admitted to being sixty years of age. He wore carpet slippers and carried a walking stick, without which he would definitely have fallen down.

The advance west met with some success. 8th Hussars captured Riede 11 miles south-east of Bremen, and 5th RTR took Syke, 3 miles further south. On 8 April, nearing Syke and Sulingen, Gordon Johnson, 5th RTR, recalled 'Major Cuckmay's lap gunner (who spoke German) popping open the door of a telephone office/kiosk and shouting to some startled German Mayor at the other end that unless he surrendered he would call up the RAF to bomb him to smithereens. I think the German thought we had a direct line to "Bomber" Harris.' Norman Smith, 5th RTR, noted that every troop, among its new replacements, always had a German speaker, and all the uniformed interpreters were young Jewish boys.

The Queens came up against the 20th SS Training Division at Sudweyne and Kirchweyne 5 miles south-west of Bremen and had a bloody little battle. They killed fifteen SS, took fourteen more prisoners but suffered thirteen casualties, including Lieutenant Wilkinson-Cox, who had won an MC in Holland, who was killed, and Captain Marsden, a Tobruk veteran, who was wounded. So Bill Crook, a platoon commander in 'A' Company since D+1, became the company commander 'after all our officers had become casualties'.

Just outside Wildeshausen on 10 April Peter Bickersteth's RB platoon captured a large German military hospital in the pine woods. The German senior doctor, a colonel, explained they had 200 patients. A search revealed some 'egg' grenades, which were blown up. One patient, an old 90th Light Division opponent, saw the Jerboa emblem, said in German: 'Der Raten, Mein Gott'. During the night the rifle platoon watched over the hospital complex, were mortared, observed in the dark several hostile SPs and infantry arrive. By dawn the 200 patients and staff had vanished – to fight another day!

The next day the Skins and Durhams took Wildeshausen where there was a vast store of gin, but the Cherry Pickers reported seeing seventeen enemy tanks in a wood that Typhoons shot up with rockets. Indeed two rare Tigers had previously attempted to recapture Syke but were seen off by the SPs of the Norfolk Yeomanry, 1st RB and a RHA stonk.

The Panzer Grenadiers were fighting tooth and nail to keep their centre lines open into Bremen, as 'Snatch' Boardman relates:

As we re-entered Wildeshausen [on the evening of the 10th] we were met by a relaxed Sgt Ted Glynn who directed us to the local school which would be our billet for the night. 'Get yourselves cleaned up. We have captured some hooch and we are going to have a party.' We told him there were 17 German tanks just up the road, but he replied 'Don't worry, the Norfolk Yeomanry [with 17-pounder SPs] are in position all round the town and we can stand down.' We were having a meal when we heard a sudden shot and a round went through the roof of the school. 'Bloody fools' said Ted, 'some stupid bastard has started on the booze and fired his main armament.' The shot was followed by another, and another and a lot of Spandau fire. 'Mount up' came the shout and we were back in our vehicles and hearing radio reports that German tanks and infantry had followed us in. The Norfolk Yeo had assumed that they were with us. The leading tank had a heyday and simply shot at unmanned tanks as he drove down the road. The only crewmen in a tank were the RHQ radio operator, maintaining a link to Brigade, and 'A' Sqn leader's gunner, who knocked the leading tank out at pointblank range. The German infantry were in among us and we could not distinguish friend from foe. The RHA was called down upon our own position. We were lucky to escape with the loss of two Scout cars and one tank slightly damaged. The SLI lost their RAP and six medical orderlies were taken prisoner.

It was a bit of a shambles. Two M-10 SPs of the Norfolk Yeo, two Cromwells, a Sherman and four trucks were knocked out. Apparently the 1st RB had spotted five SPs and forty SS moving through the woods at about 2200 hrs, but their wireless failed to work to give the alarm. Everyone was taken by surprise and Colonel Mogg, 9th DLI, was cut off for a time at Brigade HQ. One theory was that the SS troops were determined to get their gin back. It was fortunate that the Skins had not drunk it all before midnight!

5th RTR went through a small village made up of farm buildings. George Stimpson saw a long wooden building, shuttered, bolted and barred from the outside with a padlocked door. He blew the padlock off with his Sten gun:

When we looked in it was dark, and an unbelievable stench. Each wall was lined with three tier beds and a crowd of wretched people in the centre. We called some over. I asked 'Does anyone speak English?' 'Yes' said a young girl, 'I do.' I told them we were British soldiers and their troubles were now over but in the interests of safety they should stay where they were for a bit longer. The girl came forward, kissed me on the cheek and said 'Thank you for coming to help us.' This was the first time I had ever used bad language in front of a female.

The Master Race know how to treat their slaves. Norman Smith, 'B' Squadron, and his mate Trooper Jack met Fraulein Lisa and her friend. She was a nurse who lived in a cosy caravan and hated the Nazis. She baked him a cake.

5th RTR had been 'lent' on the 11th and 12th to 53rd Welch Division who had crossed the River Weser. They had run into trouble at Rethem, 10 miles further on, defended by 2nd Marine Division from Hamburg who, like most marines of any service, gave of their best and held out for four days. On the 11th and 12th 5th RTR destroyed eight 88mms and several 125mm Flack guns defending the railway line, despite two determined counter-attacks. 'B' Squadron supported the Monmouthshires and lost a number of desert veterans in the fighting. One sad event, among others, took place at Rethem. Sergeant Jack Wardrop, 5th RTR, who had written a superb book about his adventures and had been a tank driver with 'C' Squadron in the desert, later a tank commander, and had *never* missed a battle in four years and four months, was killed. He was commanding a Firefly, and the gun was strapped to the cradle over the back of the tank as action was not expected. A two-man tank-destroyer 'stay behind' party,

Leaving OP of 'A' Company 1st RB. Left to right: Lieutenant-General Neil Ritchie (XII Corps Commander), Lou Lyne (GOC 7th Armoured Division), Tony Wingfield (Brigadier 22 Armoured Brigade), Lieutenant-Colonel Desmond Fitzpatrick (CO 8th KRIH).

lurking in a pine copse, bazooka'd his tank while supporting the 6th Royal Welch Fusiliers.

Since all the bridges over the rivers Weser and Aller were blown, 3rd British Division took over Wildeshausen and Harpstedt, and 53rd and 52nd Divisions now held the western flank. It was clear that the chances of cutting off Bremen by the division without a really costly battle against 15th Panzer Grenadier and 18th SS Ersatz were now minimal. The RHA shelled the city, however, and the Cherry Pickers continued to probe the outskirts – but found all roads firmly mined and covered by SPs, roadblocks and Bazooka teams. But 1,700 prisoners had been taken in four days' fighting.

The division concentrated east of Nienburg, the Queens at Erichshagen, Cherry Pickers at Liebenau, the Skins at Lemke. There they stayed, rested, re-organized, got some sleep and waited for the final furlong. 'A 3 day rest to make proper meals, wash and change our clothing,' remembered 'Snatch' Boardman.

CHAPTER TWENTY-TWO

The Last Lap – Relief of Fallingbostel POW Camp

The BBC on 6.2 M/cs broadcast news of the Russians at the gate of Berlin, General Patton 'invading' Czechoslavkia, and American armies close to the Elbe at Magdeburg. Holland had almost been cleared of Germans by the Canadians and 30th Corps. It was all heady stuff. With the end in sight the sensible thing would have been for all the German armies in front of 21st Army Group to surrender. But obviously they were not being sensible. The Marines at Rethem, the cadets at Ibbenbüren, the SS troops in Wildeshausen – all fought like demons for a lost cause. When the Cherry Pickers resumed their 'swan' on the 17th, they had a stiff fight at Jarlingen. The SS had coerced a motley crew, which included armed labourers from the Todt organization, a policeman and some uniformed schoolboys wielding Bazookas, to fight hard. If the boot had been on the other foot would our own Home Guard (old men and young lads) have fought that well? The news of the liberation by 11th Armoured of Belsen concentration camp, a few miles to the east, percolated through. Some members of 7th Armoured visited the camp and hated what they saw there. Ricky Hall, RASC, recalled: 'You could smell Belsen from miles away. We had to take disinfectant in because they had typhoid and were burying the dead in great pits with bulldozers.' Tich Kirkham, the Skins, told Bill Bellamy of 'the horror of Belsen which he had visited and [near Soltau] of starving, mad slave workers who had escaped from camps and were bent on an orgy of destruction.'

Beyond Fallingbostel Albert Mitchell came across a concentration camp, 'thin dead bodies everywhere, some in piles. The living skeletons walking around in striped shirts and caps. I went to one – he was taking lice from his head and eating them, he was so far gone. He did not see me although we were face to face. A dreadful place.'

Colonel Victor Paley, who had commanded 1st RB since June 1943, now left to join the staff of VIII Corps and was replaced by Lieutenant-Colonel Paddy Boden.

The Devons were lent to 4th Armoured Brigade to expand their bridgehead and by the 15th had reached Kirchboizen, 7 miles from the new divisional target of Soltau. The Cherry Pickers and 8th Hussars crossed the River Aller at Rethem and moved down the road to Walsrode, a distance of

22 miles. But the 16th will linger in the memories of many Desert Rats. 'B' Squadron 11th Hussars, and the recce troop of 8th Hussars led by Tim Pierson and Major P.H. Huth, liberated a huge POW camp, Stalag XI B, in the woods south-west of Fallingbostel. 'C' Company of 1/5th Queens under Captain Crook there encountered an amazing sight.

There were two camps, one with 6,500, the other with 6,000 prisoners. Roughly half of them were British and American POWs under command of RSM Lord, Grenadier Guards, most recently with 1st Airborne Division. There were veterans from Normandy and many from Arnhem. The British wore *pressed* battledress, *scrubbed* equipment and were far better turned out than their liberators! Survivors of the disaster at Villers-Bocage turned up again from 4th County of London Yeomanry and 'A' Company 1st RB. The RB recovered five riflemen taken at Calais in 1940 and another from 9th RB captured at Derna in 1941. A leave party from Norfolk Yeo were there having made a rather peculiar detour, plus Trooper J. Walker, 'C' Squadron 11th Hussars, and several 8th Hussars taken at Sidi Rezegh in 1941. Lieutenant-Colonel H. Moore, chief admin. officer of the division, quickly organized rations, cigarettes and newspapers for the British POWs – still under command of the indomitable RSM Lord. The town of Fallingbostel was defended by mortars and A/Tank guns, and the Queens had to clear it house by house.

Peter Bickersteth's riflemen moved into the outskirts of Fallingbostel on 16 April:

50 yards from bridge a *terrific* explosion – Chapman pushes me flat. 'Get down skipper, fucking hell, etc', large chunks of concrete and flying glass everywhere. Pause, recce and then to Bridge – completely gone – dust, smoke but no living soul. Tiles still sliding from roofs, crunch over glass. Mill, left of bridge, damaged, pub on right shattered . . . Examine pub and find beer pumps working so disperse to all and sundry – free! Decide to wash feet as [Rifleman] Discipline arrives with half-tracks and my hip-bath. Sgt Saunders arranges defence and contact with 'friends.' Beautiful sunshine and hot pleasant p.m. watching sappers and their Bailey bridge. Write letter to Mum and Dad. [Later] Chris Milner arrived – very angry. 'Sure your feet need washing, but war is not over yet.' He'd found Colin playing a piano!!?? George fell in cess-pit and had to be washed in river. Colonel Mogg and Durhams arrived and floated a 6-pdr over stream.

In Germany we did not hesitate to liberate such creature comforts as luck guided us to [recalls Leslie Gosling, 3rd RHA]. April 14th I was reccing gun positions near Bremen and chanced upon a nice estate in a wooded clearing. The property was owned by a manufacturer of cars and fighting vehicles. He had a very fine cellar with thousands of bottles, but I could not carry much away on the back of a Sherman which was already laden like a Christmas tree. But the surprise was in his garage where we made him unlock a big cabin trunk and found it stacked with Cadburys milk chocolate which we had not seen for years. He said it came from his friend the German ambassador in Madrid. I went back with a 15cwt truck the next morning but too late – just in time to see the General's driver loading the last bottle into Div HQ's 3 tonner.

A feature of the appalling casualties the German armies had suffered in the last year was the number of hospitals crammed full of their wounded – there were three in Walsrode.

22nd Armoured Brigade continued their advance on Soltau. 1st RTR went north from Walsrode and at Jarlingen lost a tank to a Bazooka. On the outskirts of Soltau 11th Hussars ahead of them lost a scout car to a rare Panther tank and Sergeant F. Williams, Trooper K.C. Glover and R. Rodger were killed instantly. 8th Hussars then destroyed the Panther.

Soltau was heavily defended by infantry and 88mms and so was surrounded – 8th Hussars and Queens at Dorfmark, 4 miles south-west, 1st RTR 2 miles west and the Skins in the south. On the 17th the Skins plus the Royal Scots and 7th RTR from 4th Armoured Brigade made a frontal attack on Soltau with the assistance of Crocodile flame throwers and Wasps (mounted in carriers). Not only did the RHA regiments join in but 7.2 in heavy guns from AGRA were brought up to shell Soltau. John Pilborough, Skins recce, wrote:

The next barrage fell in the right place; two shells landed in the 75mm A/Tk gun pit itself. Then 'C' Sqn with the flame throwers went down the valley and burned out the opposition in the woods on the other side. They soon covered the two miles into Soltau which at first appeared to be clear. However the leading tank was bazooka'd and from then on full use was made of the flame throwers. The town fire brigade turned out and attempted to deal with the blaze while the battle was still on. All the same by evening the fighting was over and the town burning well.

'Snatch' Boardman continues the story:

We shared a house that night with a family of Germans. They stayed well out of the way and hid in the cellar. There was no sympathy for these people and a feeling of gay abandon as we parked the tank in the front garden. The following morning (18th) we moved through the devastated town and on to the autobahn, the first time we had seen such a road. Hitler is reported to have built them to enable his armour to speed west in 1940. It was a raised road and provided 88mm guns with marvellous targets.

Brett-Smith of the Cherry Pickers wrote in his diary: 'The enemy becoming more and more clueless, though no less fierce. It became largely a matter of finding the right road, as there weren't *quite* enough bazooka men to go round.'

It was perhaps surprising that British Army discipline continued at such a high level. One afternoon on the advance to Soltau an old German farmer, sixty-five to seventy years old, came up to Trooper Albert Mitchell, 5th RTR:

[He was] waving his arms, pointing to his farm, trying to pull me to go there. I took my rifle and foolishly went with him. One of my mates was in the barn, drunk, trying to rape the wife — also about 65–70 yrs. She was crying and upset. I said to my mate – and raised my rifle at him – 'Ted, leave her alone, or I will fire.' He verbally abused me but finally he backed off and I got him back to our line, where he slept it off.

The division's objectives were now Harburg, the southern suburb of Hamburg south of the River Elbe, and of course Hamburg itself. Bremen had been captured, 5th Guards Armoured Brigade were on the left flank, and on the right flank 11th Armoured were moving rapidly towards Lauenberg on the River Elbe. The German 1st Parachute Army was still fighting hard to escape north over the River Elbe by ferries and a few remaining bridges. Harburg lay 40 miles due north of Soltau, which in turn was close to Lüneburg Heath, the Wehrmacht/Panzer main training grounds in Germany – their Salisbury Plain. It was hoped to capture the Elbe bridges at Harburg, and before that to cut the autobahn linking Harburg to Bremen. On the 18th 1st RTR started well and captured Welle, 20 miles north. Major Freddy Pile with 'A' Squadron wrote:

The advance to Hamburg did not unfortunately leave us unscathed. We lost 3 officers and 17 ORs (either killed or wounded), a quarter of our Tank crew strength in under three weeks including Capt G.F. Cordy-Simpson the 2 i/c who was killed in the Forest of Langeloh, and Lt J. Noble badly wounded by a sniper on the autobahn. The names Holliman, Frost, MacGregor, Davies and Elsbruch and many others ensure for 1 RTR a great and unbroken tradition . . . [Founded in 1916, in Western Desert June 1940].

Several of the ill-fated 2nd Northants Yeo (of 11th Armoured Division) had joined 'B' Squadron 1st RTR in August 1944. These included Reg Spittles and Bernard Roberts. The latter wrote:

From the landings to the end, I lost four tanks and some really good mates. One of these was Sgt G. Ferguson. A great mate, he had won the MM with 2 Northants Yeo. He was in charge of the troop for a lot

Benny Branson's Cromwell, 'C' Squadron 1st RTR.

of the time, we were short of officers. That was no trouble for he was as good as any officer. He came from a village eight miles out of Northampton, called Lamport. [Near Tostedt on the 18th] a sunny hot afternoon our troop was ordered to make a dash up a B road to an embankment about ³/₄ mile away. We were told the RHA would put a smoke screen down which they did but it was useless [to us]. Prior to setting off Fergy and a few of us older ones talked it over. I can remember it well for I had a funny feeling and Fergy must have felt the same for he just quietly said to me 'Rob, this is it.' I just replied 'I know.' We made the dash flat out and all four tanks made it and hulled down behind the embankment and reported back to the Squadron Leader. The Germans obviously saw us arrive and sat there waiting for our next move. As soon as our tank got near the top [of the embankment] and our turret clear, Fergy gave the order to traverse and shoot. He said 'It's a Tiger and we've hit it.' Next he was shouting 'Reverse, Rob, he is traversing on us.' I went down as fast as possible but not quite quick enough, for Fergy's body was still out of the turret and he was cut nearly in half. We had acted fast, got hulled down, advanced and hit the Tiger with our peashooter 75mm which was useless against the big German tanks. We lost a top class chap through no fault of our own.

Bill Bellamy also mourned for the death of Wally Ryde, 'the bravest of all the Troop leaders'.

8th Hussars and 1/5th Queens were brought up to bypass the forest of Langeloh, which was swarming with Bazooka teams, and take Tostedt, 5 miles north-west of Welle. The Queens reached Schneverdingen and then joined forces with the Hussars to take Tostedt, which was manned by SPs and A/Tank guns. The next day, the 19th, the Queens and 8th Hussars, aided by a Typhoon stonk, took Hollenstedt, covered by 88mm guns. 8th Hussars then had a field day; turning east on the autobahn they destroyed eight 88mms on the way to Rade. Bill Bellamy had recently rejoined 8th Hussars recce troop 'equipped with Chaffee tanks, Honeys, Jalopys and Scout cars, operating as it did on the outer edge of the Regiment as its eyes and ears, it was very much to my taste'.

The advance towards the Elbe continued on the 20th. Harry Upward, 5th RTR, driving his Sherman Firefly, wrote: 'Somewhere near Lüneburg the whole squadron was advancing across this open plain and we were at the rear with one big gun. We got a direct hit from an 88mm. It was quite an experience. I had the hatch up. There was this great concussion. A flash and a bang to make your teeth ache and the tank was on fire.' Harry was the only one of the crew to be hurt, with burns on hands and face, and he went back to hospital in Brussels. A Bazooka killed Sergeant R.P. Atkinson and a sniper Lance-Corporal Greenside of the Cherry Pickers. Every regiment suffered a few casualties every day. With hilly wooded country and the forest trees at the edges of the road it was natural defensive country. The Skins, 2nd Devons and Queens had the unenviable task of clearing the Forest of Harburg.

The mopping up in this huge area some 25 miles west to east across and 55 miles in depth north to south, went on until the end of April. The same day the 8th Hussars and 'A' Company 1st RB had a hard little battle in Daerstorf, 8 miles west of Harburg, where the RB used their Wasps (ironically for the first time) against infantry and A/Tank guns with house to house clearance. The RHA FOOs had now worked their way up to the Elbe and had a lovely time shooting at ships in the river and trains travelling along the far bank.

The Devons were now fighting their last battles of the campaign. On the 20th they took Vahrendorf, a village 2 miles south-west of Harburg, although heavily shelled by the heavy AA guns from Hamburg. For the next five days they patrolled vigorously in the neighbouring villages of Sottorf and Sieversen, with another sharp fracas on the 24th with flame throwers, killing thirty-six enemy. But at 0230 hrs on the 26th, 12th SS Reinforcement Regiment plus SS Hitler Jugend and assorted Hamburg sailors and policemen backed by 88mm guns defending Harburg made a savage counter-attack on Vahrendorf. The fighting went on all day as two enemy 75mm SP guns worked their way into the village. They were knocked out after Colonel Brind whistled up a squadron of tanks. The enemy finally withdrew on the 27th, leaving behind sixty killed and seventy prisoners.

On the 22nd, however, two unusual events took place. 8th Hussars found a POW camp at Fishbeck, quite close to Buxterhude, and there liberated 1,700 Belgian and Dutch officers.

On the same day a rather curious non-military 'battle' was fought for Buxterhude. This was the German Naval HQ, reported to have the plans of the North Sea mined areas. An elaborate attack by the Skins, RB and a Marine Commando had been laid on. But Cherry Picker troop leader Tony Hunter MC, and Sergeant Luke of 'D' Squadron got there first and 'smartened up the town's outskirts and barracks. The Commandant surrendered before the main attack started. In the bag were the second Admiral of the North Sea Fleet, 400 German Wrens, the whole officers' Mess wine cellar and 8,800 shotgun cartridges.' When Colonel Wainman arrived he found Hunter and Luke *inter alia* comfortably ensconced in the Naval Mess, possibly checking the cellar contents.

Major Hastings' history of the Rifle Brigade mentioned:

It required all the qualities of tact at the disposal of Colonel Paddy Boden to clear these formidable women from the battlefield with no more serious damage than a bruised foot for RSM Stacey, on whom one lady elected to drop the heaviest volume in the archives of the German Navy. Eventually the whole party was marched off, many in tears as the German Admiral took the salute.

John Pilborough, Skins, was also there: 'We set off at 0500 hrs and soon arrived at the large barracks which to our delight we found to be occupied by a large number of [German] Wrens. They were hardly out of their beds and made a nice change from the sort of prisoners we had grown used to. We were not allowed very long to ogle this sight and left the Marine Commandos to search the place!' Clifford Smith, 'D' Squadron 11th Hussars, recalls: 'A headline in the *Daily Mirror* called them "Unlovely Women", but that was *not* our opinion!'

An attack on Harburg started from Jeserburg with 5th RTR, 9th DLI and 'I' Company 1st RB, via the autobahn at Hiltfeld. The main bridge 3,000 yards east of Hiltfeld was promptly blown and that, for the time being, was that. General Lyne noted that the Germans were most distinctly *not* giving up. Ships' crews, stevedores from the docks, policemen and firemen from Hamburg, submarine crews with a sprinkling of SS troops, parachutists, 'ordinary' Wehrmacht, school boys and the Volksturm Home Guard, backed by a powerful army of 88mms not needed for the AA defence of flattened Hamburg, were deployed to contest every acre of the polders and marshes around Harburg. Moreover, in the huge forests surrounding the centre line, north of Soltau, many thousands of armed enemy were still at large. Prisoners were now averaging a thousand a day with very small losses on our part. 'A' Company of the DLI took the village of Maschen, and 'B' Company took Hiltfeld. In Maschen on the 21st an 'O' group was rudely disturbed by shelling and Ted Halliday said 'It's enemy shelling', and Terell said, 'No it's the RHA dropping short.' More explosions. 'Get into that f.....g village' was the succinct end to the 'O' Group. The Durhams spent

Chaffee tanks and Honeys of the Recce Troop, 8th Hussars, south of Hamburg, April 1945.

the next ten days patrolling the vast woodlands, even the Transport Officer and Regimental QM Sergeant leading patrols, and 'A' Coy captured a platoon of Hamburg *police*!

At the southern end of the salient it took another four days of patrolling and wood clearing by 53rd Division, helped by 1st RTR, for mopping up operations against Hungarian SS, a SP tank hunting battalion and numerous Bazooka teams, in a huge area with many dumps of gas shells. Despite some casualties caused by accurate mortar fire, Spandaus and mine fields, over 2,000 prisoners were taken.

There were many bizarre incidents. The Burgomeister of Molsburg, an ardent Nazi, bit a phial of poison and fell dead at the feet of Lieutenant Hickman of the Cherry Pickers. The schoolmaster at Harsfelt included in his teaching syllabus a detailed Bazooka usage class! On the 25th, 5 miles from Harsfelt, 'D' Squadron 11th Hussars were ambushed by fifteen Bazooka men (doubtless the schoolmaster's young pupils). A White scout car was hit, a Daimler armoured car was sent up in flames and a Dingo was ditched. All crews escaped but Trooper Hartnell was taken prisoner. Two days later No. 5 Troop's Dingo, covered in *black crosses* bowled down a road towards Lieutenant Newton, who promptly *recaptured* it. It was driven by the commander of the Bazooka teams, a former officer of 21st Panzer Division, a veteran of the Afrika Corps and the Russian front, who said to his captor: 'In ten years' time we will both be fighting *together* against the Russians.'

CHAPTER TWENTY-THREE

The Surrender of Hamburg – 'the Stink of Death'

The RAF had destroyed Hamburg but the Germans had proved time and time again, at Caen and Harburg for instance, that in the rubble and cellars they would and could fight to the death. It was quite possible that they would make Hamburg their final Armageddon, in the same way as, apparently, they were doing in Berlin against the Russian armies. It was not a pleasant thought. No one was particularly keen on more casualties. The Queens had lost seventy-eight and the Cherry Pickers forty-eight casualties since leaving the Rhine bridgehead. Every unit in the division had suffered.

> The final phase was when I [Leslie Gosling, 3rd RHA] shelled the Phoenix Rubber Works in Hamburg on the 28th April. This brought about the white flag delegation followed by the surrender of the Hamburg garrison and almost immediately Admiral Doenitz sued for peace, so I claim to have precipitated the end! A most lovely day. After clearance of early mist, view from the OP on top of a windmill right across Hamburg; the factories were still working, trains and transport moving; ships still in the river, not as if the war was on at all. Ammo now available, so I used one gun to shoot up three factories including a brewery.

By 29 April 8th Corps, including 11th Armoured Division and the Americans on our right, had crossed the Elbe. Two German officers, a staff officer, army doctor and a civilian with a white flag approached 1/5th Queens with two requests: that our artillery should not shell the many hospitals across the river in Hamburg, and secondly that we should lay off shelling the Phoenix Rubber Works. Perhaps the civilian owner's Luftwaffe and submarine contracts were coming to an end? Passed along and up the line, the Divisional Intelligence Officer mooted the surrender of Hamburg itself. A letter was composed, signed by Major-General Lyne, and sent to Major-General Alwin Woltz, the army commandant in Hamburg. It contained six key points deploying logic with threats. Negotiations continued back and forth and at 1900 hrs on 1 May a large black Mercedes car with an even larger white flag arrived in 'D' Company area of the 9th DLI containing two officers from General Woltz's staff. They were escorted by the IO, Bill Bailey, who took them to Battalion HQ. Admiral Deonitz had ordered General Keitel to order General Woltz to surrender the city of Hamburg to the Desert Rats.

That night on the German radio could be heard Wagner's 'Death of Siegfried' and 'the end of Adolf Hitler fighting [sic] to the last against the Bolshevik hordes'. Next day it was 'Goebbels Kaput', or words to that effect. Hitler and Goebbels had committed suicide and Admiral Doenitz was the Führer. Negotiations were continuing with Field Marshal Montgomery for unconditional surrender of all German forces facing 21st Army Group. 11th Armoured had reached Lübeck on 2 May, 30 miles away from the Russians at Rostock.

Just after 1600 hrs on the 3rd the division set off through Harburg, flattened by the RAF, initially in pouring rain and later in the afternoon sun, to cover the 8 miles across the two remarkably ugly bridges over the Elbe into Hamburg. By 1715 hrs Lieutenant-Colonel Wainman had led the Cherry Pickers into the main square, followed by 1/5th Queens and 5th RTR. The civilians were under strict curfew and stayed indoors. The roads through the rubble were lined with the police, who presumably had just returned from the Harburg front line! The adjutant of the Queens, Captain R.G. Newell, hoisted the regimental flag over the appropriately named Rathaus (town hall), Brigadier Spurling accepted General Wolz's surrender and 9th DLI took over control of the two vital river bridges. Lieutenant Brett-Smith's diary is revealing:

The first thing that struck us was the incredible tidiness of the place. Everything that the RAF had claimed was true. Hamburg had ceased to exist. Yet the streets were absolutely clear, the telephone lines and tram wires were in perfect order and we drove down wide empty streets on either side of which were heaps of rubble which had once been houses. There was no broken glass, nothing lying about the streets: the German clearance organisation must have been brilliant. But all the same the damage was terrific. Not single houses but whole streets were flat. Sometimes you would see a row of houses standing but on looking closer they were only empty shells. In Adolf Hitler Platz the garrison commander – a rather fat man with spectacles stood outside the Town hall which was curiously intact. A water-bug of the 1/5 Queens flashed through the square obviously miles adrift. Col Wainman arrived in his Dingo dressed in an American combat jacket, a pair of corduroy trousers and an 11th Hussars cap. He produced a packet of Army biscuits and proceeded to feed the pigeons walking sedately round the square.

'Snatch' Boardman parked his tank in the car park of the Hamburg police station; others were outside all the government offices and on the Harburg–Hamburg bridges.

The ruins of Hamburg.

We then saw the terrible destruction in Hamburg. The roads were badly potholed and piles of rubble on each side had been made into temporary homes. We were told the Germans dare not try to clear the debris because so many bodies were buried under it. They had no medical supplies to fight the epidemic which would follow. Some 80,000 people had died in one night when a fireball had been created by the extensive bombing.

Bill Bellamy wrote:

We entered the dockland area, where rows of houses at first sight intact, were mere burnt out shells. The whole place stank of death, sweet and cloying . . . I have never seen such a mass of contorted metal as those huge cranes and gantries, deformed by heat and blast into the most inconceivable shapes. Knotted girders, blackened or reddened, some drooping where the enormous heat had melted the steel. It was an unforgettable scene.

Tom Ritson was a subaltern in 3rd RHA and he wrote home:

My troop as senior one in the senior regiment was ordered to form up in the central square in front of the Town Hall to impress the civilians.

5th RTR brew-up in Hamburg.

The whole place is full of armed German police, German soldiers wandering around quite lost and German cars. The rest of the regiment deployed in the zoo nearby which we all thought most appropriate. We heard the news of the surrender this evening. We had been expecting it as Gen Busch, C in C Army Gp Nord, passed through our lines yesterday to negotiate, actually calling at our HQ on his way to 21 Army Group HQ.

George Stimpson, 5th RTR, guarded a bank on the corner of Adolf Hitler Platz and Monckerberg Strasse: 'The order to unload and clear guns came over the wireless and this was followed by the sound of a shot ringing across the square. One tank of 'C' Squadron had not cleared its gun correctly. When the trigger was pressed a bullet in the chamber went off and killed the driver as he was getting out of the driver's position.' Later George went to 'a backwater of the Alster and washed my feet; it was all over, more or less.'

CHAPTER TWENTY-FOUR

Final Round-up and VE Day

'Snatch' Boardman, Skins, remembers:

Thousands of German troops surrendered and created a major problem. We herded them into fields and collected arms and equipment. Feeding points had to be arranged and many required medical attention. We pushed on and up to the Kiel Canal, where our instructions were to prevent any more potential prisoners from coming south. They must remain where they had been before the surrender. My troop motored up to a small hand-operated ferry capable of carrying small vehicles. There was a German ack-ack troop on the southern side and another troop over the canal. Two large cargo boats were tied up at a jetty – one with a cargo of confiscated radios from Norway and Denmark. We personally selected sets for ourselves . . . Our next problem was caused by all kinds of foreign labour, enforced civilians who now felt free to plunder, rape and generally attack the German population. Who could blame them? There was a mixture of Poles, Russians and Czechs and all were half starved. We gave them what rations we could. We remained at Bendorf for about a week. SSM Charlie Gower who had drilled the young Skins subalterns in Colchester proudly announced over the air that he had captured the German heavyweight boxer, Max Schmeling, dressed in civilian clothing and driving a car towing a trailer full of souvenirs.

Brett-Smith, 'C' Squadron 11th Hussars, with 8th Hussars and 3rd RHA went to Pinneburg:

It was indeed a wonderful and an astonishing sight to see the end of the German army. We had known for long how disorganised they were and that all administration had broken down completely. Even so the sight that we now saw was more than we had ever expected. Infantry, Air Force, SS, Anti-tank gunners, Kriegsmarines, Hungarians, Roumanians, Austrians, non-combatants, Labour Corps, men of every conceivable age and unit jostled one another in complete disorder: staff cars full of officers, wagons full of soldiers, trucks towing other trucks and other trucks still. (The record was 8 cars pulled by one lorry.) Motor-bicyclists, footsloggers, ambulances, even trains. Down every road the Wehrmacht marched in to give itself up, its pride broken, its endurance at an end.

Only the SS marched with confidence and arrogance. Even after initial searching a pistol or grenade would be found hidden in boots, or under a cap.

Sergeant George Stimpson recalled the incident of the 'last young hero'. When 'C' Squadron 5th RTR approached Beidenfleth, 5 miles west of Hamburg on the River Stor, they did so with caution and treated it as another hostile village to be occupied:

As the leading tank was nearing a T junction, it was met by a small ten-year old boy. He stood alone defiantly, armed with a Panzerfaust with his finger on the trigger. The sergeant tank commander dismounted quickly and disarmed the boy. When he had made the anti-tank weapon safe, he bent the boy over his knee and gave his arse a good spanking, then before he sent him back to his mother, gave him a bar of chocolate.

Lieutenant Ben Tottenham, Skins, was sent to Brunsbuttelkoog to act as local 'Gauleiter', as were scores of divisional officers in their very early twenties:

Major-General Wittkopf in command of 2,000 POWs surrendered to me as the *senior* officer present! We were a somewhat shabby and unusually dressed trio [Dickie Brett-Smith and Dick McAdam, Cherry Picker troop leaders were with him] by contrast to the General who was immaculate in field grey, red stripes and gold braid on his ample form. Our drill was impeccable thanks to RSM 'Bosom' Bland at Sandhurst. I rapidly sorted out the logistic problems of absorbing 2,000 POWs and controlling the town.

By the night of 4 May came the great news of the surrender of Germany, Denmark, Holland and Norway, and that hostilities were to cease at 0800 hrs the next morning. VE Day was to be declared on 8 May.

Bill Bellamy, 8th Hussars, wrote:

My troop had discovered [in the Gauleiter's Residence by the Altesee, the lake in the centre of Hamburg] some band instruments in the basement. As I emerged I was greeted with loud harmonious 'Oompa Music'. They were grouped around one of the Corporals in the Regimental band, some dressed in Nazi hats, or bits of Nazi uniform, all playing their hearts out in the morning sun. It was a scene of great humour and made us all feel much better. This went on with my enthusiastic support for about a quarter of an hour while the German

3rd RHA officers at Itzehoe, near the Kiel Canal. Left to right: Tom Ritson, Donald Tribe, Stanley Middleton.

civilians watched us somewhat nervously. I then noticed a staff car driving along the road with both General Lyne, our Divisional Commander and Colonel Desmond Fitzpatrick in it. They did not look pleased. I was sent for, given an imperial rocket, told to return the instruments and take my troop to the northern approaches of the city.

VE Day found 3rd RHA at Itzehoe near the Kiel Canal. Tom Ritson recalls: 'We celebrated the end of hostilities with numerous *feux de joie* and we imbibed well, if not wisely. One of the battery signallers who had survived the Desert and Normandy unscathed, fell out of a barn window and broke his arm.' 3rd RHA had liberated the Hamburg Amerika Steamship Line's wine reserves and the enterprising RHA driver signed his name as Charlie Chaplin.

'When the German currency was made legal – we had thousands of Marks in the tank – I don't think', recalls Gordon Johnson, 'the old

Cromwell ever had such a sort out looking for money in every nook and cranny – a few days before we had been lighting cigarettes with the bank notes.'

On Sunday 6 May there were regimental church services throughout the division. 'The 8th Hussars' was taken by Frank Hone. It was standard in all units and ended with a mighty singing of 'Now thank we all our God'. 'Very satisfying,' wrote Bill Bellamy. 'VE Day itself seemed almost an anticlimax and only rated ten lines in Regimental Orders.'

Richard Brett-Smith wrote of VE evening:

Formal Cease Fire was blown, a rum punch to toast the victory, bonfires lit with swastikas on top to perish in the flames. That wonderful night will never be forgotten by anyone who was there, with hordes of strange fur coated figures swigging rum punch and singing their hearts out. Verey lights ricocheting all over the place and the Colonel going round to each squadron in turn, and each squadron striving to produce a bigger and better brew-up for him than the last and succeeding only too well.

But Lieutenant Osborne, 11th Hussars, wrote in his diary: 'I don't think anybody was too festive, we were merely damn glad that we had got through OK and that was all.' And General L.O. Lyne CB, DSO, ended his Special Order of the Day of 7 May by saying: 'It will be a great honour in the future to be able to say *"I was a Desert Rat."*'

CHAPTER TWENTY-FIVE

Victory Parade in Berlin

'About the middle of June a rumour spread around the Regiment,' wrote Bill Bellamy, 8th Hussars, 'that we were to go to Berlin. About the same time a load of battleship grey paint appeared from German Naval Stores, Lübeck, to enable us to clean up the tanks.' And Tom Ritson wrote:

> we drove down the autobahn near Helmstedt ready for the long drive to Berlin. We had spruced up somewhat, guns cleaned, uniforms pressed and brew cans removed from sight. We drove for much of the day in a downpour through the Russian occupied area past Magdeburg and on to the western part of Berlin. From the Grünewald, a large city park full of burned out buses, we drove into the Charlottenburg district, pulling up at the Olympic Stadium.

To Bill Bellamy 'it appeared to be more like a journey into enemy territory than a meeting with friends. Sergeant Alan Howard, a dedicated communist/socialist whose uncle had fought in the International Brigade during the Spanish War, told us what a joy it would be to meet our Russian allies.' And Trooper Clifford Smith, 11th Hussars wrote: 'Amidst the ruins a feeling of isolation as being on an island surrounded by Russians.' Verdon Besley, Queens, recalls the Olympic Spandau barracks, 'a lovely barracks but in a filthy condition with huge bugs going up the walls and human excrement on the floor. We tried to clean it up until the MO shut it down and fumigated it. We bivouacked down outside.'

> Berlin in July 1945 beggars description [wrote Tom Ritson]. It was then two months since the Russians had stormed the city street by street in bitter fighting. No serious attempt had been made to clean it up. At least half of all the buildings had been destroyed. There was no electricity, water or drainage and the weather was hot . . . the stench of the dead bodies in the ruined buildings and the corpses coming to the surface in the various lakes within the city area. We were continuously warned of the dangers of polluted water, mosquitoes and rats.

Bobby Wolfson remembered that rats 'the size of a cat would climb up the outside pipes into the sleeping quarters jumping from bed to bed'.

'A' Squadron 1st RTR Comets during the victory parade in Berlin, 1945.

Major Derrick Watson,'A' Company 1/5th Queens, who had been wounded on 28 March and evacuated to England, had rejoined his battalion just in time for the Victory March on 21 July:

> A joyful re-union took place with Captain Ted Sargenson who was the *other* survivor of the 32 officers of the 1/5th Queens who had fought at Alamein. Appropriately Ted carried the Regimental Colours, and a 'desert' rollcall brought Sgt Majors Parkin and Orpin, Sgts Gershon, Honeymen, Jeffries, George, Bill Longley, Frank Walker, Signaller Peter Knight and Driver Campbell as survivors from the 1,200 men of 1/5th Queens RR (TA) who were plunged into battle in Aug 1942 straight from the ships bringing them from England.

Peter Hogg, 1/5th Queens, obtained a visa signed by Marshal Zhukov to visit the Berlin Chancellery 'where it all began. Arriving by jeep I was shown round by some Russian officers and saw Hitler's study.'

A whole series of parades then took place, with bags of spit and polish. 'Our Brigadier [Spurling] visited us, a really bull parade – all went well,' recalled Sergeant Lodge of 2nd Devons, 'until our CO was ready for inspection, eyes front, was given in turn by all platoon sergeants. Support Co (mine) was head of parade. I gave the final eyes front . . . and froze to the spot.' It had been a terrible night in the Sergeants Mess!

The first parade took place on 6 July. The Union Jack was hoisted in the Grosse Stern at the foot of the Franco-Prussian War memorial and

Major D.J. Watson, 1/5th
Queens, July 1945.

Lieutenant-General Sir Ronald Weekes inspected the 1st Battalion
Grenadier Guards (borrowed for the occasion), 1/5th Queens, 2nd
Devons and the Canadian Composite Battalion (also borrowed). 5th
RHA arrived on 10 July, and moved into Kladow barracks and
Divisional HQ on the 18th. Field Marshal Montgomery arrived on the
12th to invest the three Russian commanders, Marshals Zhokov,
Rokossovsky and General Sokolovski. They all gave each other colourful
and appropriate medals! This time the Grenadiers and 8th and 11th
Hussars lined the route as Guard of Honour. Bill Bellamy recalled: 'We
travelled the length of the Charlottenburger Chausée as far as the
Brandenberger Tur, the great Triumphal Gate, marking the divide
between British and Russian zones. Then the Tiergarten (zoo) and the
Siegessaule. The trees in the parks on both sides of the avenue were
stripped of their leaves – the aftermath of a first world war battle. The
fighting must have been horrific.' On the 13th the first full scale
Divisional Parade, a rehearsal for the Victory Parade, took place. Two
days later the delegates for the Potsdam Conference started to arrive,

Victory parade, Berlin.

including of course the Prime Minister, Winston Churchill, Anthony
Eden and Clement Attlee. Then followed another frenetic week of last
minute rehearsals, flag poles and stands being erected for the great day –
Saturday 21 July. The bands were provided by the Royal Marines, 11th
Hussars and 2nd Devons, and the troops on parade were found from
3rd RHA, 5th RHA, 8th Hussars, 11th Hussars, 1st Battalion Grenadier
Guards, 1/5th Queens, 2nd Devons and representatives from the Navy,
RAF and RAF Regiment.

3rd RHA fired a nineteen-gun salute in honour of the Prime Minister and
Field Marshals Montgomery, Brooke and Alexander. As Tom Ritson recalls:
'A few days later Mr Churchill was dismissed by the electorate and Mr
Attlee returned to Potsdam in his place.' Verdon Besley, 1/5th Queens,
wrote: 'We were all ready, the Queens right in front of Churchill waiting to
start when there was a cascade of motor bikes escorting President Truman,
with their sirens sounding, and the parade started.'

Bill Bellamy observed:

the Russians outnumbered the British. They were quite smart in their
loosely cut service dress, flat hats, gold or silver epaulettes, and
polished jack-boots and they all had so many medals! As we
approached the saluting base, being leader of the 8th Hussars column I
had a very clear view. Mr Churchill stood slightly to the fore wearing a
light coloured Service Dress and a peaked dress hat. He was standing,

5th RHA Sexton Rams on the victory parade, Berlin.

looking directly up the Chaussée and saluted us in answer to the Colonel's salute. Standing next to him was Mr Attlee in civilian clothes and bareheaded. Then Field Marshals Alan Brooke and Montgomery with the tall bare-headed figure of Mr Anthony Eden to the left. General Lyne was standing to the PM's left, together with a senior Naval Officer. I also spotted Mr Morrison. Then it was all over and we were past.

The new 'Winston' Club for 7th Armoured Division Other Ranks was later opened formally by Winston Churchill, where he made his famous speech that included *inter alia*:

Now I have only a word more to say about the Desert Rats. They were the first to begin. The 11th Hussars were in action in the desert in 1940 and ever since you have kept marching steadily forward on the long road to victory. Through so many countries and changing scenes you have fought your way. It is not without emotion that I can express to you what I feel about the Desert Rats.

8th Hussars pass before the prime minister, Mr Attlee, Berlin victory parade, 21 July 1945.

Dear Desert Rats! May your glory ever shine! May your laurels never fade! May the memory of this glorious pilgrimage of war which you have made from Alamein, via the Baltic to Berlin, never die!

It is a march unsurpassed through all the story of war so far as my reading of history leads me to believe. May the fathers long tell the children about this tale. May you all feel that in following your great ancestors you have accomplished something which has done good to the whole world; which has raised the honour of your own country and which every man has a right to be proud of.

Acknowledgements

Practically every unit of the Desert Rats has provided editorial contributions to the making of *Churchill's Desert Rats*.

Special thanks, however, are due to Leo Cooper, Pen and Sword Books, for permission to use extracts from Peter Roach's *8.15 to War* (1st Royal Tank Regiment) and to Random House (UK) Ltd for permission to use extracts from Rex Wingfield's *The Only Way Out* (1/6th Queens Royal Regiment). I am grateful also to Captain L.G. Bellamy MC, 8th Kings Royal Irish Hussars for permission to use extracts from his book *A Schoolboy's War* and for the loan of many interesting photographs. The 5th Inniskilling Dragoon Guards have several literary heroes. *Tracks in Europe* by Captain C.J. Boardman, and *First In, Last Out*, by John Pilborough and P.A. Duckworth have provided good coverage of the famous Skins. Captain Boardman has also provided several interesting photographs. Major Derrick Watson, 1/5th Queens Royal Regiment, has sent me many helpful articles, letters and photographs, and for the 1st Battalion Rifle Brigade Major Christopher Milner MC, Major Bill Apsey and Peter Bickersteth kindly produced a number of anecdotes. Norman Smiths' book *Tank Soldier*, about the 5th RTR, has also been invaluable.

In addition letters, advice, diaries and photographs have been incorporated into the book from Verdon Besley (1/5th Queens), Major B.E. Burton (1/5th Queens), Richard Brett-Smith (11th Hussars), Major John Evans DSO (1/5th Queens), Trooper Geoff Ferdie (5th RTR), Leslie Gosling (3rd RHA), Trooper W. Hewison (1st RTR), George W. Hinde (1/6th Queens), Lance-Corporal Harry Hopkins (1st RB), Gordon Johnson (5th RTR), Lance-Corporal James A. Kay (1/7th Queens), Signaller Peter Knight (1/5th Queens), Albert Mitchell (65th A/Tank Regiment RA, Norfolk Yeomanry), Lieutenant W.E. Mason (13th Medium Regiment RA), Major F.D. Pile MC (1st RTR), Major Tom Ritson (3rd RHA), Trooper Bernie Roberts (1st RTR), Sergeant George Stimpson (5th RTR), Trooper Clifford Smith (11th Hussars), Corporal Reg Spittles (1st RTR), Captain A.F. Perdue (1/6th Queens), Captain Bobby Wolfson (3rd RHA), and many others.

Index of Places and Names